Catherine, the Princess of Wales

Catherine, *the* Princess *of* Wales

A Biography of the Future Queen

Robert Jobson

PEGASUS BOOKS

NEW YORK LONDON

CATHERINE, THE PRINCESS OF WALES

Pegasus Books, Ltd.
148 West 37th Street, 13th Floor
New York, NY 10018

First Pegasus Books cloth edition August 2024

ISBN: 978-1-63936-712-2

10 9 8 7 6 5 4 3 2 1

Printed in the United States of America
Distributed by Simon & Schuster
www.pegasusbooks.com

Contents

There is no rule book, no right or wrong – you just have to make it up and do the very best you can to care for your family.

CATHERINE, THE PRINCESS OF WALES, FROM A SPEECH
ABOUT BEING A MOTHER AT THE ROYAL COLLEGE OF
OBSTETRICIANS AND GYNAECOLOGISTS,
23 MARCH 2017

Preface

For everyone facing this disease, in whatever form,
please do not lose faith or hope. You are not alone.
CATHERINE, THE PRINCESS OF WALES

Thursday, 22 March 2024, 6 p.m.
***BBC News at Six*, with Sophie Raworth**

'The Princess of Wales has just announced that she is undergoing treatment for cancer. Here now is a very personal message from her, which has just been released, in which she explains what has been happening in recent weeks.'

I wanted to take this opportunity to say thank you, personally, for all the wonderful messages of support and for your understanding whilst I have been recovering from surgery. It has been an incredibly tough couple of months for our entire family, but I've had a fantastic medical team who have taken great care of me, for which I am so grateful.

In January, I underwent major abdominal surgery in London and at the time, it was thought that my condition was non-

cancerous. The surgery was successful. However, tests after the operation found cancer had been present. My medical team therefore advised that I should undergo a course of preventative chemotherapy and I am now in the early stages of that treatment.

This of course came as a huge shock, and William and I have been doing everything we can to process and manage this privately for the sake of our young family. As you can imagine, this has taken time. It has taken me time to recover from major surgery in order to start my treatment. But, most importantly, it has taken us time to explain everything to George, Charlotte and Louis in a way that is appropriate for them, and to reassure them that I am going to be ok. As I have said to them; I am well and getting stronger every day by focusing on the things that will help me heal; in my mind, body and spirits.

Having William by my side is a great source of comfort and reassurance too. As is the love, support and kindness that has been shown by so many of you. It means so much to us both. We hope that you will understand that, as a family, we now need some time, space and privacy while I complete my treatment. My work has always brought me a deep sense of joy and I look forward to being back when I am able, but for now I must focus on making a full recovery.

At this time, I am also thinking of all those whose lives have been affected by cancer. For everyone facing this disease, in whatever form, please do not lose faith or hope. You are not alone.

After weeks of speculation, this is how a shocked nation learned that Catherine, The Princess of Wales, was having treatment for cancer. In her televised address, the future queen appeared resolute, a testament to her courage not in the absence of fear, but in the face of it. The world watched as the princess spoke of her concern for her family, some on their phones or TV screens, others at Canada Gate next to Buckingham Palace, where television crews had gathered to report the breaking news live. In a video filmed by a BBC cameraman two days earlier in Windsor, Catherine sat alone on a bench surrounded by daffodils and spring blossom, wearing a black-and-white crew-neck sweater and with minimal make-up, as she revealed that she had started a 'course of preventative chemotherapy'.

The next day the British newspapers spoke of the princess's courage and the cruel indifference of fate, reminding us all of the human frailty beneath the crowns and titles. *The Times* ran an editorial entitled 'Catherine's Courage', commenting that 'the Princess of Wales deserves compassion and privacy as she recovers from cancer.'

It went on: 'The news, which was calmly delivered to the public by the princess herself in a brief video, is a chastening reminder of cancer's capriciousness in striking without regard for age, rank or circumstance. Following so closely on from King Charles's disclosure of his own cancer diagnosis last month, no one should now begrudge the Royal Family the privacy and consideration that are their due at this doubly challenging time.'

The *Sun* ran with similar words for its own editorial, with the paper writing: 'Our hearts go out to Kate, as well as to William, to George, Charlotte, Louis and to the rest of her wider family.'

Messages of support for the princess flooded in following the announcement. The British prime minister Rishi Sunak was among the first to react to the news. 'The Princess of Wales will have the love and support of the whole of the country as she continues her recovery,' he said. 'She has shown tremendous bravery with her statement today.' Sir Keir Starmer, the leader of the Labour Party, stated, 'Any cancer diagnosis is shocking. But I can only imagine the added stress of receiving that news amidst the lurid speculation we've seen in recent weeks.' President Joe Biden issued a heartfelt statement too: 'Jill and I join millions around the world in praying for your full recovery, Princess Kate.' His wife, Dr Jill Biden, tweeted simply, 'You are brave, and we love you. Jill.'

Catherine's retreat from the public eye, and the tumult it stirred, laid bare her foundational role within the Royal Family. The news of her hospital stay captured global attention, with the revelation that she planned to return to royal responsibilities post-Easter sparking a wildfire of conjecture about her health and the solidity of her marriage. The Palace's call for privacy amidst this storm of speculation only highlighted the intensity of the public's fascination and concern. The retraction of a Mother's Day photo due to digital tampering, and Catherine's subsequent apology, added even more layers to the unfolding drama.

The blaze of conjecture intensified with news of an attempted breach into her medical records at the London Clinic, reaching its zenith with Catherine's valiant video declaration. Her dignified announcement cut through the maelstrom of rumours with the truth. Social media and certain mainstream media segments seemed to corner the princess in their frenzy. But the aftermath of her video was profound, prompting apologies from those who had taken her circumstances lightly. Stephen Colbert, host of the CBS TV programme *The Late Show with Stephen Colbert*, expressed his regret over comments when he had poked fun at the princess and the rumours. On his show, Colbert reflected on the nature of his job, acknowledging the fine line between comedy and sensitivity.

In Catherine's vulnerability, a collective strength and compassion emerged, uniting the nation and beyond in hope and solidarity with her, William and their family.

Introduction

When Kate Middleton was a child, becoming a princess would have been seen as very unlikely. It was a position reserved for foreign royals or the daughters of nobility, aristocrats like Lady Diana Spencer, who wed Prince Charles five months before Catherine was born.

This century, though, the perception of monarchy at home and overseas has undergone a seismic transformation. Princely marriages, once 'a brilliant edition of a universal fact and, as such, it rivets mankind', according to the Victorian writer Walter Bagehot, are no longer restricted to unions between a certain class.

In May 2004, Australian-born commoner Mary Donaldson, of Scottish parentage, married Danish Crown Prince Frederik in a ceremony attended by dozens of royals and dignitaries from around the world at Our Lady's Church in downtown Copenhagen. The prince met the student from Tasmania during the 2000 Olympics in Sydney, when he stopped in at the Slip Inn bar where she was working. As the new King Frederik X's wife, she became Queen Mary of Denmark on 14 January 2024 after the unexpected abdication of Queen Margrethe II, then Europe's longest-reigning living monarch after fifty-two years on the throne.

In neighbouring Norway, the marriage in August 2001 of Crown Prince Haakon, the heir apparent to the Norwegian throne, to a commoner who became Crown Princess Mette-Marit, was rather more controversial. The royal bride, previously known as Mette-Marit Tjessem Høiby, was a former waitress and a single mother to her then four-year-old son. She met the prince through mutual friends in 1999 and they announced their engagement in December 2000. They lived together until their wedding took place eight months later, which was also considered to be controversial. The princess spoke openly about living a 'wild' life in her past and asked the media to give her a fresh start.

Then it was Britain's turn. At the University of St Andrews in 2001, art history undergraduate Kate Middleton became reacquainted with and later fell in love with her future husband Prince William, heir apparent to the British throne. They had known of each other from schooldays, when they were both at private schools: he at Eton and she at Marlborough. 'There was plenty of socialising back then and they were known to each other,' a senior source close to the family said. They too broke with 'tradition' and enjoyed a long courtship and lived together before they wed on 29 April 2011 in Westminster Abbey.

Throughout British and European history, royal marriages have been used by monarchs and governments alike as a useful tool to secure strategic alliances. They were often unions arranged for political reasons and signed off while those involved were still minors and even very small children. Betrothals by proxy were commonplace throughout the courts of Europe in medieval times and later. Love between the two participants, if it developed at all, was seen as an unexpected bonus and certainly not a necessity.

Often the feelings of the individuals were totally disregarded, leading to mismatches and sadness for those trapped in such unions. Others simply made the best of the situation. It perhaps explains why so many princes had mistresses and their wives enjoyed secret, illicit affairs. It was largely accepted as part of the arrangement. All parties were expected to be discreet and not to upset the status quo.

In British nobility terms, a commoner refers to somebody who does not hold a hereditary title or belong to the nobility, essentially a person who is not part of the aristocratic family or the peerage system. For centuries it was seen as unacceptable for royalty in the UK or in Europe to marry commoners. Therefore, such marriages – usually borne out of love – were rare, and frowned upon in society when they did happen. Called 'morganatic' marriages, these unions came loaded with legally binding caveats, the most draconian being that the spouse or any children from the union were prevented by law from inheriting royal rank, status or privileges.

At the dawn of the twentieth century, however, the political tide and social landscape was turning. The First World War practically ended the power game of royal matchmaking, as practised by Queen Victoria. After all, she had enjoyed her role as Europe's matriarch and the power it afforded her and her country in the latter third of the nineteenth century. As the end of her long reign approached, she had more than thirty grandchildren and their marriages, many of which she had influenced personally, had helped to retain Britain's global influence.

Victoria's death in 1901 marked the end of such meddling marriage diplomacy. Her successor Edward VII was more focused on diplomatic treaties such as the Entente Cordiale in 1904, in which he played a key role and helped to end antagonisms between Britain and France. It later paved the way for their diplomatic cooperation against German pressures in the decade preceding the First World War.

Before Britain entered the war on 28 July 1914, there were well over twenty countries across Europe governed by a monarchy, with a king or queen or a regal figure of equivalent stature as its head of state. After the war, in which more than nine million of the 60 million combat troops were killed, those returning home from the trenches and those at home who had lost loved ones demanded radical political change.

Monarchies toppled like dominos, with four great empires collapsing: the Russian Empire in 1917, the German and the Austro-Hungarian in 1918, and the Ottoman in 1922. Independent republics were formed in Austria, Czechoslovakia, Estonia, Hungary, Latvia, Lithuania and Turkey. The working class wanted a voice and demanded elected leaders who were answerable to them in place of the old order. As republics were formed, those monarchs still on their throne agreed to begin to change, or risk being overthrown as Tsar Nicholas II was in Russia.

The usual pool of German princesses seen as suitable royal brides was dwindling along with the rights of the landed nobility. Given that Britain had spent the previous four years fighting the Hun in relentless battle, King George V was strongly advised to ditch his Saxe-Coburg-Gotha family name and change it to Windsor. He also felt it was better if his sons picked British brides, not the daughters of fallen 'despots'.

It meant that Lady Elizabeth Bowes-Lyon, a Scottish aristocrat descended from the Royal House of Scotland, was seen as the perfect choice to marry the King's second son Albert, known to the family as Bertie, Duke of York, and later George VI. It was a great match, as Elizabeth was seen as the strength behind her stammering and painfully shy prince, the saviour of the monarchy after the 1936 abdication crisis and a beacon of hope during the Second World War.[1]

Kate Middleton's forebears were predominantly from the English working- and middle-classes. Her ancestors included coal miners, carpenters, and farm labourers, whose lives were a far cry from her own advantaged childhood. But her family tree also contained influential establishment figures like William Petty Fitzmaurice, the Earl of Shelburne, the Anglo-Irish Whig statesman. He was the UK prime minister who successfully negotiated a peace treaty with George Washington in 1783, thus ending the American War of Independence and Britain's control over the American colonies.

When Kate married Prince William in 2011, the royal naysayers against marrying outside of the pool of aristocracy were distant memories, but the spotlight was still on her as a 'commoner'. She became Her Royal Highness Catherine, The Duchess of Cambridge, as William had been made the Duke of Cambridge by Queen Elizabeth II. Then on 9 September 2022, she became only the tenth Princess of Wales since 1328 when her husband William was created Prince of Wales by his father, Charles III, on his accession. The courtesy title, given on marriage, is typically but not always held by the wife of the heir apparent to the English, and later the British throne. The bearer of the title is destined to become the nation's next Queen Consort.[2]

CHAPTER I

A Happy Childhood

As children we spent a lot of time outside and it's
something I'm passionate about.

CATHERINE TALKING TO GIOVANNA FLETCHER
ON HER PODCAST, *HAPPY MUM, HAPPY BABY*

The evolution from Kate Middleton to the Duchess of Cambridge and now to HRH Catherine, The Princess of Wales, is truly remarkable by anyone's standards. If she had been born fifty years earlier such a journey would have been impossible, the stuff of fairy tales. She may not have had a glass slipper that only fitted her slender foot, but in many ways, hers is a modern-day Cinderella story.

Catherine was not a downtrodden youth exploited by her wicked stepmother, and there is not a fairy godmother in sight, but her rise has been nonetheless meteoric. She was born on a cold winter's day on 9 January 1982, at the Royal Berkshire Hospital in Reading. Her parents, Michael and Carole, waited until the summer to arrange the baptism of their first child, Catherine Elizabeth Middleton, on 20 June 1982, at St Andrew's, Bradfield,[3] a quaint Grade II listed, fourteenth-century parish church in Berkshire.

That summer, Adam Ant's hit single 'Goody Two Shoes' was

the soundtrack of the season and could be heard blasting from car radios across the country. Power suits with big shoulder pads were all the rage for women, along with big bouffant hair, while mullets were in vogue for men, along with double denim. In the news, Britain's first female prime minister Margaret Thatcher, the Conservative Party leader, was basking in the apparent glory of the British military victory over Argentina in the Falklands War. Inflation had hit 9.1 per cent and unemployment was on the rise to over three million.

Amidst all the turmoil on Fleet Street, where most national newspapers were based back then, the editors remained singularly obsessed with one story, the imminent arrival of Charles and Diana's first child. Right on cue, the royal couple welcomed their fair-haired baby boy into the world on 21 June 1982, weighing in at 7lb 1.5oz.

The prince and princess looked the picture of happiness on the steps of the Lindo Wing of St Mary's Hospital, Paddington, but that was far from true. Diana was in pain and had needed to be induced because she could not handle the press pressure any longer, as in her words 'it was becoming unbearable'. She confided, 'It was as if everybody was monitoring every day for me.'[4] A few days later, after informing the Queen, the prince and princess announced that they had named their son William Arthur Philip Louis. He was second in line to the throne and Britain's future king.

There were no steel barriers or photographers outside the hospital when Michael and Carole Middleton took baby Catherine home, but she was equally cherished and celebrated by her own family. A bright, pretty child, she was raised by her hard-working parents, who both had solid jobs in the burgeoning airline industry. When Catherine was around the age of two, her father Michael received a significant promotion to take up a senior management position as a despatcher with British Airways. The only catch was that the post was based in Amman, Jordan. With a two-and-a-half-year contract in hand, they faced this challenge head-on, viewing it as an exciting adventure, and after thorough consideration, Michael and Carole made the decision to uproot their family and embrace the expatriate life.

It was a bold move, as Jordan was experiencing considerable political disquiet. There was widespread unrest and Amman was the centre of serious mass protests, especially at the Yarmouk University, where students were demanding change *en masse*. These cries about poverty and inflation threatened to destabilise King Hussein's reign. Although he was a constitutional monarch, not an absolute ruler like those in neighbouring countries, Hussein retained significant executive and legislative powers, and if pushed, he had shown that he was not afraid to use them.[5]

Although Michael was on a decent salary as a senior manager, bolstered by a relocation allowance, his family were not exactly living the high life. From May 1984 they rented a modest three-bedroom villa costing £300 a month in the Um Uthaina neighbourhood, an elegant neighbourhood in the Zahran district located in south-west Amman, which was turned into a paediatric clinic after they left. It was, however, a 'very happy time' for the family, despite Michael's role with British Airways being very demanding. One Christmas season he had to remain in Jordan while Carole and their young daughters, Catherine and Pippa, returned to the UK and their home in the village of Bradfield Southend, in Berkshire.[6]

Nicola Nijmeh, the building's owner who became a paediatrician working from the old villa, had fond memories of Michael when he was based mainly at Amman Airport. She recalled, 'He always wore white shorts and drove a white Toyota with a prominent BA emblem.' Hana Hashweh, a Jordanian BA agent who collaborated with Mr Middleton, said he was, 'active, profoundly honest, and a beacon of integrity.'[7]

At the age of three, Catherine found herself immersed in a vibrant tapestry of cultures at her innovative nursery school. Her classmates hailed from various corners of the world, including Jordan, Britain, Japan, India, Indonesia and America, providing her with exposure to a rich array of backgrounds and traditions. Although her daily class consisted of only twelve students, every morning the larger group would come together to explore the basics of Arabic, further enriching her early cultural education.

Sahera al Nabulsi, the visionary teacher behind the Assahera nursery, said these children would form a circle together, reciting versions of 'Incy Wincy Spider' in both English and Arabic. 'To improve their Arabic, we'd delve into a verse from the Qur'an,' Sahera recalled. 'And then we'd share tales of the Prophet's companions, like Omar Bin Khattab, underscoring values of respect and love.'[8] Understandably, school celebrations of religious holidays were a colourful cocktail of cultures. Christmas saw Ms al Nabulsi donning the role of Santa Claus. In contrast, Eid al-Fitr, marking the culmination of Ramadan, was enlivened with the sounds of drumming.

It meant that Catherine, who has argued that a child's experiences in their early years shape their adult life, spent half that time in a foreign country, immersed in diverse cultures with peers from a multitude of countries and faiths. Experts say that children introduced to such diversity at a young age acquire enhanced, stronger social skills and are more receptive to those who speak a different language than their parents and show greater cultural awareness and acceptance of a global world.

While Carole was usually the parent who did pick-ups at the nursery, Ms al Nabusi said that when Michael arrived instead, his two girls' faces would light up with joy and they would race excitedly to greet him.[9] Beyond the nursery's walls, adventures awaited at places like the Haya Cultural Centre, a hub opened by King Hussein in 1976 that offered a planetarium, culinary classes and vibrant play zones. It was specifically established for the purpose of developing the skills and the capacities of children in the fields of art and culture, and clearly had an impact on the adult Catherine.

When Prince William attended a reception at the British ambassador's residence to Jordan's residence in Amman in June 2018, he met Rania Malki, chief executive of the Save the Children Fund in Jordan, who said she knew the house where Catherine lived while she was in Jordan, because it is now the home of her children's paediatrician. 'No way!' he replied. 'She will be thrilled. She loved it here, she really did. She is very upset that I am coming here without her.' Catherine has had a strong affection for Jordan ever since and her young family holidayed there in 2020.

The Middleton family enjoyed living overseas and were determined to make the most of it. They threw themselves into the expatriate lifestyle and were keen to get as much from the experience as possible. Michael took the family on regular family excursions to some of the many ancient historical sites in the country. After the announcement of Catherine's engagement to William in 2010, a sweet family photograph was officially released of the Middleton family visiting the first-century Roman ruins at Jerash.

When William made a solo visit to Jordan in June 2018, he toured the same ruins that his wife had visited as a child. Along the route, he and Jordan's Crown Prince Hussein stopped in front of an enlargement of the Middleton family photo on an easel. Standing in the spot where the photo was taken, he said, 'I need to come back with the family for this shot.' He then pointed at his father-in-law in the photo, saying that 'Michael's looking very smart in his flip-flops.'

After a few mostly happy years, as planned, the Middleton family returned to their West Berkshire home in September 1986. Shortly afterwards Catherine was enrolled at the fee-paying St Andrew's preparatory school in Pangbourne, where she stayed until July 1995. Her teachers described her as a dedicated pupil, a hard worker and very conscientious, not only towards her studies but sports activities too, and she was a noted athlete and swimmer.

In 1987, when Catherine was five, her mother Carole started a business on her kitchen table called Party Pieces, supplying items such as hats, plates, balloons and decorations for children's parties. The business grew to become a successful company, selling its products nationwide by mail order and online, and employing forty people at its base in Ashampstead, Berkshire.[10] Catherine would later enjoy the benefits of this commercial success by receiving her education at two of the finest independent schools in England.

In 1990, she and her sister Pippa joined the local Brownies club, where again they were popular on field trips, playing sport and earning badges. 'She was quite easy-going,' Brownie pack leader June Scutter said. 'They were just ordinary children, nothing different from any others.'[11] Catherine developed her love for the dramatic arts while she was at St Andrew's and was so good that at eleven, she was handed the lead role of Eliza Doolittle in the school production of *My Fair Lady*. Aged thirteen, she had a starring role in the school production of the Victorian play *Murder in the Red Barn*.

Catherine recalled, 'I had a very happy childhood. It was great fun and I'm very lucky I come from a very strong family. My parents were hugely dedicated. I really appreciate now as a parent how much they sacrificed for us. They came to every sports match, they'd be the ones on the sideline shouting, and we'd always have our family holidays together.'[12]

Independent and driven, Carole Middleton was not only a terrific entrepreneur, but a parent who was determined to give her children the opportunity to be the best they could be. She ensured that Catherine set her standards high from an early age. 'I was lucky,' Catherine acknowledged later. 'My parents and teachers provided me with a wonderful and secure childhood where I always knew I was loved, valued and listened to.'

The only setback in her young life came when she failed to settle after being enrolled as a day-pupil at the independent Downe House School. An archetypal all-girl, selective English boarding school, it is consistently in the top five of all UK schools for academic attainment. Originally sited within Charles Darwin's former house, the school moved to Cold Ash, near Newbury, in 1921. The whitewashed, Moorish-inspired school building, The Cloisters, was built during the First World War by the architect Maclaren Ross, with later additions and further buildings across more than 110 acres of grounds. It is a traditional school with a sharp focus on the future, it says.

There has been widespread speculation that Catherine suffered some bullying while she was a pupil there, although it is something she has never spoken about publicly and has not been confirmed. That said, whatever happened there, she struggled to assimilate with other pupils. She felt like an outsider, which is understandable as her peer group had been together at the school since they were eleven and had already bonded.

Catherine, who had shown herself to be a first-class schoolgirl hockey player, had always enjoyed team sports and this had helped her make friends easily. Unfortunately, Downe House did not have a hockey team and offered lacrosse as an alternative. Again, it was unfamiliar to her and she felt excluded. When she had a try-out for the team it did not go well and proved another major disappointment for her.[13]

But that competitive edge stayed with her and remained important. It was part of who she was and of her family dynamic. 'I suppose as a family we were just very active. And I can always remember being physical, using our bodies, whether it's walking, climbing in the Lake District, in Scotland [or] swimming from a young age,' she revealed in September 2023 on Mike Tindall's podcast 'The Good, The Bad & The Rugby'.[14] She went on, '[My parents] always encouraged us to be physically active and sporty and they always encouraged us into doing team sports and trying things.'

Speaking about her love of sport in general and its importance to her, Catherine said that her favourite childhood memory of sport was 'coming back in having played hockey or netball in the freezing cold rain and thinking that we were all totally mad, but it has been great fun, and off the back of it that sense of achievement that you've come through. It's not adversity in its full sense, but it's been tough.'

While Catherine tried her best to settle in to Downe House School, Michael and Carole had taken soundings about Marlborough College as a precaution. After listening to their daughter, they believed that the environment and the ethos of the school suited her better. Catherine left Downe House for Marlborough College after just two terms in 1996.

The co-educational, £39,930-a-year independent school Marlborough College, established in 1843, was much more to her liking. The institution, whose motto is *Deus Dat Incrementum*, which translated means 'God gives the increase', coincidentally had some royal links. Princess Eugenie, her future husband's first cousin, as well as Lord Janvrin, the Queen's Private Secretary from

1998–2007, were former pupils. Other famous alumni included the infamous KGB spy and art historian Sir Anthony Blunt, who was also Surveyor to the Queen's Pictures, and the former Poet Laureate, Sir John Betjeman.

Within weeks of starting at Marlborough, the wan expression left Catherine's face and she began to blossom. She felt at home and slowly but surely her natural exuberance returned. The girls in Elmhurst House were much more welcoming than Downe House and she soon settled in. Within weeks she began to thrive. Contemporaries recall her as the perfect pupil, listening to her Walkman, watching the US television show *Friends* and indulging in Marmite sandwiches.

Her turnaround came during a summer break when at sixteen she morphed into a beauty. Her demeanour changed too when she was finally able to ditch the dreaded teenage braces on her teeth. She was soon top of the schoolboys' so-called 'Fit List', which at the time they would circulate and pin on their walls.

Much like other girls her age, Catherine experienced a few innocent teenage romances. Her first 'love' was Harry Blakelock, a fellow student at Marlborough College, who later pursued a career as an insurance brokerage partner after studying at Exeter University. Their youthful relationship had its ups and downs, but ultimately ended before the start of her gap year. Friends said she felt a close attachment to him and when they parted it was her first taste of heartbreak. Another one of her schooltime beaus was the dashing Willem Marx, who pursued a degree in Classics at Oxford University and later became a business and broadcast journalist. Although their relationship did not develop into something more, they remained friends.[15]

There were reports that Catherine had a schoolgirl crush on Prince William when he was at Eton College and her former housemate

Jessica Hay even claimed she had a picture of him on her wall at school.[16] During the ITV interview with Tom Bradby to mark their engagement, however, Catherine firmly quashed this rumour, telling him, 'No, I had the Levi's guy on my wall, not a picture of William, sorry.'[17]

Once again, she enjoyed her school life and excelled at her studies and sport. She soon made friends and showed her prowess at hockey, tennis and athletics, where she was a top high jumper. She did well in class too. Studious Catherine attained eleven GCSEs and went on to get three A-levels with A grades in Maths and Art and a B grade in English.

Reflecting on her early years, Catherine spoke of how they impacted on her personally. She said:

What resonates the most is the simple things. I see that now with my own children. Life now is so busy and distracting and sometimes simple things like watching a fire on a rainy day provides such enjoyment. I remember that from my childhood, the simple things, like going for a walk together. I try to do this with my children.

It totally strips away complications and pressures. I think those experiences mean so much to children and the world they're in, which is a real adventure at that age. As children, we spent a lot of time outside and it's something I'm passionate about. I think it's so great for physical and mental wellbeing and laying those foundations. It's such a great environment to spend time in, building those quality relationships without the distractions of 'I've got to cook' and 'I've got to do this'. And it's so simple.[18]

Marlborough College, with its more open-minded community, had helped her to develop, both emotionally and academically.

At the age of eighteen, perhaps still pining a little for her first love Harry Blakelock, Catherine set off on her gap year adventure in July 2000. There was some structure to it. At first, she studied Italian and Art History at the British Institute of Florence, in the Palazzo della Strozzino, where she joined eleven other girls in her class.

While studying in Florence, she shared an apartment with several girls above a delicatessen near Piazza degli Strozzi, a short walk from her place of study. She socialised with friends at nearby cafes and bars in her free time and said later that she really benefited from the experience. Of course, she missed her mother and father, but they did travel out to spend time with her in the city, taking in its breathtaking sights such as the Duomo, Giotto's Campanile, Michelangelo's David and Ponte Vecchio.

After three months in Italy, she joined up with a Raleigh International programme in Chile. Again, she worked well alongside her peers and was noted for her maturity and presence. Group Leader Rachel Humphreys recalled that Catherine was popular and friendly while retaining a certain aura. 'She was always very in control of herself and impeccably behaved,' she added.

After returning to Britain, Catherine threw herself into a job working on Round the World Challenge boats in the Solent. She waited tables, cleaned the boat and performed other deckhand duties for a £40 daily wage. During this time, she befriended another deckhand, Ian Henry, who was set to go up to Oxford University the following year. They became close enough for her to invite him on a Middleton family holiday in Barbados later in 2001. Ian later said they were just 'very good friends' and nothing more, although a fellow crewmate said that Catherine, who was dubbed 'fit Kate' by the boys, enjoyed a 'summer romance'.[19]

That said, true romance would soon be within her grasp.

CHAPTER 2

From Friendship to Love

I think I went bright red when I met you and
sort of scuttled off.

CATHERINE ON MEETING WILLIAM AT UNIVERSITY

Catherine had initially set her sights on Edinburgh University to pursue a History of Art degree after completing her A-levels at Marlborough College. Confirming her place through the Universities and Colleges Admissions Service, she was set to take her next step in her academic journey immediately. But doubts had crept in at the eleventh hour, prompting her to take a step back and reassess what she wanted to do. Instead, after discussing it with her parents, she opted to take a gap year, giving her a chance to mull over her options.

Eventually she reapplied to study Art History at the University of St Andrews on her return. Catherine rightly believed that a year abroad would enrich her experiences and broaden her educational horizons. Years later, erroneous reports surfaced suggesting that her change of heart was solely influenced by William's decision to attend St Andrews and that somehow her mother had been involved in this process. 'Utter nonsense' is how one source close to the family described that fanciful theory.

Indeed, it had been expected that the prince would attend Trinity College, Cambridge, like his father, but he took a conscious decision to veer away from the Oxbridge path. Like Catherine he opted for St Andrews, as he felt studying there was better aligned with his aspirations. He bypassed freshers' week, choosing instead to slip quietly into undergraduate life and avoid the media circus. Reflecting on his decision in a 2019 interview, he said, 'It would have been a media frenzy and that's not fair on the other new students.' But his absence was primarily due to concerns raised by his Scotland Yard security team leader, who cited safety fears as the paramount reason for him not to attend.

William made it clear that one of the reasons he wanted to attend university was not only to broaden his mind but expand his social circle too. 'I just hope I can meet people I get on with. I don't care about their background,' he said. He sounded sincere enough, but if that was his intention, he had probably selected the wrong seat of learning, as St Andrews had the highest percentage of privately educated undergraduates in the UK apart from Durham University.

If William was nervous, he put his best foot forward and did not show it. He arrived on 24 September 2001 dressed casually in jeans, trainers and a pastel sweater and seemed a little surprised by the size of the welcome. Thousands lined the streets of the small town, which revolves around a 'town and gown' divide and, of course, golf, to greet him. He acknowledged that he would have to pick his friends carefully and rely on their discretion. 'People who try to take advantage of me and get a piece of me, I spot it quickly and soon go off them. I'm not stupid,' he said.

The prince had chosen modules in History of Art, Geography and Anthropology for his first year after enrolling as plain 'William Wales'. Among friends he decided to use the pseudonym 'Steve' in a bizarre attempt to stay under the radar. Romance was in the air too. He struck up an intimate friendship with a stunning student, Carly Massy-Birch, who was in the year above him. The two met when he auditioned for the role of Zooey in a play based on J.D. Salinger's *Franny and Zooey*, and they dated in the Martinmas semester, from September to December.

A country girl from Devon, Carly clicked with the prince straight away. They kept their romance low-key and she would cook for him at her home. 'I'm a real country bumpkin,' Carly told the journalist and author Katie Nicholl, in an article for *Vanity Fair*. 'I think that was why we had a connection. William was in the year below, and we just happened to meet through the general St Andrews mêlée,' she said.

The pair had shared interests. They talked about literature, played board games together and attended dinner parties with pals or drank pints of cider at the Castle pub. 'We tended to go to pubs and bars, and there was always a good dinner party going on,' Carly told *Vanity Fair*. She added, 'We got on well, but I think we would have got on well even if nothing had been going on romantically. It was very much a university thing, just a regular university romance.'[20]

Their relationship was fleeting, however, after William admitted he felt torn between Carly and another girl, Arabella Musgrave, the daughter of Major Nicholas Musgrave, who managed the Cirencester Park Polo Club. He had fallen for Arabella at a party in 2001 and they enjoyed a passionate summer romance just prior to him going up to St Andrews. He was smitten, but before he left for Scotland, they mutually agreed it would be better if they cooled their relationship as he was going to be away for long periods at university.

In his early undergraduate days, William was homesick and he missed her. When he went back to Highgrove for weekends, they would meet. It was perhaps this ardour for Arabella combined with his being bored in Scotland that led to his university wobble, when he wanted to quit St Andrews after just one term following doubts about his choice.

He had, of course, dated a few girls before Carly and Arabella, such as Davina Duckworth-Chad, the daughter of a Norfolk landowner, who joined him on a cruise along the Aegean Sea in 1999. He also had a close relationship with Jecca Craig during part of his gap year in Kenya in 2000 and briefly dated Olivia Hunt, an Edinburgh University student. His angst caused him to question if he was on the right course or even university, and he thought about quitting. 'I think the rumour that I was unhappy got slightly out of control. I don't think I was homesick. I was more daunted,' he explained later.

Whatever the reason behind William's uncertainty, it led to a serious heart-to-heart about his immediate future with his father at Highgrove. 'We chatted a lot and in the end we both realised, I definitely realised, that I had to come back,' he said. It was the right call. Quitting college was not really viable and Charles urged his son to give it time and persevere with his studies. On his return to university, the prince spoke to his module coordinator so that he could major in Geography and almost immediately felt happier.

His private life took a positive turn, too. William and Catherine (whom at that stage he still called Kate) were already friends. A close source told the author that they had first become aware of each other much earlier than university. 'Boys from Eton and girls from Marlborough knew each other. She was part of that, and I understand he invited her on a few things.'

Reflecting on that period of her life, Catherine said, 'Actually, William wasn't there for quite a bit of the time initially; he wasn't there for freshers' week, so it did take a bit of time for us to get to know each other, but we did become very close friends from quite early.'[21] The two had met again at St Salvator's Hall and Gannochy House, their hall of residence known to the students as 'Sallies'. 'Well, I think I went bright red when I met you and sort of scuttled off, feeling very shy about meeting you,' Catherine said.[22]

The pair rekindled their friendship and began to socialise more, playing the odd game of tennis and drinking together. They really enjoyed spending time with each other. As William wrestled mentally about what to do next, Catherine sensed his angst and the two bonded. 'We were friends for over a year first and it just sort of blossomed from then on. We just spent more time with each other, had a good giggle, had lots of fun and realised we shared the same interests and just had a really good time,' he said in their engagement interview.[23]

William was captivated, not only by her beauty, but her infectious energy that set her apart. He found himself smiling every time she laughed. While other first-year undergraduates struggled with the transition to life at university, Catherine embraced it and flourished, throwing herself into all aspects of student life. Unlike William, who initially felt like a fish out of water and struggled to adapt, she quickly found her circle and a routine.

Most afternoons, if Catherine did not have a lecture or seminar, she would nestle comfortably in an armchair in the common room with a mug of tea and read the newspaper clippings that had been lovingly cut and sent to her by her dad, or simply join in the banter with the friends she had made. She became an active member of the all-female, invitation-only Lumsden Club, a registered charity founded in 2001, which supports women and children's charities and the arts, both locally and overseas. While attending university, she also achieved a Gold Duke of Edinburgh Award.

Though they were good friends, Catherine surely stirred stronger feelings in William after she strutted down the catwalk as a model in the now-infamous charity fashion show, held at the Fairmont Hotel on 27 March 2002. Dressed in a daring, black-lace ensemble by designer Catherine Todd, she captivated him. 'She wore a risqué sheer black-lace dress over a bandeau bra and black bikini bottoms,' he recalled. As she moved with grace along the runway, William found himself unable to look away. He had secured a front-row seat at the 'Don't Walk' event, paying £200 for the privilege. If her idea was to catch his attention, she succeeded admirably.

Around the time of the fashion show, Catherine had been casually involved with Rupert Finch, a distinguished fourth-year law student. Tall and handsome, Rupert's subsequent silence about their romance was telling. 'It's not something I'll ever talk about. It's between Kate and me and was a long time ago,' he remarked cryptically in 2006. Shortly afterwards, Catherine and Rupert went their separate ways, clearing the path for William.

From that pivotal moment, William knew he wanted to be more than just friends with Catherine; he was seeking something more meaningful. However, his initial attempts at romance, such as preparing intimate dinners for her, often ended in mishaps. 'When I was trying to impress Kate, I was trying to cook these amazing, fancy dinners and what would happen was I would burn something, something would overspill, something would catch on fire,' he admitted. Catherine, ever the capable presence, would step in to salvage the situation. Humble in his culinary skills, William acknowledged, 'I am the first to admit that I am not an excellent chef.'[24]

In their second academic year, in September 2002, William and Catherine embarked on a new chapter by moving into a student house along with two other undergraduate friends, Fergus Boyd and Olivia Bleasdale. The comfortable maisonette, nestled in the heart of town at Upper Flat, 13a Hope Street, offered a cosy base. Their rental agreement, priced at £400 a week (£100 each), seemed a fair deal for the accommodation, so they signed up.

Landlady Charlotte Smith, recounting the story, admitted she had nearly turned down William and Fergus as tenants, because she was not keen on letting the property to boys. 'We had not allowed boys to rent it in the past due to bad experiences,' she disclosed in an interview with online platform ivillage. However, upon learning that one of the prospective tenants was the future king, she relented. 'It had the reputation for being one of the best flats for comfort in St Andrews,' she noted, justifying her decision.

Reflecting on their first encounter, Mrs Smith shared, 'We arranged to meet Kate Middleton, Fergus and Olivia before they moved in, but we thought we'd better not ask to see Prince William, because we thought his credit rating must be quite good. But he insisted on meeting us.' Catherine's demeanour left a lasting impression. 'She was very friendly,' Mrs Smith recalled. 'She had her younger brother there at the time – I think just visiting – and she was very caring, making sure that he knew what was going on. They came across as a very nice group of people.'

In a television special with chef Mary Berry titled *A Berry Royal Christmas* in December 2019, Catherine revealed, 'In university days [William] used to cook all sorts of meals. Bolognese and things like that.' Their private bliss, however, was soon exposed after a tip-off to a national newspaper. Once the *Mail on Sunday* broke the story, their relationship took on a life of its own, beyond William's control.

Among the student community, it was an open secret that they were a couple. They could often be spotted walking or cycling to lectures, browsing the aisles of the local Safeway supermarket, or spending quiet evenings at home, listening to William's R&B tracks or Fergus's jazz on their music systems. Their routine rarely deviated during the week, except for Wednesday afternoons when they indulged in sports. William, now the university's water polo captain alongside his friend Fergus, dedicated two hours every Thursday night to training in the pool of St Leonards girls' school.

Back then, their relationship remained shrouded in secrecy, but a revealing moment occurred during a dinner party with friends attended by Carly Massy-Birch. It unfolded amidst a spirited drinking game called 'Never Have I Ever', a playful activity where participants disclose their experiences, when perhaps unwittingly Carly exposed William's secret love affair with Catherine, much to the prince's chagrin.[25]

In May 2003, Catherine's father, Michael, attempted to quell speculation when their family home became besieged by reporters. He denied reports of William and Catherine being a couple. 'I spoke to her just a few days ago and can categorically confirm they are no more than just good friends,' he asserted. 'They are together all the time because they are the best of pals, and yes, cameramen are going to get photos of them together. But there's nothing more to it than that.'

He had simply tried to dampen speculation, even jesting about the idea of becoming in-laws to Prince William. Yet, the media remained relentless, convinced of Catherine's significance in William's life, despite her father's well-intentioned attempts to downplay the situation.

It is conceivable that Catherine had not fully disclosed the depth of her friendship with William to her father at this stage. However, the scrutiny from the media persisted, with speculations continuing to swirl. When Catherine celebrated her twenty-first birthday, her parents hosted a lavish champagne party at their expansive family home, followed by a themed dinner in a marquee reminiscent of the 1920s. In a spontaneous gesture, William slipped into the marquee unannounced, their affection for each other unmistakable to all in attendance, further confirming the true nature of their bond.

In a BBC interview marking his own twenty-first birthday in June 2003, William was guarded when it came to discussing his personal life. 'I don't have a steady girlfriend,' he asserted. 'If I fancy a girl and I really like her and she fancies me back, which is rare, I ask her out. But, at the same time, I don't want to put them in an awkward situation, because a lot of people don't quite understand what comes with knowing me.' Lamenting the intrusive speculation that surrounded his relationships, he expressed concern about the impact that dating him might have on these girls.

Their journey was not all smooth sailing. At university, like many young couples, they experienced their first relationship break. When asked about this during their engagement interview with ITV news anchor Tom Bradby in 2010, William explained, 'We were both very young. It was at university, we were sort of both finding ourselves as such and being different characters and stuff, it was very much trying to find our own way and we were growing up.'

The exact timing of this cooling-off period remains unclear, but by the following August, their romance was back on again. Catherine had already become a familiar face at Highgrove and Sandringham, with William whisking her away for weekends at various retreats, including a cottage on the Balmoral Estate. Reflecting on her nerves before meeting William's father, Catherine recalled, 'I was quite nervous about meeting William's father, but he was very, very welcoming, very friendly, it couldn't have gone easier really for me.'

While their friend Fergus opted to remain at Hope Street, William and Catherine moved to Balgove House, a cottage on a private country estate just outside the town centre, for their third year in September 2003. Owned by a distant cousin of William's,

Henry Cheape, the cottage served as their sanctuary for the final two years of undergraduate life. Complete with CCTV cameras, it provided a haven. William and Catherine were now embracing their newfound independence, handling chores like shopping, cooking and entertaining guests together.

These salad days were idyllic, filled with romantic walks and quiet evenings together, shielded from the prying eyes of the press. However, this private bliss was shattered four months after the Mermaids Christmas Ball, when the *Sun* newspaper splashed photographs of them in a romantic embrace on the Swiss ski slopes of Klosters, prompting a furious response from the prince. Yet, despite the media frenzy, their relationship continued to flourish. They immersed themselves in undergraduate life, frequenting local spots like Ma Bells and the West Port Bar and enjoying the annual May Ball festivities. William was adamant about not rushing into marriage, asserting to tabloid journalist Duncan Larcombe, 'Look, I'm only twenty-two, for God's sake,' as he revealed his reluctance to settle down.

Their university journey culminated in May 2005 with both William and Catherine achieving impressive upper second-class honours degrees. As they graduated, surrounded by family and friends, their love was palpable, with exchanged glances capturing the depth of their closeness. Following the ceremony, William introduced Catherine's parents to the Queen, who had attended the ceremony with Prince Philip, marking a significant step forward in their relationship. The couple were now poised to embark on the next chapter of their journey together.[26]

CHAPTER 3

The Waiting Game

Kate makes the grade too.
DAILY MAIL

As potential royal brides go, Catherine appeared to tick all the requisite boxes. By September 2005, she had met the Queen on several social occasions alongside William and received the nod of approval. To onlookers, it appeared their relationship had reached a new level. While Catherine went about her daily life, frequenting shops along the fashionable King's Road in Chelsea before returning to her nearby apartment, media speculation swirled about a royal engagement.

In William's company, she danced at the trendiest clubs and enjoyed the VIP treatment that came with dating a prince. Any intrusive paparazzi were swiftly dealt with by his armed Scotland Yard protection officers, ensuring minimal fuss. It could have turned the heads of some young women, but Catherine was unfazed by the trappings of royalty. Astute and discerning, she remained steadfast, unaffected by the apparent glamour. She loved William for who he was, not his royal rank. Her grounded nature and unaffected demeanour at this time stood as a testa-ment to her resilience and authenticity in the face of intensified media scrutiny.

When her royal boyfriend was not at her side, however, it was a different story. She no longer had William's bodyguards around to watch over her, yet the media harassment intensified. It unnerved her and her family to such an extent that they decided to act. The situation also forced the prince to show his mettle. He did not want the woman he loved to face the unacceptable level of paparazzi intrusion that his late mother had experienced.

After talking it over with Catherine and her parents, he stepped in. Michael and Carole Middleton instructed lawyers to contact national newspaper editors, urging them to give their daughter and her family privacy. They argued forcefully that photographers had followed her almost every day and night since she had left university and according to the code of conduct, they should not be persistently pursuing her. The level of unacceptable intrusion, they said, had reached breaking point.

But with speculation about a possible royal marriage reaching fever pitch, the paparazzi refused to back down. When the *Mail on Sunday*'s diary editor (and later, royal author) Katie Nicholl wrote that palace courtiers had started making 'contingency plans' for a wedding, it added fuel to the flames, heaping even more pressure on William to formalise the relationship. He knew he loved Catherine, but equally he was struggling with committing himself fully to her, as he felt he was too young to wed. Was it, he feared, a case of the right girl at the wrong time? It certainly seemed that way.

While he wrestled with relationship doubts, Catherine had to deal with the daily reality of being a high-profile royal girlfriend. Despite the Palace trying to dampen down tabloid speculation, the articles about a pending wedding kept on coming. When the serious-minded *Independent on Sunday* published an article describing how 'commoner' Catherine, a real princess of the people, could soon be replacing William's mother Diana as 'The People's Princess', it became open season for the tabloids.

'For republicans who prefer to be citizens rather than subjects and who hoped, after Diana's death, that the demise of the monarchy was imminent, it's not the happy-ever-after they envisaged. But it might yet be for William,' read the report in the *Independent on Sunday*. But as one source close to Catherine's family said, 'There is nothing common about her; she is a one-off, a truly remarkable woman.'

The couple had always known that leaving the safe St Andrews' bubble was going to be a challenge. In the run-up to their finals, they had avoided the issue and simply focused on their exams. But the trials that lay ahead of them would test the love they undoubtedly shared to the very limit.

In July 2005, after their graduation ceremony, they flew to Kenya for a romantic holiday at the Lewa Gowns game reserve, owned by the parents of the prince's friend Jecca Craig. The magic was still there, and William and Catherine knew they were both very much in love. As they savoured the stunning landscape from the terrace of the Maasai-owned Il Ngwesi Eco-Lodge, in the Mukogodo Hills, they could not possibly have imagined the dramas on the horizon.

Within weeks of their returning, the media scrums were back. Catherine's lifestyle had become surreal. One day she could be taking tea with the Queen at Windsor Castle or meeting with Prince Charles, the next she was catching a ride on a red London bus trailed by paparazzi. She was not about to let that stop her being with the man she loved, but it was taking its toll on her. It never seemed to wane. William, conscious that the constitutional clock was ticking, was also beginning to feel the pressure of expectation.

That October, Catherine's lawyers, the same ones used by Charles, pleaded with newspaper editors to grant her some respite, claiming she was being hounded relentlessly by paparazzi photographers. November brought a glimmer of hope when William, amidst swirling rumours of their cooling relationship, told one of the All-Blacks rugby players at a Palace reception that their love was still thriving. Then in January 2006, they were photographed publicly kissing during another ski break in the Swiss resort of Klosters. Could their relationship really be on the rocks?

Days later, as Catherine celebrated her twenty-fourth birthday, William set out on his military career by starting his 44-week training as an officer cadet at the Royal Military Academy, Sandhurst. Accompanied by his father Charles, he joined 269 others. Cadets were banned from leaving the camp for the first gruelling five weeks of intensive training. Sleep was scarce. Lieutenant Colonel Roy Parkinson made it clear at a press conference that special treatment was not countenanced, not even for a prince who would one day become Commander in Chief of the British Army, Royal Navy and Royal Air Force. It also meant his contact with Catherine was off limits.

While he was away training, Catherine continued to face mounting unwelcome media pressure. Some newspaper editors, who had previously been largely positive about her, began to label her 'Waity Katie'. It seemed as if the press, almost overnight, had turned on her. Without foundation she was called 'desperate' for waiting so long for William to propose. Some writers even began to question her interests and lifestyle, wondering: 'Exactly what is the point of Kate Middleton?' The barbs stung, but she continued to be resolute, masking her pain.

Catherine had considered working in an art gallery and even

contemplated starting her own business. Media scrutiny was not the only obstacle, the Royal Family and even Queen Elizabeth harboured reservations. There were also 'raised eyebrows' over Catherine's frequent trips to Mustique, a private island in the southern Caribbean.

She continued working for the family business, Party Pieces, resenting the misconception that she was not putting in a shift. She was given her head there and was considering ventures like designing children's wear. In response, she told friends, 'I think I know I've been working very hard for the family business.' The broadsheets, not just the tabloids, were fuelling the 'Kate' narrative, highlighting the story's momentum. Even the hairdresser she used, Richard Ward's upscale hair and beauty salon in Chelsea, was featured in the gossip pages.

Another significant moment came on 17 March 2006, during the Cheltenham Gold Cup race meeting. Camilla, alongside Charles, was scheduled to present the winner's trophy in an official engagement. Royal photographer Mark Stewart spotted Catherine in the crowd and brought it to the attention of a Clarence House press officer.

During the second race, Catherine mysteriously appeared on the balcony of the royal box. There, she joined a gathering that included Camilla's daughter Laura and her fiancé Harry Lopes, Tom Parker Bowles and his then-wife Sara, Zac Goldsmith, Ben Elliot and Thomas van Straubenzee, one of William's closest friends. Catherine, relaxed and conversing casually with Prince Charles, drew everyone's gaze and ignited fresh speculation about an impending royal engagement. 'It was astonishing to see how relaxed Kate was around the heir to the throne,' remarked Mark Stewart. The bookies quickly shortened the odds on a royal engagement.

Media speculation went off the scale when Catherine next appeared at the wedding of Laura Parker Bowles and Harry Lopes on 6 May 2006, at St Cyriac's Church in Lacock, Wiltshire. Her presence alongside William at an occasion attended by the Prince of Wales, Prince Harry and Princess Margaret's daughter, Lady Sarah Chatto, sent the media into overdrive. Surely a proposal was now imminent, the press speculated.

Then, on 15 December, William graduated from Sandhurst, a momentous occasion graced by the presence of Queen Elizabeth, Prince Charles and the Duchess of Cornwall, as well as Catherine's parents. While at Sandhurst, William made a point of retreating to the Middletons' five-bedroom home in the Berkshire village of Bucklebury every Friday evening, finding solace in Catherine's loving arms. His insistence on her presence and that of her parents at the graduation ceremony spoke volumes about the strength of their bond, but was it going to be enough?

Catherine arrived just moments before the Queen and the royal party, who included Prince Philip, Prince Charles and Camilla. All the other guests were pre-seated as Catherine was ushered into her place in the front row accompanied by William's friend Thomas van Straubenzee and two of his godfathers, King Constantine II of Greece and Lord Romsey. The ITV network had hired lip-reading experts, who worked out that Catherine had said, 'I love the uniform, it's so sexy.'

It was William's big day, but the newspapers inevitably focused on Catherine and the significance of her appearance alongside the royals. The *Daily Mail* summed it up best with the headline, 'Kate Makes the Grade Too', while the *Sunday Times* went further a few weeks later, publishing a lengthy article about Catherine under the headline, 'The Girl Who Would be Queen'. It all heaped more pressure on William.

After his Sandhurst graduation in December 2006, William took up his role of a 2nd Lieutenant in the Blues and Royals Regiment, leading an armoured reconnaissance unit and undergoing training in Devon for the next four months. As Catherine approached her twenty-fifth birthday in January 2007, William unexpectedly cancelled plans to attend a New Year gathering at Jordanstone House, arranged by her family in the snowy countryside near Dundee in Scotland. Understandably, Catherine let him know she was disappointed. Instinctively, she sensed that something was wrong.

The day before her birthday, on 9 January 2006, William left to join his regiment at Bovington Barracks in Dorset. The three-hour drive meant they had less time together than expected and the cracks in their relationship began to show. As Valentine's Day approached, William gifted Catherine a Van Cleef & Arpels make-up compact; a classy present, but one that might have felt to her like an empty gesture.

Overwhelmed and unsure about her future, she decided to get a job at the women's fashion chain, Jigsaw, as an Accessories Buyer at their head office in Kew. Again, it felt like a stop-gap move. Why was she putting her life on hold while William figured out his feelings? Only she knew the answer. With all this uncertainty circling, speculation about an impending engagement in the press was the last thing either of them needed. By the time of Catherine's twenty-fifth birthday, it had reached fever pitch. More than fifty press and photographers besieged her Chelsea apartment. She emerged with a smile, sporting a £40 Topshop dress that sold out within hours, but inside she was a mess, shaken by what she was having to cope with.

When William saw the TV footage of the media scrum encircling her, he was appalled. He feared that Catherine was now enduring the same unacceptable intrusion that his mother had faced. Compelled to act, he issued a statement asking the media to back off in the strongest terms. Her parents' lawyers, Harbottle & Lewis, also urged the media to exercise restraint.

This time, it was not simply a few freelancers at Catherine's door, but staff representatives from newspapers and respected news agencies like Associated Press and the Press Association were also present. Multiple TV crews, including one from ITN, joined in. While the BBC refrained from sending a camera crew, they used footage supplied by the agency APTN, who were with the paparazzi. Sky News did the same.

Palace officials took note of the situation, but could do nothing. Catherine's lawyers stopped short of making an official representation. Diana's former personal protection officer Ken Wharfe, however, went public and expressed his serious concerns, stating that Catherine's safety was clearly at risk: 'History appears to be repeating itself, despite claims that lessons have been learned after the loss of Diana. As far as I can see, the warnings have not been heeded.'

Ken even reached out to Carole Middleton, offering to protect Catherine for free until the chaos subsided. Patrick Jephson, Diana's former and only private secretary, echoed Wharfe's sentiments, emphasising the importance of proper ground control. Dickie Arbiter, a former press secretary to Diana, joined in. He cautioned that the intrusive behaviour must cease immediately to prevent another tragedy. Arbiter told the BBC that the press's treatment of Kate Middleton was utterly unreasonable.

The Press Complaints Commission entered the fray. A spokesman reiterated that it was unacceptable to photograph individuals in private places without their consent. Clearly these boundaries had been crossed. Some media commentators pushed back against the chorus of disapproval, suggesting that lawyers were exploiting Catherine's situation to introduce harassment laws through the back door, which could limit the activities of legitimate news photographers.

In the eye of this storm, the Murdoch-owned News International (later, News UK) publishers of the *Sun*, *The Times* and the now-defunct *News of the World*, made a significant decision, announcing they would cease using paparazzi photographs of Catherine after the backlash. With Diana's tragic death still fresh in the memory, no one wanted history to repeat itself.

Post Diana, politicians wanted to be seen to be doing something about the excesses of journalism, especially where the privacy of the young royals and those close to them were concerned. On 6 March 2007, the House of Commons Culture, Media and Sport Select Committee felt compelled to examine the matter of press privacy invasion by calling various experts. However, it was not the details of press regulation that made the front pages, but remarks made by royal photographer Arthur Edwards. During a Q&A with Mr Edwards, the respected newspaper man told MPs that the prince had spoken openly about wanting to get married. 'She's in love with Prince William,' Edwards said. 'I'm sure one day they'll get married. I have talked to him about that and he's made it clear . . . he wants to get married.'

His comments to MPs were splashed across the front page of the London *Evening Standard*, forcing Clarence House to issue a statement, saying bluntly, 'Prince William has no plans to get engaged.' It did not matter what the truth was, this inevitably sparked another media and betting frenzy. Bookmakers William Hill even stopped taking bets on a royal engagement.

In an article in 2008, Adam Helliker, the *Sunday Express* columnist, disclosed that Catherine had privately expressed her desire to be called Catherine instead of Kate. He wrote, 'I hear that in the past few weeks the former accessories buyer has quietly informed friends that she would like to drop the informal "Kate" and in future wishes to be known by her full name: Catherine.'

This request was made through a humorous email to her close friends. It was unclear whether she did not like being called 'Kate' or whether it was all part of a bigger preparation for her formal public role as Prince William's future wife, but it appears that she had a genuine desire to go by her full name. It only added to the speculation.

Inevitably all this led to a flurry of speculation about a potential royal title in the future, but Prince Charles's communications secretary, Paddy Harverson, flatly denied that too. Further reports surfaced, suggesting that Catherine's lack of career options had caused some disquiet among senior royals, including Queen Elizabeth. Media commentators wrote that she should secure full-time employment, ignoring the fact that she had been busy working for her parents' company Party Pieces, preparing catalogues in Bucklebury.

Caught between growing expectations of a future royal role and the lack of official guidance, Catherine found herself between the devil and the deep blue sea. She knew William was in no hurry to propose and while she would obviously have liked him to give her an engagement ring, she was prepared to wait. They were in love after all; but it was a precarious position.

Despite the paparazzi's relentless pursuit, the consensus was that Catherine was handling the media attention well. She largely remained composed, smiling and not overreacting. If she was handed a parking ticket, she reacted with dignity. Not wanting to let herself down, she always tried to look her best before leaving a nightclub, because she knew the paparazzi would be waiting to catch her out. Some lensmen were inevitably cynical in how they viewed her. One unnamed photographer, who often took pictures of her and William leaving London clubs, told the *Guardian* newspaper that she was actively playing their game. 'She dresses for it. She makes a special effort,' he said.[27]

Her one-time boss at Jigsaw, Belle Robinson, who had hired Catherine in 2006 when she first moved to London after graduating from university, portrayed her as down-to-earth and unpretentious. The successful businesswoman, who gave Catherine the use of her luxurious villa on Mustique for private romantic holidays with the prince, highlighted her adaptability and resilience in the face of media attention.

Belle Robinson, in an interview for the London *Evening Standard*, said, 'She [Catherine] sat in the kitchen at lunchtime and chatted with everyone from the van drivers to the accounts' girls. She wasn't precious.' Talking about her pragmatic approach with the media, Belle said, 'There were days when there were TV crews at the end of the drive. We would say, "Listen, do you want to go out the back way?" And she'd say, "To be honest, they're going to hound us until they've got the picture. So why don't I just go, get the picture done, and then they'll leave us alone."'

Belle added, 'I thought she was very mature for a 26-year-old, and I think she's been quite good at neither courting the press nor sticking two fingers in the air at them. I don't think I would have been so polite.'

Catherine got no official support at this time, despite the senior royal rank of her boyfriend. But she showed great maturity in handling the increased media attention. It would undoubtedly stand her in good stead for her future role. Belle and Catherine's working relationship ended when she quit her part-time job, saying she needed 'some time to herself'. There were no hard feelings. Belle witnessed the demands made on Catherine and applauded her strength of character in having to deal with them.

When Catherine and William were together, they maintained a low profile, although they were often photographed on holidays, leaving nightclubs or on the polo field. If any of the paps overstepped the mark, she relied on media lawyer Gerrard Tyrrell to address press harassment issues promptly.

Her love for William remained constant and her confidence grew steadily. It was now, or so she thought, simply a case of playing the waiting game.

CHAPTER 4

Our Way

*At the time I wasn't very happy about it, but actually
it made me a stronger person.*
CATHERINE TALKING ABOUT HER SPLIT FROM WILLIAM

E ven though Catherine was not anticipating an immediate
marriage proposal and engagement ring from William, it
is perhaps understandable that she wanted some form of greater
commitment for their future together. It did not materialise, and it
left her feeling unsettled, particularly as the newspapers were filled
with speculative reports of a pending royal engagement.

Then, seemingly out of the blue, William telephoned to initiate a
split, telling her that he felt they needed 'a bit of space' to 'find our
own way'. In the emotionally charged thirty-minute conversation,
they both acknowledged being on 'different pages'.[28] William
admitted his inability to commit to marriage, deepening Catherine's
sense of disappointment and loss. It was a devastating blow to her,
after all their years of companionship. She also felt let down by
William's decision to handle the situation over the phone rather
than face to face.

It was not the first time William had brought their relationship to an end, but this time it felt different, more definitive. They had parted ways briefly in 2004 during their student days at St Andrews, which William later attributed to their youthfulness. His rationale for the second breakup seemed more perplexing. Had he fallen for the right person, but at the wrong time? Despite their years of intimacy, William felt he was too young to commit to marriage, a sentiment that left Catherine feeling frustrated. Why should she be treated as an afterthought because he could not make up his mind? After all their time together, William was not only her romantic partner; he was also her confidant, closest companion and best friend.

Until now, Catherine had never questioned his intentions. In the wake of the breakup, however, such doubts began to creep in. Had she been led on? Despite the hurt and the emotional turmoil that followed, she resolved to maintain her composure. She shielded her pain from the outside world. As the media swarmed, she sought solace in her mother's embrace.

Carole Middleton acted swiftly and decided that her heart-broken daughter needed a change of scenery. She arranged for them both to escape the media onslaught by flying to Dublin on 3 April 2007 to attend a private art exhibition at the Urban Retreat Gallery, hosted by her friend, Gemma Billington. Amidst a champagne reception, Catherine mingled with local celebrities including the Irish professional footballer Niall Quinn. Afterwards they took in the sights of the city, including a visit to the National Gallery of Ireland. It proved a welcome respite from the tumultuous storm of media scrutiny.

William chose the predictable path, opting for an alcohol-fuelled night at the Mahiki nightclub in Mayfair with his close pals. Still unsure that he had made the right decision, he threw himself into celebrating being single again. 'I'm free!' he shouted as he slipped into his drunken version of the robot dance. He then declared to his friends that they should all 'drink the menu', which they made a good fist of doing.

The gossip columnists had a field day, speculating on why the pair had split. Some claimed that William had 'had his head turned' by another girl, the beautiful socialite Isabella Anstruther-Gough-Calthorpe.[29] It is true that the two had met years before on holiday in Greece and were friends. But despite being single at the time of William and Catherine's break, apparently Isabella was not keen on becoming a royal girlfriend and felt it would limit her career prospects as an actress. This did not cool William's ardour and he reportedly tried to woo Isabella and visited her family home several times. Despite his crush, she decided to let the prince down gently and reportedly rebuffed his advances.

On Catherine's return from Dublin, she felt emboldened, especially when she saw the photographs in the press of her royal ex-boyfriend falling drunk out of nightclubs. She decided she was not going to be seen sitting around moping; what was good for the goose was good for the gander. She turned for support to her old friends, such as Emilia Jardine-Paterson, whom she knew from Marlborough College. Emilia, who later became one of Prince George's godmothers, accompanied Catherine on a holiday to Ibiza during the split. They hit the late-night social circuit with gusto and partied hard long into the night. There were so many paparazzi photos of Catherine leaving nightclubs and other venues, often with her sister Pippa alongside her, the media dubbed them the 'sizzler sisters'.[30]

Catherine also joined an all-female dragon boat racing crew called the Sisterhood for a charity challenge. She was encouraged to join by another loyal friend from Marlborough days, Alicia Fox-Pitt, younger sister of Olympic equestrian star William Fox-Pitt.

Alicia told the press at the time: 'She [Catherine] has been training with us. All being well she will be in the boat. She is a very gifted sportswoman, and we played a lot of sport together at school.' They boasted that they were an 'elite group of female athletes, talented in many ways, toned to perfection with killer looks, on a mission to keep boldly going where no girl has gone before.'

Pippa Middleton, who had just graduated from Edinburgh University, moved into Catherine's Chelsea apartment at the time. With her sister as her wing woman, the attractive singles hit the town. Catherine accepted a slew of invitations and, in public at least, appeared more vibrant and sociable than she had been for some months. One evening she was at luxury jeweller Asprey for the launch of the book *Young Stalin* by Simon Sebag Montefiore, and on another night, she went to a party to promote *Rabbit Fever*, a movie about women obsessed with a brand of vibrator, where she put on a pair of pink silk *Playboy* bunny ears.

The gossip columns were still captivated by her and chronicled her every move, making it difficult for William to put her out of his mind. Being single appeared to suit Catherine. After years as the loyal girlfriend, she was letting her hair down and seemed much freer. Her heels were higher and the outfits she wore were racier. Gone were the frumpy tweeds as she stepped out in a slinky off-the-shoulder top and silky skirt, with a bare midriff and caramel tan. It was even speculated that Catherine started dating again and went out with shipping heir Sir Henry Ropner.[31]

For William, after his initial wave of drunken nights out, it was a different story. As an army officer his free time was restricted and he was holed up in his barracks for most of the summer. Apart from when he was granted leave to carry out a few royal duties and the odd quiet evening out with friends, his commanding officers left him in no doubt that he had to focus on his military commitments.

Seeing photographs of his ex-girlfriend in newspapers and magazines having fun and looking sensational must have been a bitter pill to swallow. If he had not realised it already, he had made the wrong call ending their relationship and soon began having serious second thoughts. He knew too that after the way he had treated Catherine, if he wanted her back, it was not going to be easy. She was no pushover. He had broken her heart once, now he would have to prove that he was worth another chance. He also recognised he would need to give her cast-iron assurances about their future together. But how and when would he get that chance to tell her his true feelings?

He did not have to wait too long, thanks to their mutual friend Sam Waley-Cohen, the amateur jockey who went on to win the Aintree Grand National in 2022. Sam invited them individually to his 'Freakin Naughty' themed fancy dress party at his family's seventeenth-century manor house and the chemistry between William and Catherine did the rest. She arrived dressed as a nurse and William made a beeline for her. They spent the first part of the evening deep in conversation before hitting the dance floor and inevitably they ended up kissing. They could not keep their hands off each other and when friends joked they should get a room, they sloped off together.

Sam Waley-Cohen said later, 'There's an idea that I was like Cupid with a bow and arrow. People love the idea that somebody put them back together, but they put themselves together far more.'[32] There is no doubt, however, that sending them both invitations and the timing of the party certainly helped.

Meanwhile, William and Harry had long wanted to take control of their mother's legacy and the tenth anniversary of her death in

August 2007 gave them that opportunity. The brothers decided on a two-pronged memorial; a charity pop concert at Wembley Stadium held on her birthday, followed by a special service of thanksgiving. It was also a chance for William to acknowledge quietly that Catherine was back in his life.

They decided to play it cool in public at the *Concert for Diana*, not wanting to overheat the media speculation. Catherine sat two rows behind William with her sister Pippa, while William sat alongside his friend Thomas van Straubenzee, with Harry and his girlfriend Chelsy Davy next to him in the front row. But the press took note later, when both William and Catherine joined in the singing of Take That's song 'Back for Good' with gusto. On 31 August, a decade after the princess's death in Paris, her sons jointly paid tribute to her at a memorial service at the Guards' Chapel in Westminster. William and Catherine then enjoyed a romantic holiday together in the Seychelles, where they made a secret pact to marry in the future. They also agreed to keep as low a profile as possible.

After twelve weeks more training, in April 2008 Prince William followed in the footsteps of his father, Prince Charles, his grandfather, Prince Philip, and great-grandfather, King George VI, to qualify as a pilot.[33] The Prince of Wales awarded his son his wings as Royal Air Force pilot at a ceremony held at RAF Cranwell, with the Duchess of Cornwall also in attendance. The press was more interested in the fact that Catherine was his guest at the ceremony, the first time she had appeared with the prince at a major official event since he had graduated from Sandhurst in December 2006, fuelling more speculation that the couple were closer than ever.

William then announced he would spend the next five years working as an RAF Search and Rescue pilot. Some questioned how this would impact his relationship. Would Catherine really wait that long? Sneering reports claimed that Queen Elizabeth and other royals thought Catherine was 'something of a show-off'. The *Daily Mail* claimed his career choice had given Catherine the perfect chance to walk away. 'The truth is that Kate will be 27 in January and in the three years since leaving St Andrews, where she and William first lived together, she has done little to establish herself in a career. Perhaps, with William away in the RAF, she will at last get a proper job,' they concluded.[34]

Privately, William had already given Catherine an assurance that he would commit formally when he felt the time was right. One of the issues was her security, or the lack of it when he was not with her. Even the Royal Protection Department at Scotland Yard, SO14,[35] sought official clarification about their position regarding Catherine. For in early September 2008, the police ensured that an experienced officer was assigned to keep a watchful eye on her when the couple flew to Salzburg, Austria, to attend the wedding of Chiara Hunt to Rupert Evetts. Officially, Catherine would only be assigned her own PPO once they were engaged.

Carole Middleton, meanwhile, was reportedly growing anxious that her daughter's on-off relationship with William had run its course. In 2009, Catherine largely kept out of the public eye, while William carried out solo royal engagements to Australia and New Zealand. In 2010 he was posted to RAF Valley, Anglesey, after completing his search and rescue training. This time, however, Catherine ruled out a long-distance relationship and once he had settled on the base, they decided to find a home nearby where they could live together; another first for a royal couple. They were still not engaged, but the strength and direction of their relationship was not in doubt.

Catherine chose to work remotely as a web designer and photographer for the family's firm, while William carried out his duty and worked on base. They rented Bodorgan Hall for approximately £750 per month, a four-bedroom farmhouse on Lord and Lady Meyrick's Bodorgan Estate with views of Llanddwyn Island and Snowdonia and its own private beach. Surrounded by thick woodland, it is a short walk from the beach, where the couple walked their new cocker-spaniel puppy, Lupo. William would potter around making tea and toast and the locals were protective of them if the paparazzi came snooping.

Catherine did their shopping at the local supermarkets, Waitrose or Morrisons. They kept fit, running on the nearby shingle beach. Both enjoyed a healthy diet, with Catherine doing most of the cooking herself, especially William's favourite supper, roast chicken. She has always been a big fan of smoothies, green ones, with kale, spirulina, matcha, coriander, spinach and blueberries. She is not a vegetarian, but favours meat-free dishes and lentil curry is a popular meal. The couple also love sushi.

Catherine enjoys baking too, particularly cakes, and was an avid follower of recipes by *The Great British Bake Off*'s icon, Mary Berry. Healthy eating is still part of their daily regime today. Catherine is said to favour slow-burn energy oats for breakfast and both are light eaters at lunch, enjoying salads and fruits. She also has healthy snacks and once told a child at Great Ormond Street Hospital that she ate a lot of olives. Given her model figure, her sweet tooth is a surprise to some and apparently she loves sticky toffee pudding for dessert. Neither of them are big drinkers; William favours a pint of cider over beer and Catherine's aperitif of choice is a gin and tonic.[36]

Back then they had no staff apart from a regular cleaner. Their Scotland Yard protection officers slept in the farmhouse's converted outbuildings. Sometimes they would go out for a drink at the local White Eagle pub. William, mindful of his future public role, revelled in this domestic bliss and the privacy afforded them both by the position of the property. He reflected later about their first home together, describing it as an 'immensely special place for us both'. When William was on duty with the RAF, though, and away from their home, Catherine admitted that she had sometimes felt alone.[37] 'It was so isolated, so cut off, I didn't have my family around me, he was doing night shifts.'

Soon that peace and harmony would be over. What lay next for the couple was the real world.

The proposal finally came during a holiday in Kenya. Lake Alice, a hidden gem nestled five miles from the equator and elevated at 11,500 feet, was a sight to behold. Its turquoise waters shimmered against the lush green hills, while the snowy peak of Mount Kenya loomed in the distance. It was a paradise untouched by the hustle and bustle of civilisation, a place where only a select few with the deep pockets to reach it have had the privilege to witness its astounding beauty. For William, the romantic adventurer, it was the perfect setting to ask his beloved Catherine for her hand in marriage.

The couple had been discussing it for a while, so the question was not entirely unexpected. Yet, the moment was still magical. 'I took her up somewhere nice in Kenya and I proposed,' William shared in his engagement interview with ITV's Tom Bradby. The journalist, then a friend of William's, turned to Catherine and asked, 'And he produced a ring there and then?' Catherine's face lit up with a radiant smile as she confirmed, 'Yes.'

William laughed as he recalled his nervousness about carrying the ring in his rucksack for three weeks. He had been terrified of losing it, knowing the trouble he would be in if it disappeared. But his careful planning paid off. 'You hear a lot of horror stories about proposing and things going horribly wrong. It went well and I was really pleased she said yes,' he said with a relieved grin.

William explained, 'It was my mother's engagement ring, so I thought it was quite nice because obviously she's not going to be around to share any of the fun and excitement of it all – this was my way of keeping her close to it all.' It was a touching gesture that had taken Catherine's breath away when William produced the precious ring, consisting of fourteen diamonds surrounding a 12-carat oval blue Ceylon sapphire set in 18-carat white gold, created by then-crown jeweller Garrard & Co for Diana in 1981.

Why had he waited so long to propose? Bradby asked. 'I'm trying to learn from lessons done in the past,' he said. 'I wanted to give her a chance to see in and to back out if she needed to before it all got too much.' His father, Prince Charles, had released a statement earlier that day saying he was 'delighted' to announce the engagement. At last, the marathon courtship of the second-in-line to the throne, more than eight years in all, was over.

'It's obviously nerve-racking,' Catherine added, almost shaking as she said it. She said the Queen had been 'welcoming' to her as was Charles. Now, with the late Princess of Wales's famous blue sapphire ring on her finger, she tried her best to maintain her poise. They looked deeply in love.

After they returned from Kenya, the pair were determined to keep the engagement a secret, so they did not lose control of it all. Even the Queen did not know for over two weeks. 'We're like sort of ducks,' said William. 'Very calm on the surface with little feet going under the water. It's been exciting because we've been talking about it for a long time, so for us it's a real relief and it's nice to be able to tell everybody. Especially for the last two or three weeks – it's been quite difficult not telling anyone, keeping it to ourselves. I was torn between asking Kate's dad first and then the realisation that he

He can't really say no.'[38]

Catherine was going into the marriage with her eyes wide open. She had experienced great highs and deep lows with her prince during the years they had been together and was stronger for it. 'I think if you do go out with someone for quite a long time you do get to know each other very, very well . . . You go through the good times, you go through the bad times, both personally and within a relationship as well,' she told Tom Bradby.

On 30 October, William invited Kate's parents to Birkhall on the Queen's Balmoral Estate. It was there that the prince – knowing his bride-to-be had accepted his proposal – asked Michael Middleton for his daughter's hand in marriage. They were preparing to announce the news on 3 November, once he had told the rest of his family, but the death on the day before of Catherine's ninety-year-old paternal grandfather, Peter, at his home in Hampshire, caused them to delay. Catherine explained that the confusion meant she did not even know if her mother, Carole, knew about the proposal.

On 23 November 2010, the Palace announced the engagement, only hours after William had told the Queen of his plans. She was 'thrilled' as was Prince Charles, who famously joked, 'They've been practising long enough,' before adding he was also 'thrilled, obviously.' The Palace announced that the marriage would take place on Friday, 29 April 2011 at Westminster Abbey. They said the Royal Family would pay for the wedding, but that Catherine's parents would also contribute.

Jamie Lowther-Pinkerton, the former SAS major-turned-courtier, revealed it would be a 'classic' royal wedding with all the pomp and pageantry the world expected of the British. He said the couple, who were 'over the moon', were very much in charge of the arrangements. They wanted it to be *their* wedding and, even though it would take

might say no dawned upon me. So, I thought if I ask Kate first, then he can't really say no.'[38]

Catherine was going into the marriage with her eyes wide open. She had experienced great highs and deep lows with her prince during the years they had been together and was stronger for it. 'I think if you do go out with someone for quite a long time you do get to know each other very, very well . . . You go through the good times, you go through the bad times, both personally and within a relationship as well,' she told Tom Bradby.

On 30 October, William invited Kate's parents to Birkhall on the Queen's Balmoral Estate. It was there that the prince – knowing his bride-to-be had accepted his proposal – asked Michael Middleton for his daughter's hand in marriage. They were preparing to announce the news on 3 November, once he had told the rest of his family, but the death on the day before of Catherine's ninety-year-old paternal grandfather, Peter, at his home in Hampshire, caused them to delay. Catherine explained that the confusion meant she did not even know if her mother, Carole, knew about the proposal.

On 23 November 2010, the Palace announced the engagement, only hours after William had told the Queen of his plans. She was 'thrilled' as was Prince Charles, who famously joked, 'They've been practising long enough,' before adding he was also 'thrilled, obviously.' The Palace announced that the marriage would take place on Friday, 29 April 2011 at Westminster Abbey. They said the Royal Family would pay for the wedding, but that Catherine's parents would also contribute.

Jamie Lowther-Pinkerton, the former SAS major-turned-courtier, revealed it would be a 'classic' royal wedding with all the pomp and pageantry the world expected of the British. He said the couple, who were 'over the moon', were very much in charge of the arrangements. They wanted it to be *their* wedding and, even though it would take place at the high altar in Westminster Abbey, a royal church, it still had the feel of an English parish church. 'This is their day,' Lowther-Pinkerton said. 'They are calling the shots.'

Queen Elizabeth had monitored her grandson's romance from a discreet distance as William and Catherine's relationship had developed. She did not interfere, but she was delighted by his choice. She knew that there was far more at stake than a broken heart if this marriage failed. Indeed, the reputation of the monarchy would be severely dented if there was to be a repetition of the past indiscretions that had wrecked Charles and Diana's marriage. She knew too that the institution and those who worked for it would have to be far better when it came to welcoming and nurturing any newcomers to the Firm.

Princess Diana had repeatedly complained to the Queen personally that she always felt like an outsider. Writing in her book, *The Queen and Di: The Untold Story*, acclaimed author Ingrid Seward revealed how Diana felt particularly 'isolated' while the Royal Family performed their numerous Christmas traditions and rituals. After they opened their presents on Christmas Day, following Diana and Charles's return from their honeymoon, the downward spiral began for the young princess. The problem ran far deeper than feeling sidelined in a few parlour games.

Queen Elizabeth and Prince Philip had stressed the importance to William that Catherine should be well acquainted with the idiosyncrasies of the family and what public life would be like. She wanted to ensure that her future granddaughter-in-law was immersed in royal life and as a result able to cope with what lay ahead once the flag-waving and cheering had stopped. Her Majesty liked the lack of drama that came with Catherine.

'The duchess always appeared to be calm and circumspect. Her Majesty was drawn to her sensible approach when she arrived on the scene,' a former courtier said. 'She found her very polite and good-natured, and she liked the way she interacted with members of the family. She seemed very at ease.' In turn Catherine described William as a 'great teacher'. There is little doubt that he did his best to protect his wife from both the excesses of his family and the distracting commotion, the 'white noise' that seems to come with the Royal Family.

This time the Queen wanted no surprises or mistakes, and she quietly let it be known among the family that they should welcome Catherine with open arms. Prince Philip was relieved William had found such a 'level-headed' girl to marry. According to author Gyles Brandreth, a friend of Philip and his official biographer, the duke had some blunt but sage advice for Catherine: not to believe her own publicity.

He told her never to believe the attention she was about to receive was for her personally, but for what she was supporting, Brandreth said. He also warned her against looking at the camera, like celebrities. 'You are representing the Royal Family. That's all. Don't look at the camera. The Queen never looks at the camera. Never. Look at who you're talking to,' the duke told Catherine.[39]

In return, with Charles's blessing, the Queen promised the couple a two-year 'grace' period from the excesses of public life after the wedding, so that they could enjoy the early years of their marriage, just as she and Prince Philip had done when he was serving as a lieutenant commander in the Royal Navy in Malta.

On 24 February 2011, two months before their wedding was due to take place, Catherine got a taste of real royal life with her first engagement at Trearddur Bay, in Anglesey. Her royal debut was a lifeboat-naming ceremony on the promenade of the quaint Welsh coastal village, and heeding his grandmother's advice, William took the lead. In the crowd, a handful of devoted royal enthusiasts clutched gifts for her, including a rather odd offering, a framed picture of a young William. As she stepped from the Range Rover, Catherine stuck closely to William's side, braving the winter chill and wind with poise.

The media swarm had descended. Overnight police had erected steel barriers to shield the couple from the frenzy and the roughly 2,000 well-wishers watching on. Dressed in a smart, plain coat, one she had been seen in before, Catherine sent a clear message that she intended to be down to earth. William gave a speech and joked, 'I do the talking, she does the fun bit,' before she drew cheers as she poured champagne on the lifeboat, *The Hereford Endeavour*. He was very protective of Catherine throughout, shielding her from any public speaking, which is something she took time to feel comfortable doing.

On her bachelorette party night, Catherine let her hair down. She reportedly dressed up in a figure-hugging bodysuit and carried out an exaggerated impersonation of pop star Cheryl Cole during the soiree. Maid of honour Pippa Middleton is said to have organised the private event at a mutual friend's house, with a minimal guest list. Her university housemate Olivia Beasdale attended, along with Marlborough schoolfriends Alicia Fox-Pitt and Rose Astor.

At the Diamond Jubilee concert two months later, when William met Cheryl Cole, he is said to have told her, 'Did you know you've got a bit of competition?' Kate is said to have confessed that she performed the star's 2009 hit song, 'Fight for This Love'. Cheryl added, 'She even learnt the dance routine and was step-perfect by all accounts, as her sister Pippa and brother James also came over and told me all about it.'[40] A few years after their encounter, Cheryl spoke about Catherine in an interview with *Closer* magazine, saying, 'We had this amazing moment. She's so ordinary! I mean, obviously she isn't because she's a princess, but she's easy to get along with.'

Meanwhile, William celebrated his stag night in what was thought to be a low-key event with about twenty friends. They went clay pigeon shooting before going surfing during a weekend at a Devon mansion named Hartland Abbey.

It was a moment of peace, a lull before the tempest of royal grandeur when the eyes of the world would be upon them both.

CHAPTER 5

Sealed With a Kiss

I am so proud you are my wife.
**PRINCE WILLIAM TO CATHERINE
ON THEIR WEDDING DAY**

In the gothic grandeur of Westminster Abbey, a royal love story for the ages unfolded as Prince William and Kate Middleton were united in holy matrimony, mesmerising a global audience of millions who came together to celebrate on 29 April 2011. London was abuzz with anticipation that spring morning.

Guests from all walks of life started arriving hours before the 11 a.m. service was due to start. The congregation was a tapestry of friendships, families, celebrities and starry-eyed admirers, from John Haley, landlord of the Middleton family's local pub, to the singer Sir Elton John and David and Victoria Beckham.

As she stepped out in public, the bride looked breathtaking in an ivory-and-white-satin wedding dress with lace sleeves and shoulders, designed by Sarah Burton of Alexander McQueen. She topped it off wearing a Cartier tiara, known as the 'Halo Tiara' loaned to her by Queen Elizabeth, and carried a bouquet of lily-of-the-valley, Sweet William, ivy, myrtle and hyacinth. When the Archbishop of Canterbury, Dr Rowan Williams, asked her, 'Catherine Elizabeth, wilt thou have this man to thy wedded husband?' she answered with the barely audible words, 'I will.' Then William placed the gold wedding ring on his bride's finger, and in her marriage vows she promised 'to love and to cherish' her husband but did not agree to obey him. As they walked down the aisle, the candle version of her signature scent, Jo Malone London Orange Blossom Cologne, was lit.

Before the ceremony, ecstatic crowds had gone wild as William's car took him from Clarence House to the Abbey while the bells pealed. William had earlier accepted the title of Duke of Cambridge bestowed upon him by his grandmother the Queen. It meant that when Catherine stepped outside the Abbey, she was no longer a commoner but a royal duchess.

Although Catherine had chosen not to ride to the ceremony in the 1881 Glass Coach, one of the principal State carriages, the newlyweds travelled back to Buckingham Palace for the Queen's luncheon reception in a horse-drawn carriage, the 1902 State Landau coach that also transported Charles and Diana during their 1981 wedding.

'Are you happy?' Catherine asked her husband, as she climbed into the open-topped carriage amidst a cacophony of joyful background noise. 'It was amazing, amazing,' replied the newly ennobled Duke of Cambridge. 'I am so proud you're my wife.' They were totally at one with each other. The Queen agreed. 'It was amazing,' she said as she left the service.

Five horse-drawn carriages transported the royal wedding party to Buckingham Palace, accompanied by numerous well-rehearsed riders on horseback. That did not stop one of the horses from getting spooked and throwing his rider to the ground while the Cambridge newlyweds looked on in shock. Fortunately, no one was injured.

William wore the red tunic of a colonel of the Irish Guards and a Garter Sash, with the wings of the Royal Air Force and the Golden Jubilee medal. He also wore the Garter Star with St George's cross indicating that he is a Knight of the most Noble Order of the Garter. His cap displayed his regiment's motto, *Quis Serabit?*, meaning 'Who shall separate us?' Not one for jewellery, he chose not to wear a wedding ring, like his grandfather Prince Philip. Catherine not only proudly wore his late mother's sapphire and diamond ring, but in keeping with royal tradition her wedding ring was created from a large nugget of Welsh gold, which had been used to make royal wedding bands since 1923.

Inside Buckingham Palace, the wedding party gathered in the Centre Room before emerging onto the famous balcony to greet the massive crowd in The Mall and a wall of noise. One of the more memorable moments for those watching on television was the expression of one of the young bridesmaids, Grace van Cutsem, Prince William's three-year-old goddaughter, who was not amused by the loud cheers and clearly showed this by scowling and covering her ears.

Once out on the balcony, William looked at his wife and asked, 'Are you ready? OK, let's . . . ' He then drew her close and they kissed, not once, but twice, to the delight of the huge crowd, which stretched all the way down to Trafalgar Square. But this was not just a kiss for the cameras; it was true love, and everyone watching knew it, including the estimated two billion glued to their television screens around the world. Everyone present could feel something special was beginning.

Minutes later, there was the traditional flypast of Second World War aircraft – a Lancaster, Spitfire and Hurricane – followed by four Royal Air Force jets flying over the crowd and the Palace in formation, the official climax to the royal wedding celebration.

It was all timed to military precision. The prince and Catherine then went inside to a lunchtime reception for 650 people, hosted by Queen Elizabeth II, which featured an eight-tier wedding cake.

They left about two hours later in an open-topped, dark-blue Aston Martin DB6 with a licence plate reading 'Just Wed', with William at the wheel. The car is one that Charles had owned since 1969 and he had converted in 2008 to run on biofuel made from English wine wastage. The prince had his father's permission to use the classic convertible, but got off to a shaky start and the car lurched forward. Charles later joked about it, saying, 'Yes, because he didn't take the handbrake off.' Fortunately, no great damage was done to Charles's beloved Aston Martin. Finally, as the newlyweds left the Palace, an RAF Search and Rescue Force helicopter took part in an aerial display, after his colleagues had asked if they could pay tribute to the prince by holding a display in his honour.

For the evening reception, Catherine changed into a second dress, which she wore with a bolero, also designed by Burton for McQueen. It, too, was white, but with a strapless neckline and shorter train, better suited to the more relaxed atmosphere of the evening festivities.

William's best man, his brother Harry, was on fine form. In his speech, he said his mother Diana would have been 'proud' to witness the marriage of her son to the 'beautiful' Catherine. His words were heartfelt, as he had grown to love her like a sister. Harry went down the kind and affectionate route with the address, calling William the 'perfect brother'. Wisely, he opted to drop a reference to Catherine's killer legs on the advice of then girlfriend Chelsy Davy, who said it was inappropriate. Instead, Harry referred to William as 'dude' several times during the Buckingham Palace reception.

Described by one guest as 'the most magical party imaginable', the after-party celebration, to which only the couple's inner circle were invited, took place in the Palace's Throne Room, with a live band led by Ellie Goulding, one of their favourite artists. She sang Sir Elton John's hit 'Your Song' as their first dance. 'I did their first dance and like, talk about scary,' Miss Goulding said afterwards. 'I was so nervous, my hands were shaking.' The singer went on to perform several more songs, including her hit single 'Starry Eyed' and a cover version of the Killers' 'Mr Brightside', another on the royal couple's playlist.

The newlyweds had something special for a finale. They stood holding hands in the middle of the dance floor grinning, then suddenly the opening bars of the song 'You're the One That I Want' from the musical *Grease* came booming out. William and Catherine then began dancing around, pointing at each other, and mouthing the words with the style of the lead characters Danny and Sandy. It brought the house down. Guests were then transported home from the party at 3 a.m., leaving the newlyweds as the only guests at the Palace.

After spending their wedding night in the Belgian Suite, the extravagant suite of rooms on the ground floor of the Palace – so-called because it was first decorated for Prince Albert's uncle Leopold I, first King of the Belgians – the young couple emerged next morning looking remarkably fresh. Catherine was in a cobalt, blue-belted dress, topped by a black jacket with three-quarter length sleeves, with black and beige wedge heels and her long hair styled casually, while William wore a navy blazer over a finely striped shirt, chinos and brown shoes.

The pair, who often used the pseudonym Mr and Mrs Smith when checking into a hotel when they were students, looked just like any other young couple heading off for a weekend away, as they emerged from the garden entrance walking together and holding hands. The difference was that the media was there to capture the moment and they were flying off by private helicopter. In an instant, they were gone, but the whirlwind of goodwill they had created was not forgotten. Together, William and Catherine were the Royal Family's new golden couple, ready to take the world by storm.

The pair sent a message of thanks to the nation for their support on the 'most wonderful day of our lives' and Catherine said, with characteristic understatement, 'I am glad the weather held off. We had a great day.'

'Beforehand, I had a lot of time to think about it,' William said in an interview for the 2017 documentary *Diana, Our Mother, Her Life and Legacy*, as he reflected on his mother's absence in the run-up to his wedding. 'When it came to the wedding, I did really feel that she was there,' he added. 'There are times when you look to someone or something for strength, and I very much felt she was there for me.'

Married couples usually jet off on honeymoon straight after their wedding, but William's work schedule with the RAF prevented that. Instead, they spent a weekend privately in the UK. Then they were soon on their way back to Anglesey. Within days, William was again stationed at his Welsh base RAF Valley and involved in two mountain rescues as a search and rescue pilot.

A few weeks later in May, the royal couple did escape on their ten-day honeymoon to the idyllic £5,000-a-night on North Island in the Seychelles. The destination, the most exclusive of the 115 islands on the archipelagic island country, was soon leaked to the press, who largely left them alone. They had arrived on 10 May by private jet at 7.30 a.m., before transferring by helicopter to North Island. The Seychelles government got in on the act, with a spokesman for the Department of Tourism not only confirming the arrival of their famous visitors, but capitalising on it.

'We are obviously delighted that Prince William and his new wife have decided to honeymoon in the Seychelles. We know they will want some peace and quiet and there couldn't be a better place for them to find it, so we will leave them to enjoy themselves throughout their stay.'

There were only eleven luxury villas with 24-hour service at the exclusive tropical resort, including everything from top cuisine to escorted diving, so it was a total escape from the outside world. It also had a special place in their hearts, as four years earlier in 2007, on the nearby island of Desroches, it was where they had rekindled their romance after they had separated, and where they had committed to spending the rest of their lives together. On their return, the couple issued a statement saying how much they had 'thoroughly enjoyed their time together, and they are grateful to the Seychelles government for their assistance in making the honeymoon such a memorable and special ten days'.

Catherine stepped into the royal world with a sun-kissed radiance. Her first engagement as a Royal Family member could not have been bigger – a rendezvous with the US President, Barack Obama, and the First Lady, Michelle Obama. It took place in the same opulent suite of rooms where the Cambridges had spent their first night as a married couple and where the American leader and his wife were staying during their historic US state visit.

The meeting at the Palace on 24 May came after the Obamas had been officially welcomed by Queen Elizabeth at the start of their three-day state visit. Although it was designated as a 'private audience', photographs of the occasion were later released and the Palace did give the media an insight into what happened. Officials revealed that the two couples hit it off immediately and spent a remarkable twenty minutes together, twice the originally allotted time. Catherine's cap-sleeved, caramel-coloured dress by Reiss that she wore for the occasion, which retailed at £175, sold out in a matter of hours of the photographs appearing online.

Prince William spoke to the president about his job as an RAF search and rescue pilot, while Catherine and the US First Lady had what was described by palace aides as some 'typical girly chat' about the royal wedding. Like most women, Mrs Obama wanted to know all about it. It was a baptism of fire in the game of soft power diplomacy. The late Queen, who as host had final sign off on the itinerary, knew that using Catherine in such a high-profile media opportunity so soon after the royal wedding had attracted such global media interest, would inject much-needed glamour and youthfulness into the programme. She was right and the photographs made a splash all around world.

Catherine's schedule, while carefully managed, meant that she hit the ground running with royal engagements coming thick and fast. On 9 June she and her husband carried out their first official public engagement as a married couple, at a charity gala in London for Absolute Return for Kids, also known as ARK. She wore a dusty pink, embellished Jenny Packham gown, accessorised with matching suede shoes by LK Bennett and understated drop earrings. What the new duchess wore, as far as the press were concerned, was just as important if not more than what she did or said. It irritated her. 'I am not a clothes horse,' she complained. She soon realised, however, she would have to get used to it. The media's obsession with her wardrobe went with the job.

They were back on the Palace balcony days later for Trooping the Colour. Then at the end of the month with William at her side, Catherine honoured servicemen and women on Britain's third Armed Forces Day, presenting operational medals to the Irish Guards, including the newly instituted Elizabeth Cross to the families of three servicemen who were killed during the six-month tour of duty in Afghanistan.

From the very beginning of her royal journey, Catherine displayed an unwavering commitment to maintaining a balance between her royal obligations and what she held most dear: a loving marriage and a happy family life. She made it unequivocally clear to her advisors that, while her official duties and charitable work were important, her foremost role was that of a devoted spouse and, when the time arrived, a devoted mother. With a steely determination, Catherine confided that she intended to chart her own course, to avoid spreading herself too thinly. She made a conscious choice from the outset to extend her support to causes that resonated deeply with her and those where she believed her patronage could genuinely transform lives for the better.

Before any announcements were made about her patronages, she discreetly participated in meetings behind closed doors, actively contributing to the formulation of effective strategies to champion the causes closest to her heart. This approach was wholeheartedly backed by William, Charles and the Queen, who were all determined not to overwhelm her, only too aware of the challenges faced by Princess Diana and the impact it had upon her.

In fairness, Catherine, who was a decade older than Diana when she entered the Firm, possessed a greater degree of maturity and wisdom compared to her late mother-in-law. That said, the prospect of royal engagements and interaction with the public remained a daunting challenge for anyone without any prior experience.

Nobody wanted history repeating itself.

CHAPTER 6

First Steps

You know, over the years William has looked after me, he's
treated me very well . . . he is very supportive of me through the
good times and also through the bad times.

CATHERINE, THE PRINCESS OF WALES

Catherine's baptism in the royal world had gone well, but
William continued to watch over her and media commentators noted that she never put a foot wrong. William took the lead
while she observed him in action at close quarters. Catherine was a
fast learner and she needed to be, because her next big test would be
her first overseas visit and it would be full-on. The late Queen knew
that if the people of the Commonwealth realms were to continue
their long-term affiliation to the monarchy and affection for the
Royal Family, they would need to reinforce trust.

With this in mind, the Cambridges set off to Canada for a tour
from 30 June to 8 July 2011. It was a well-trodden path and an
important one. In 1939, George VI and his wife Queen Elizabeth
had toured Canada from coast to coast. The tour was designed to
bolster trans-Atlantic support as war loomed. During a walkabout,
a Boer War veteran asked the Queen Consort, 'Are you Scots or are
you English?' to which she replied, 'I am a Canadian.' The Queen
Mother was always going to be a hard act to follow.

The nine-day royal visit to Canada was a spectacular success and left an indelible mark on the country and the couple. From the grandeur of joining Canada Day celebrations on Parliament Hill in Ottawa to the culinary adventure of preparing lobster soufflé in Montreal; from the adrenaline rush of racing in dragon boats on Prince Edward Island to the serene canoeing experience in the Northwest Territories; and finally, donning cowboy hats and immersing themselves in the fervour of the Calgary Stampede in Alberta. Each day created another spectacle and another headline as the couple charmed their way across the huge country.

Through it all, Catherine demonstrated a remarkable poise. If she was nervous, she did not show it, embracing her role as a roving royal ambassador with ease and naturalness. Side by side with her husband, she navigated the rollercoaster of events with an unflinching composure. There were none of the emotional displays in public that had marked Princess Diana's 1983 Australia debut tour. Her smile remained fixed and her focus unwavering. Catherine embodied the quintessential image of a picture-perfect princess, captivating enthusiastic crowds wherever they went. That said, William made clear he supported her, holding her hand and sharing affectionate hugs in public. They were a team and he wanted to show her and the world that he was there for her.

Despite polls suggesting that nearly half of the citizens of Canada, where the Queen still reigned, felt the monarchy was a relic of a colonial past, the warmth of the welcome the royal couple received seemed to contradict this sentiment. Thousands gathered to witness their arrival in the Canadian capital, Ottawa, and even more lined the route leading to Rideau Hall, the residence of the Governor-General, David Johnston, waving Canadian flags. Some had travelled for hours, a testament to the fascination for the newlyweds.

The crowds were huge and the reception ecstatic. Jasmine Starks, aged fourteen, from Waterloo, Ontario, said, 'We love Kate. She's so down to earth and very beautiful. We got up at four in the morning to watch the royal wedding. I can't wait to see what she's wearing as it's what everyone will be talking about.' Pat Cook, from Hamilton, Ontario, aged sixty-four, said, 'I think William and Kate have really renewed interest in the monarchy in Canada. They seem very in love and Kate has so much self-confidence and will fit right in with the royals. We've been here since nine this morning to get a good spot.'

In the moments leading up to their arrival in Ottawa, the anticipation among the 300 distinguished VIP guests was high. The exclusive gathering comprised military families and individuals deeply involved in charities close to the hearts of the royal couple, and as they took their seats, the military guard of honour added a touch of grandeur to the scene. The official car, bearing the Duke and Duchess of Cambridge, pulled up alongside the red carpet and Canada's prime minister at the time, Stephen Harper, and his wife, Laureen, were there to welcome them.

The air was electric with excitement and a deafening roar of approval erupted from the approximately 10,000-strong crowd as William and Catherine emerged from the vehicle. Catherine, sporting a healthy tan, seemed taken aback by the warmth of the welcome and waved at the jubilant well-wishers. After paying their solemn respects at the war memorial, they embarked on the first of many joint walkabouts.

At first, Catherine looked a little apprehensive for the first time on the visit, but she soon began to relax as she was handed armfuls of flowers and gifts. Each time, she said, 'Thank you so much. We are so delighted to be here.' She later admitted that there was a real art to doing walkabouts. 'Everybody teases me in the family that I spend far too long chatting. I still have to learn a little bit more, and to pick up a few more tips, I suppose.'[41] William himself smiled as one woman told him, 'Canada is so happy you are here,' to which he replied, 'Thank you. That is so kind.'

As she waited for the prince to finish, Catherine chatted with Prime Minister Harper and his wife, Laureen, telling them, 'That was so amazing, there were so many people there . . . We have been on the go since 7.30 a.m. this morning, so it's been a long day.' As the couple got into their official car, her first test over, she leaned into her husband's shoulder and grinned broadly.

Royal aides, led by William's private secretary Jamie Lowther-Pinkerton, were keen to pace the duchess on her first ever tour, so they ensured that the itinerary built in some periods of private time. For a few hours, William and his new bride were alone. Five miles from Ottawa, he rowed her across to the Harrington Lake Estate near Lake Meech, where the prime minister Stephen Harper had a private retreat, to an island where they spent hours together in a 1920s romantic log cabin, complete with a packed picnic.

They even managed to ditch their Scotland Yard bodyguards, who gave them radios and kept a discreet distance so that the young couple could wander off into dense woodland completely alone. 'They took food and drink with them and just disappeared together,' an official explained to the media at the time.

Later, the duchess, wearing a purple Issa jersey dress, created a wave of excitement among the crowd of more than 300,000 at an open-air pop concert on Parliament Hill, Ottawa, as she arrived with William, who was casually dressed in an open-necked shirt. Catherine was by now getting a reputation as a natural royal performer. She looked relaxed and happy as they took their seats in the VIP section, belying her hidden nerves. As the TV panned onto them, showing the couple on the big screen for the crowd, the show's host, CBC radio star Jian Ghomeshi, joked, 'We have to keep introducing you because we like having you here.'

In his speech marking Canada's 144th birthday, William spoke in French and English of Catherine's family ties to Canada. Warming up the crowd, he said Catherine had learned about Canada from her late grandfather, 'who held this country dear to his heart for he trained in Alberta as a young pilot during the Second World War.' He also spoke of his grandmother, Queen Elizabeth II. 'The Queen,' he said, 'has asked me to convey her warmest good wishes to the people of Canada and her happy and abiding memories of being on Parliament Hill with the Duke of Edinburgh one year ago.' He referred to his grandmother as 'the Queen of Canada', since she was Canada's head of state, getting a loud cheer from the crowd.

The royal couple completed their trip to Ottawa, with her being dubbed 'Catherine the Great' by the Canadian media, by visiting veterans at the Canadian War Museum. After planting a tree at Rideau Hall, they paid their respects at the headstone of the Unknown Soldier. Inside, they mingled with 150 veterans of the Second World War, the Korean War and Afghanistan, together with their families.

At every turn, however, Catherine found herself compared to Princess Diana, once a beloved figure in Canada. It was during a visit to the Sainte-Justine University Hospital in Montreal, the nation's largest mother-child centre, that these comparisons came to the fore when she appeared overwhelmed by the experience. William, her rock, touched her arm as they chatted with a shy two-year-old named Jak Kilow in the hospital's playroom. Seated alongside the young patients on small chairs, they both mirrored Diana's empathetic style as they crouched down to their level to ask them questions.

One patient, Laurence Yelle, a brave fourteen-year-old who was battling a brain tumour, said afterwards, 'Kate was so lovely, she spent a lot longer talking to me than I thought she would. She asked me questions about the artwork I was doing and about my illness. It was easier than I thought to talk to her, she was the most normal person.' In this tender moment, the duchess proved that while comparisons to Diana were inevitable, her own innate compassion and humanity shone through as she embraced her own unique legacy as a royal figure.

On 3 July, after spending the night aboard the Canadian frigate HMCS *Montreal*, in which they sailed up the St Lawrence from Montreal to Quebec City, William made his first major speech of the trip on Prince Edward Island. 'It is quite a moment for Catherine and me to be standing here in Atlantic Canada, in front of Province House, where the Canadian Federation was forged,' he said. 'Here, in the crucible of Canadian nationhood, we look forward to meeting many of you. We have both so looked forward to this day and discovering more about your beautiful island.'

Following this, they set off by helicopter for the beautiful Summerside Harbour where there was a spectacular search and rescue demonstration, made extra special by having William at the controls. The backdrop was straight out of one of Catherine's favourite childhood books, *Anne of Green Gables*, which is set there in 1870.

In what would become a feature of their future royal tour style, the couple later rolled up their sleeves and gave the waiting photographers exactly what they had been waiting for. Each climbed into separate boats to join crews in a dragon boat race on Dalvay Lake. This was the new, young and vital Royal Family for all to see. Both gave it their all – William was given a position as a rower, while his wife oversaw steering in her boat. The prince seemed delighted that his team emerged victorious, despite the wet and miserable conditions. Heather Moyse, the Olympic bobsled gold medallist, said, 'Both he and Kate are very competitive.'

From there they flew to Yellowknife, the sparsely populated capital of the Northwest Territories, where they were welcomed with traditional drumming by the Dene people at the Somba K'e Civic Plaza. Members of the Inuktitut and Chipewyan people were among the greeting party too. After a quick change out of formal wear and into casual clothes – Kate wearing an olive, fitted shirt, skin-tight jeans and cream-and-white deck shoes – they took a floatplane to Blachford Lake, a remote Ranger outpost in the vast wilderness of the north, situated right on the edge of the tundra.

Two days later, William and Kate joined the colourful Calgary Stampede, in Alberta, complete with white Stetsons and their best country garb, including jeans and checked shirts. The tour was a spectacular triumph. William agreed: 'I can only say that the experience has exceeded all our expectations.'

The royal couple departed Canada on 8 July and then travelled south to California for a three-day visit to Los Angeles. It was Catherine's first visit to the United States and she would soon be the toast of Hollywood. Their short stay included meeting with British and American entrepreneurs, a polo match in Santa Barbara, a visit to an inner-city school in downtown LA's Skid Row area and a job fair for military veterans. They were also the guests of honour for a reception in the garden of the British consul general, Dame Barbara Hay's residence in Los Angeles. Among the 200 guests were David Beckham and the actor and comedian Stephen Fry.

The highlight, undoubtedly, was the star-studded, black-tie BAFTA Brits to Watch gala at the Belasco Theatre. For that event, Catherine drew gasps of admiration as she walked along the red carpet in a stunning lavender gown by Alexander McQueen, while William looked dapper in a double-breasted tuxedo. Stepping onto the stage amidst Hollywood royalty like Jennifer Lopez, Tom Hanks and Barbra Streisand, Prince William, BAFTA's president, expressed his pride for British success in the competitive entertainment industry. Catherine, however, was the star of the show.

As they prepared to depart the country, the couple and their team breathed a collective sigh of relief. It was a case of mission accomplished. They had all, including William and Catherine, learned invaluable lessons and their household team were now acutely aware that in the duchess they had a burgeoning global star, who needed very careful handling. The genie was out of the bottle and there was no putting it back.

Catherine's arrival on the world stage had ignited an entirely new audience. Young and old alike were fascinated by what she wore, how she enticingly flicks her hair and carries herself. Her wardrobe, a fusion of modern elegance and timeless tradition, showcased her evolving role as a global fashion trendsetter. She also won praise for her deft ability to seamlessly blend high street and haute couture, while also paying diplomatic homage to local designers and choosing just the right colours.

One standout outfit, a royal blue lace dress crafted by the Montreal-born designer Erdem Moralioglu, captured her diplomatic approach; a nod to local talent and a gesture that resonated deeply with the fashion aficionados and designers on both sides of the Atlantic. Her 'Tourdrobe' specials, like the red Catherine Walker coat dress worn on the tour's last day, and her navy blazer, jeans, blouse and slingback wedges ensemble at Yellowknife airport, were also noted. The Palace faced a new challenge: managing the immense demand for the new star they had unveiled.

Everywhere Catherine went from then on the crowds grew larger and so it seemed did her media entourage. On 5 October, it was announced that she had taken on her first charity role when she was named a patron of the Royal Foundation that William and Harry had established as their charity funding vehicle. The Palace said that her position had been approved at a board of trustees meeting on 29 September. A few days later, she stood in for her father-in-law, Prince Charles, at a charity dinner at Clarence House thanking supporters of the charity In Kind Direct.

She was the media focus again when, dressed in an all-black outfit designed by Diane Von Furstenberg adorned with two poppy pins, she took part in her first Remembrance Day as a member of the monarchy, watching from a balcony at the Foreign Office, alongside Camilla, Duchess of Cornwall, and Sophie, Countess of Wessex. Earlier, William and Catherine had announced that they had chosen their permanent home, Apartment 1A at Kensington Palace, the former residence of Princess Margaret, which underwent an £850,000 renovation by the time they moved there in 2013.[42]

Catherine's first Christmas as a member of the Firm was spent at the main house on the Sandringham Estate, but before that the couple visited the London charity Centrepoint, of which the late Princess Diana had been patron and which helps homeless youths.

Catherine had been agonising about what to get the Queen as a gift but eventually decided to prepare her a homemade present, chutney made from her own grandmother's recipe. 'I thought, I'll make her something, which could have gone horribly wrong,' she told ITV in a documentary to mark Her Majesty's ninetieth birthday. 'I was slightly worried about it, but I noticed the next day that it was on the table. I think such a simple gesture went such a long way for me and I've noticed since she's done that on lots of occasions and I think it just shows her thoughtfulness, really, and her care in looking after everybody.'[43]

Catherine's thirtieth birthday marked a second milestone in January 2012, when it was announced she had taken on some new charity patronages, accepting honorary positions as royal patron of East Anglia's Children's Hospices and the Art Room, and patron of Actions on Addiction. She also became a volunteer for the Scout Association.

When Prince William – then referred to as Flight Lieutenant Wales in the RAF – was deployed to the Falkland Islands for a six-week deployment as a Sea King co-pilot, providing search and rescue cover for both the military and civilian population, Catherine soon got the chance to step out among the public on her own. She carried out her first proper solo public engagement on 8 February, when she attended an exhibition at London's National Portrait Gallery, another one of the charities she had chosen to support. It was followed by further engagements in Liverpool on Valentine's Day and then Oxford, also to see the work of her charities. She was now beginning to find her feet.

It was wrapped up in March when she accompanied the Queen on two engagements. The first, along with Camilla, to the London luxury department store Fortnum & Mason, where they met military personnel and staff, viewed the store's product ranges for the Queen's Diamond Jubilee and unveiled a plaque for the regeneration of Piccadilly.

Almost a year after her wedding, Catherine joined the Queen again on 8 March 2012 for the start of the monarch's Diamond Jubilee UK, taking the train to Leicester, where she viewed a student fashion show at De Montfort University, visited Leicester Cathedral and met the crowds of waiting well-wishers. Perfectly turned out as ever, Catherine, who had checked with the Queen's office about the proper dress code for the visit, wore a teal peplum suit by LK Bennett and a pillbox hat by James Lock. Years later, she revealed, 'The most memorable engagement for me, I suppose, was an away day to Leicester. I went without William, so I was rather apprehensive about that.'44

Her first solo military engagement followed on St Patrick's Day when, dressed in green, she went to the Aldershot barracks of the 1st Battalion Irish Guards to hand out shamrocks to officers. The regimental mascot, an Irish wolfhound named Conmael, also got a sprig of greens to his collar. After an eleven-month-long apprenticeship came a highly significant moment in her royal career, the delivery of her first public speech. It came when Catherine addressed volunteers at East Anglia's Children's Hospice in Ipswich. She knew it would not only be all eyes on her that day but all ears too.

Graham Butland, the chief executive, recalled how nervous she was, not just talking to the 200 people in the audience, but knowing the television cameras were showing her performance live. She need not have worried, as she was calm and clear throughout, with no ad-libs. Referring to her absent husband, who was still in the Falklands, she said, 'I am only sorry that William can't be here today; he would love it here.' Afterwards, she told a guest, 'I find doing speeches nerve-racking.'

What she witnessed when she visited the hospice in Cambridgeshire surprised her. 'When I first visited the Hospice in Milton, I had a pre-conceived idea as to what to expect. Far from being a clinical, depressing place for sick children, it was a home. Most importantly, it was a family home, a happy place of stability, support and care. It was a place of fun.'

Days after attending Harry and Meghan's wedding on 19 May 2018, Catherine released a letter to mark the UK's Children's Hospice Week, in which she reaffirmed her wholehearted commitment to children's hospice care. Supporting these seriously ill children and ensuring that they experience precious family moments is vital and she felt a real affiliation to her charity.

In the letter, which was shared on social media, she candidly shared her most cherished moments as a parent. In a few words, she touchingly summed up her warmth. Her words came from her and from the heart. She wrote: 'Spending quality time together is such an important aspect of family life and for me, as a mother, it is the simple family moments like playing outside together that I cherish.'

These words summed up what truly matters to Catherine. For her, it will always be to put family first.

CHAPTER 7

The Cynical Hunt

She's a young woman, not an object.

AURÉLIEN HAMELLE, A FRENCH LAWYER
REPRESENTING WILLIAM AND CATHERINE

Catherine politely refused the offer of an umbrella outside Westminster Abbey as she talked to a group of children, because her hands were already full with a bouquet of flowers. A few moments later, William, in the background, quietly asked one of his palace aides for the umbrella, which he promptly unfurled and then held over his wife as they finished greeting crowds of well-wishers. The optics said it all. A video clip of the moment after the Commonwealth Day Service on 14 March 2022, showing the touching interaction between the couple, went viral.

It was of course a gentlemanly act. But those close to the couple say William views his role as far more than that. He is her champion. He believes that if anyone oversteps the mark regarding Catherine, whoever they are, it is his duty to step in and protect her. This extends to defending his wife against press intrusion too. His stance was clear from the start of their relationship: he would not tolerate the media crossing the line.

William's resolve was tested to the limit during an overseas tour of Malaysia in September 2012, marking the Queen's Diamond Jubilee, when the French magazine *Closer* published intrusive topless photos of Catherine. Despite the importance of the tour, William insisted on an immediate response.

In the British High Commission in Kuala Lumpur, Catherine remained composed when the couple were confronted with news of the impending publication of the photographs. Once they were alone, a maelstrom of emotions must have swirled within them. William then took decisive action. He reached out to both his father, Charles, and Queen Elizabeth, apprising them of his intentions. He then issued a formal statement, denouncing the magazine unequivocally for what he described as a 'grotesque breach of privacy'. He also expressed the couple's profound sense of violation during what they believed should have been an entirely intimate moment.

The overseas tour had started positively. Catherine had successfully delivered her first overseas speech at Hospice Malaysia, emphasising the pivotal role of palliative care in transforming the lives of ailing children. It earned widespread acclaim, particularly when she announced a ground-breaking UK–Malaysian partnership that would provide support to children and their families during times of profound need, hailed as truly life-changing.

Yet the media focus of the tour flipped as the couple grappled with how to react to the intrusion, while being thousands of miles away in a different time zone to Europe, where the story was breaking.

William, overcome with anger and frustration, assessed his legal position. He had the option to sue the photographer from the regional newspaper *La Provence* and the magazine that had originally published the intrusive photographs. Above all, the royal couple wanted to prevent the photographs from being syndicated and published by other media outlets across the world.

They knew the photographs violated their privacy, as they were taken without their consent while they relaxed just days earlier at Chateau d'Autet, the private retreat in Provence belonging to William's second cousin, Viscount Linley (now the Earl of Snowdon). The fact that the images had been captured in direct contravention of privacy laws in France added a layer of complexity to their case. They also recognised they needed to act now if they were to protect their privacy and uphold their rights.

After consulting lawyers, they announced on 14 September that they had launched legal proceedings against the publisher of the French magazine *Closer*. They then did their best to carry on regardless with the tour. Catherine remained assured and composed in public, but it had clearly unsettled William and he became, albeit temporarily, withdrawn and unhelpful in media situations.

It marked their first significant confrontation with the press. The couple were mindful that their action was overshadowing their overseas visit, but it was tough to for them to regain their focus. When they reached their next destination, the Danum Valley deep within the untamed Borneo jungle, they tried to put the topless picture controversy behind them. As they crossed the rain-forest canopy bridge at dusk, they could see the wonders of nature unfold in this mystical, spiritual place. They watched in awe as a giant flying squirrel, a Pteromyini, leapt from tree to tree. An adult orangutan wandered nearby, seemingly oblivious to the humans close to them. However, the media hunger for the story continued unabated.

As they received a briefing at an academic research centre in the Danum Valley, William's then official spokesman, Miguel Head, a well-respected, former Ministry of Defence communications officer, spoke candidly about how the couple were feeling. He did not hold back. William, the aide said, felt so strongly about privacy and harassment that, if necessary, the prince would pursue a criminal prosecution against the photographers who had snooped on his wife.

'It's part of a very long-standing and heartfelt position by the duke and Prince Harry, given their past, to do everything they can to protect themselves. They've always said they don't have an issue with the mainstream media just doing their job, but they have always had an issue with paparazzi whose work intrudes on their privacy,' the senior member of his team said. They were 'livid' and felt 'violated', he added.

The scandal played out in Britain and across Europe, with more photographs being published as every day passed. Even the Irish edition of the British tabloid the *Daily Star* broke ranks and published them. As William and Catherine spent the day smiling and joking while they photographed orangutans and admired exotic flowers 7,000 miles away, the privacy story raged. They did their best to block out the noise. At one point, the young couple were fitted with special harnesses and helmets before being hoisted 138 feet up into a giant *Parashorea tomentella* tree using a simple counterweight pulley system, which had been set by technicians to their combined weight, believed to be about twenty-three stone.

As they waited in their harnesses, the prince looked at his wife and quipped, 'Girls don't have the same wardrobe malfunctions as men do. I hope I don't have any wardrobe malfunctions.' To their great credit, even while they must surely have been seething with anger, the pair could make light of the events in front of the cameras.

Back in the UK, the royal lawyers were working tirelessly to prevent further publication of the photos. Simultaneously, they sought an injunction in a French court and tried to halt the publication of what was being billed as a '26-page photo special' in an Italian magazine.

In France, criminal barrister Aurélien Hamelle was instructed by William and Catherine and argued in the Tribunal de Grande Instance in Nanterre that the snapshots were clearly a 'grotesque breach of privacy'. In a powerful statement, he said of the future Queen of England, Catherine, 'She's a young woman, not an object.' Adding insult to injury, Hamelle argued that the photos were taken within days of the fifteenth anniversary of the death of William's mother Diana, caused largely due to 'the useless, cynical and morbid hunt' by paparazzi to take pictures of her in Paris.

In the court he argued for an injunction to have all copies of the magazine removed from stores and to prevent further distribution of the photos by any means. But the cat was out of the bag. The photos were being sold and published across Europe, with Italian magazine *Chi* going ahead and publishing additional topless photos in a 26-page supplement. The couple's worse nightmare was unfolding and the more they kicked back against the intrusion, the more the fascination with the photos grew.

The female French photographer who took pictures of Catherine sunbathing at the chateau tried to distance herself from the entire affair. Valerie Suau's only work, which she insisted was 'decent', had been published in *La Provence* newspaper the previous weekend with no complaint from the Royal Family. Months later, she would be forced to go before a French magistrate and face the consequences of her actions.

Back in the UK, the Archbishop of York, Dr John Sentamu, for some reason decided to have his say. 'It would be a very sad day when we are taken into the gutter of believing that every woman wants to flaunt her body for all to see,' he said. 'The only time we cannot escape revealing our nakedness is when we are born. Beyond that our culture has said that the only other time should be in the privacy of our homes.'

William was reportedly furious when Donald Trump tweeted, 'Kate Middleton is great – but she shouldn't be sunbathing in the nude – only herself to blame. Who wouldn't take Kate's picture and make lots of money if she does the nude sunbathing thing? Come on Kate!' Once they had instructed their lawyers, William and Catherine did not say any more publicly, but their spokesman repeated that the entire affair had left the duchess feeling 'violated'. William, he said, would go 'all the way' legally.

He did and the level of the couple's anger emerged in a written statement he submitted to the court ahead of the trial in 2017. William wrote, 'My wife and I thought that we could go to France for a few days in a secluded villa owned by a member of my family, and thus enjoy our privacy. We know France and the French, and we know that they are, in principle, respectful of private life, including that of their guests. The clandestine way in which these photographs were taken was particularly shocking to us as it breached our privacy.'

In a significant legal decision, the judge ruled that the paparazzi's intrusive photographs capturing Catherine topless during a private holiday constituted an unwarranted invasion of the royal couple's privacy. In a courtroom in Nanterre, situated west of Paris, *Closer* magazine and two photographers were found guilty and William and Catherine were awarded €100,000 (£91,000) in damages and interest. In addition, the magazine's editor and the CEO of its publisher faced additional penalties of €45,000 each, the maximum allowable under the law.

While the awards were notably substantial by French court standards, they fell considerably short of the €1.5 million that the couple's legal team had initially been seeking. However, the royal couple said they were satisfied that justice had been served for what they described as 'unjustified intrusion'. Paul-Albert Iweins, the lawyer representing *Closer*, argued that the fines were 'exaggerated'.

By the time they arrived on the Solomon Islands and Tuvalu for the last leg of their overseas tour, the mood had changed. William and Catherine were immediately crowned with headdresses of fresh flowers. In an instant, the lingering tension lifted and the couple seemed in a much brighter mood. They first headed for an overnight stay at a remote luxury resort for some much-needed and well-deserved downtime before leaving the next day for their trip to Tuvalu. The nine coral atolls that make up the tiny nation of Tuvalu, where the British Queen is still monarch, boast a population of just 10,000 – but that day it seemed as though most of them had come out to see their future king and queen.

The couple arrived in Tuvalu by plane. Then William was carried through the streets on a 'carriage' with a thatched roof made of leaves, hoisted on the shoulders of twenty-five strapping young islanders. He greeted their hosts by saying, 'Talofa', a traditional Samoan greeting, and described Tuvalu as the highlight of their nine-day Diamond Jubilee tour, which came to an end that day. He told them the whole world remembered the warmth of their welcome for the Queen when she visited in 1982. It was one of the 'iconic images of her reign'.

The couple seemed to cast aside their recent drama at a casual state dinner hosted by the island chief. There, the royal pair tried hula dancing, Polynesian style, in grass skirts and flower crowns, as if they had no worries and with a few vibrant sways of the hips. Over the nine-day tour Catherine had showcased sixteen different looks. The only hiccup was when she wore a sundress she thought was made by a local Tuvalu designer, but was actually by a designer called Ellena Tavioni from the Cook Islands.[45] Still, they had passed their first big test. Now, at last, it was time to head home.

The next big challenge came when they answered Queen Elizabeth's call to champion the London Olympics in 2012, after she launched it with her spectacular James Bond moment for the opening ceremony. Along with Prince Harry and other senior royals, the Cambridges did not disappoint. Catherine attended many events to cheer on Team GB, including tennis and hockey.

One of the most special moments was when the royal couple let themselves go as they celebrated Britain's gold medal cycling success in the Velodrome at Stratford. They could not contain themselves when legendary cyclist Sir Chris Hoy won the sixth gold of his Olympic career and Team GB rode to victory. With Catherine dressed casually in a white Adidas polo shirt and jeans, her hair in a loose ponytail, the pair embraced with delight in front of the crowd. The Royal Family had not previously been known for such public displays of affection yet William and Catherine's unguarded reaction felt spontaneous and natural, setting a new precedent for the future of the monarchy.

CHAPTER 8

Boy George

I was also relieved that he was a happy, healthy boy. Also seeing your husband and seeing pure joy on his face, it's special.

CATHERINE ON THE BIRTH OF HER
FIRST SON, PRINCE GEORGE

Catherine could not contain her laughter when she received a 'Baby on Board' badge during an official visit to Baker Street Tube station alongside Queen Elizabeth and Prince Philip. The occasion marked the 150th anniversary of the London Underground in March 2013 and she was over three months pregnant. Her blossoming baby bump was on full display as she sported a stylish teal coat by designer Malene Birger, much to the delight of the assembled photographers.

After Howard Collins, the CEO of London Underground, presented the lapel badges, typically used on the Tube to encourage passengers to offer their seats to expectant mothers, Catherine held up the badge to show the Queen and quipped, 'I will have to wear it at home!' Collins said later, 'She told me she used to use the Tube on a regular basis. She doesn't travel on the Tube now because of her new role, unfortunately.'[46] She had looked radiant that day, her first significant outing following a debilitating bout of gastroenteritis that had incapacitated her for three weeks.

Three months earlier, William had faced a difficult situation when he was forced to make a flurry of urgent calls to Queen Elizabeth, Prince Charles and Prince Harry to inform them of Catherine's pregnancy, so they knew before it was announced in the press on 3 December 2012. They had wanted to keep the news secret, but fate had other plans when Catherine suffered severe morning sickness while staying at her parents' home in Berkshire. She was immediately transferred to London's King Edward VII's Hospital, favoured by the royals, with William at her side. She had not yet completed her twelfth week.

Following a comprehensive examination by Queen Elizabeth's surgeon-gynaecologists, Alan Farthing and Sir Marcus Setchell, it was decided that Catherine should remain hospitalised while undergoing necessary checks. She remained there for seven days. Later, the duchess shared her reflections on the experience, revealing the inner strength she discovered during her battle with severe morning sickness throughout her pregnancies.

'It was utterly challenging,' Catherine recounted on Giovanna Fletcher's *Happy Mum, Happy Baby* podcast. 'I was unwell, unable to consume the nourishing foods I should have been, and yet, miraculously, my body continued to extract the essential nutrients required to nurture new life. I find that absolutely fascinating.'

She continued, 'It was through this period of *hyperemesis*, this severe morning sickness, that I truly grasped the incredible power of the mind over the body. I had to explore every avenue, employing various techniques, meditation, deep breathing and the like, to navigate through it. There are different degrees of it, mind you. I won't say that William was standing there chanting sweet nothings at me! He wasn't,' she chuckled. 'I didn't even ask him to. It was something I wanted to do for myself. I witnessed the potency of these techniques, particularly hypnobirthing, when I was unwell.

It dawned on me that this was something I could harness, a source of empowerment, especially during labour. It was tremendously influential.'[47]

Catherine went on to discuss with Giovanna Fletcher how her illness impacted her husband, explaining, 'William didn't feel he could do much to help and it's difficult to watch someone you love suffering without the means to alleviate their discomfort.' She then shared her preference for the labour experience, noting, 'Because pregnancy had been so challenging, I actually found labour quite enjoyable . . . because I knew there was an end in sight! But I acknowledge that not everyone has the same experience. Every pregnancy is unique, every birth is unique.'

Her father-in-law Charles, upon hearing the news, expressed his delight, remarking, 'I'm thrilled, marvellous. A very welcome thought of grandfatherhood at my age, if I may say so. That's splendid. And I'm very relieved that my daughter-in-law is recovering, thank goodness.' The Archbishop of Canterbury, who had officiated at the couple's wedding, added his blessings, saying, 'The entire nation will want to join in celebrating this wonderful news.'

It subsequently emerged that the duchess had received treat-ment for an extremely severe form of morning sickness known as *hyperemesis gravidarum* and had been severely dehydrated, necessitating intravenous fluids. She left the hospital with instructions to ensure rest. From then on, she divided her time between her parents' Berkshire estate and Kensington Palace, while William continued his day job as an RAF search-and-rescue pilot in North Wales.

No official due date was given for the birth. All Kensington Palace would repeat was what the duchess had let slip during a public walkabout earlier: that the baby was expected in 'mid-July'. The press was taking no chances. The first photographer's ladder, used to hold a media position, had already been put up at the end of June outside the Lindo Wing of St Mary's Hospital, Paddington, in West London, where it was known the royal baby would be born. The great 'Kate Wait', as it became known, had started.

Soon television crews were arriving there from all over the world. Tape was placed on the ground with the names of TV networks, marking their spots. But there was very little to report as Catherine was not even in the hospital. Television anchors became so bored that they all started interviewing each other.

When their baby son was born on 22 July 2013, the royal couple decided to delay the official announcement for four hours and ten minutes after the delivery. In a mark of a modern Royal Family, Catherine's hairdresser Amanda Cook Tucker was one of the first people to meet the baby, as she was called into the hospital to style the duchess's hair for her post-birth appearance outside the Lindo Wing.

William decided not to make what has become a traditional appearance on the hospital steps to tell the world about his new son and how happy he was. They wanted to do it as a family. Speaking about the moment she and William held little George for the first time, Catherine recalled, 'He was very sweet. And I was also relieved that he was a happy, healthy boy. Also, seeing your husband and seeing pure joy on his face. It's special.'[48]

Giving an insight into why they made the highly anticipated steps appearance with their newborn baby, Catherine explained, 'William and I were really conscious that this was something that everyone was excited about and you know we're hugely grateful for the support that the public had shown us, and actually for us to be able to share that joy and appreciation with the public, I felt was really important. But equally it was coupled with a newborn baby and inexperienced parents, and the uncertainty of what that held, so there were all sorts of mixed emotions.' It was far more difficult than the consummate performers made it look.

At 7.14 p.m. on 23 July, twenty-seven hours after the birth, an exhausted but beaming Catherine emerged through the door with her proud husband, William, who could hardly keep his eyes off his son and heir as he stood by her side. In her arms, Catherine showed off their 8lb 6oz bundle of joy amidst tumultuous cheers from hundreds of well-wishers and hospital staff crammed into every vantage point. Simultaneously, television transmitted the picture-perfect image of the new royal family to the world.

William stood protectively close to his wife and baby, saying, 'It's very special.' Then, seeming to confirm that their son had been born after his due date, the topic of much media speculation, the prince joked to the press, 'I'll remind him of his tardiness. I know how long you've all been standing here, so hopefully the hospital and you guys can all go back to normal now and we can go and look after him.'

Barely visible, a wisp of hair peeping from the £45 merino shawl made by Nottinghamshire firm G.H. Hurt & Son, the royal baby underwent his baptism into the mayhem of the demanding modern media world, which will chronicle his life from the cradle to the grave. After just a few seconds, Catherine, wearing a bespoke cornflower-blue crêpe-de-Chine dress by Jenny Packham, carefully passed their baby boy to her husband, who was looking relaxed in an open-necked blue shirt and casual trousers.

Then, as the cameras whirred, they walked forward to speak to the waiting press, who were hungry for more information about the day-old prince. At this moment the baby, hardly awake, managed to free his hands. The auto-drive cameras clicked and clattered in unison. The following day, the newspapers would record on their front pages, it was as if he had perfected his first royal wave.

'He's got a good pair of lungs, that's for sure. He's a big boy, he's quite heavy,' said William, adding in his typically self-deprecating way, 'He's got her looks, thankfully.' Catherine chipped in, 'No, no, I'm not sure about that.' Asked what colour the boy's hair was, the prince gazed adoringly at his firstborn and the smattering of fair hair on the child's head, before joking, 'He's got way more than me, thank God.' The duchess revealed, too, that her husband was a hands-on father. 'He's done his first nappy already,' she said. When asked how he had got on, William said, 'Good,' and his wife added, 'Very, very good.'

The couple then returned to the hospital briefly before re-emerging with their son strapped into his first 'throne', a Britax baby car seat. As Catherine got into the back of their black Range Rover, William put the seat containing his son and heir into the car for the first time. He let out a mock sigh of relief that he had managed to do this without a hitch. With only their Scotland Yard personal police protection officer accompanying them, William then got in his car and drove his new family off to their temporary Kensington Palace home, the two-bedroomed Nottingham Cottage. It would be their secure sanctuary for the next couple of days since their new home at the Palace, Apartment 1A, was not yet ready.

As William prepared to drive his new family from the hospital, one of the BBC's team of royal reporters, Peter Hunt, asked him whether he would name his son George, in line with the bookmakers' predictions. He laughed and said, 'Wait and see . . . we're still working on a name, so we will have that as soon as we can.'

They had a few names in mind, but given their little boy's status and what he represented, they wanted to be sure their choice met with the monarch's approval. Huge sums of money had been wagered at bookmakers with George being the odds-on favourite at 7/4. Then, at 6.18 p.m. on 24 July, Kensington Palace issued its last royal baby statement. Under the headline, 'The Duke and Duchess of Cambridge Name Their Baby', it read: 'The Duke and Duchess of Cambridge are delighted to announce that they have named their son George Alexander Louis. The baby will be known as His Royal Highness Prince George of Cambridge.'[49] One month later, they debuted their first official royal portrait as a family-of-three, with baby George in his mother's arms.

After Prince George had been introduced to the Queen, she headed to Scotland to start her delayed annual holiday at Balmoral. The royal couple then stayed for the next few weeks with their baby at Catherine's parents' home and after his short period of paternity leave was up, William returned to work as an RAF search and rescue pilot based in Anglesey, leaving Catherine in the care of her mother, Carole.

'For me, Catherine and now little George are my priorities. And Lupo [the couple's family dog],'[50] William said in an interview with CNN anchor and royal correspondent Max Foster about fatherhood. 'I find again it's only been a short period, but a lot of things affect me differently now.'

Her early months of motherhood were a whirlwind for Catherine – exhilarating yet overwhelming. When she spoke at the Royal College for Obstetricians in March 2017, she took the opportunity to disclose her personal struggles despite having a robust support system at home. She acknowledged the immense challenge of motherhood, saying, 'Nothing can truly prepare you for the sheer, overwhelming experience of becoming a mother.'

She spoke of her complex tapestry of joy, exhaustion, love and worry all intertwined. 'Your very essence undergoes a profound transformation overnight. You transition from primarily seeing yourself as an individual to suddenly assuming the mantle of motherhood as your foremost identity. Yet, there exists no rule book, no definitive right or wrong; you simply must navigate this uncharted territory and strive to provide the best care for your family.'

Expressing the full range of emotions that come with mother-hood, she went on, 'While it is essential to celebrate motherhood as a beautiful and rewarding journey, we must also acknowledge the inherent stresses and strains it carries. It is perfectly acceptable not to find it easy.' She had addressed the elephant in the room, the need for new mothers to care for themselves mentally as well as nurturing their newborn babies.

The baptism of Prince George was relatively low-key considering his royal rank. Just three months after his birth, and once the Queen was back from Scotland, he was baptised on 23 October in the tiny Chapel Royal in St James's Palace by the new Archbishop of Canterbury, Justin Welby, with a congregation of twenty-two. It comprised the Queen and Prince Philip, Charles and Camilla, Harry, Catherine's parents Michael and Carole, her brother James and sister Pippa, and the seven godparents and their spouses. William's uncles, the Duke of York and the Earl of Wessex, and his aunt, Princess Anne, were among those who had been left off the list so that the Cambridges could invite close friends.

It was in stark contrast to William's own christening at Buckingham Palace back in 1982. Then, a large crowd had gathered outside the Palace and the Queen Mother appeared on the balcony before the ceremony. This time it was completely private, a closed event. Photographer Jason Bell was invited to take the historic photographs at Clarence House, including one of the monarch and the three direct heirs to the throne, Princes Charles, William and George, the first time such a picture had been taken since 1899, when an eighty-year-old Queen Victoria posed with her direct successors, Edward VII, George V and Edward VIII.

George wore a replica of the christening gown first worn by Queen Victoria's eldest daughter Victoria in 1841. It was created by the late Queen Elizabeth's dresser Angela Kelly, who had been commissioned to make a new gown after the old one, which had been passed down for generations, had been deemed too fragile for further use. The christening took just forty-five minutes and the guests returned for tea at Clarence House, hosted by the proud grandfather, Charles.

George's godparents comprised a mix of schoolfriends, those from William and Catherine's childhood and others who had made a positive impact on their lives. William's long-time aide, Jamie Lowther-Pinkerton, was named one of George's godfathers. Julia Samuel, who had been a close friend of Diana, was named one of George's godmothers. She had founded the charity Child Bereavement UK, which helps youngsters struggling with the loss of a parent or loved one.

The couple also turned to William's childhood friend William van Cutsem and their schoolfriends Emilia Jardine-Patterson and Oliver Baker. Zara Tindall, Princess Anne's daughter and William's first cousin, was asked to be another of George's godmothers and Earl Grosvenor, also a family friend, rounded off the list.

At this time, Catherine relied on her mother to help care for George as she adjusted to motherhood. The young couple had never employed a large domestic staff. Catherine did most of the cooking, although just prior to George's birth they hired Italian housekeeper Antonella Fresolone from Buckingham Palace, where she had spent thirteen years on the staff before applying for the post. The advertisement stated that the position needed somebody with 'discretion, loyalty and reliability'. It stressed that 'attention to detail, together with a flexible and pro-active approach is essential'.

Once George had arrived, Catherine soon realised that her busy public schedule meant she would need extra staff as she juggled parenthood and high-profile royal responsibilities. Palace officials guided the media that the couple would at first rely on their doting grandparents and loving families for hands-on help. 'They have both got families which will care hugely for this baby,' a statement said.

A month after George's birth, they began making enquiries about part-time help. When they still could not find a suitable person, William reached out to his former nanny Jessie Webb, who was then seventy-one, to see if she would consider coming out of retirement for a short time. William believed that Jessie, who had stayed in touch with the prince and attended the royal wedding, would provide the stability and had the experience that was needed to help with the little prince. The appointment was initially part-time to assist the Cambridges as they returned to royal duties, splitting their time between William's posting in Anglesey and Kensington Palace in London. Jessie agreed, but stressed they must find somebody else for the long term.

Six months later, they found the perfect candidate and hired Maria Teresa Turrion Borrallo for the position. Maria, forty-three at the time, wore a traditional 'Norland Nanny' uniform and bowler hat, having been trained at the prestigious childcare institution Norland College in Bath, where she qualified in taekwondo, avoiding paparazzi, anti-terrorism measures and driving in extreme weather, among other practical skills. Maria was born in Madrid and had worked for other high-profile families before joining the Cambridges, where she soon developed a close relationship with her new boss, Catherine. The arrangement meant that she would accompany them and care for George during their forthcoming overseas royal tour to New Zealand and Australia.

While William served out the remainder of his service in the RAF before eventually bowing to the inevitable and quitting operational military service for good in September 2013, Catherine divided her days between her parents' Berkshire home and Kensington Palace. A nursery was established at the Middletons' home so that she could focus on motherhood cushioned by her loving parents. In January 2014, she joined her family on an annual holiday on Mustique, making it George's first overseas trip. Meanwhile, William stayed in the UK to complete an agriculture course at Cambridge University.

Giving some insight into their private life, Catherine penned a foreword for a publication about life as an RAF wife, *Living in the Slipstream*, where she touched on her time in Anglesey and her concern for William in his role. 'I loved my time in Anglesey, but I can't pretend I didn't feel anxious when William was flying in challenging conditions. He loved it and I felt incredibly proud of him.'

That year Catherine received an unexpected accolade when the influential American magazine *Time* listed her in their 100 Most Influential People list in 2013. Famous for its covers featuring Albert Einstein (*Time*'s Person of the Century in 1999), Martin Luther King Jr, Steve Jobs and Barack Obama, the editorial on Catherine read: 'In an age of celebrity breakdown and public self-destruction, the Middleton family's ethos of betterment by effort and respect for others provides a tonic. Catherine's choice of husband and calm, conservative-with-a-small-c and careful progression through the rituals of public life prove this.'

The publication continued, 'The Duchess of Cambridge is an independent woman in this generation, stepping into a difficult role with grace and a cool head, and she is doing it in her own quiet way. Her ability to remain dignified under the constant spotlight, whilst continuing her work with charities and representing the Royal Family, makes her one of the most influential figures today.'[51]

It was high praise indeed and signalled a time to come that would demand a stoic acceptance of her role, one where only authenticity would prevail.

CHAPTER 9

New Royal Family

It is fantastic having a lovely little family and I am so thrilled.
WILLIAM'S COMMENTS FOLLOWING THE
BIRTH OF PRINCESS CHARLOTTE IN APRIL 2015

There was a tremendous amount riding on their first overseas visit as a family to New Zealand and Australia. The three-week tour was also to be eight-month-old Prince George's first public appearance since his christening in October 2013 and the anticipation from press and public was palpable. Local and international press could not get enough of it. Billed as the most significant royal tour for a generation, it was no wonder the principles themselves were a little apprehensive. 'The duchess really didn't know what to expect in terms of the size of the crowds. It was daunting to the say the least,' one ex-household staff member recalled.

On 7 April 2014, New Zealand's prime minister John Key welcomed William and Catherine at the foot of the aircraft steps in Wellington. Catherine looked stunning in a scarlet Catherine Walker coat and matching pillbox hat by Gina Foster, accessorised with a diamond brooch in the shape of New Zealand's national symbol, the silver fern, loaned to her by Queen Elizabeth.

Two days later, it was George who was the star attraction at a baby group held in his honour at Government House, the official residence of Governor-General Sir Jerry Mateparae and his wife, Lady Janine. The event had been arranged by a parent support group, Plunket, and the babies chosen to play with George were born within a few weeks of him, their ten families including a single mother and a gay couple.

The idea behind the event was to give William and Catherine the opportunity to introduce George to the world in a less formal way than usual. Dressed in blue dungaree shorts with a ship on the front, a white shirt and soft, blue pre-walking shoes, he showed he was a lively youngster, waving his arms and kicking his legs in excitement as his mother frequently shifted him from hip to hip. He clearly wanted to play with the others, so Catherine set him down upon the soft carpet. In an instant, George was off, embarking on a miniature journey of exploration.

The young prince, whose first two bottom teeth had recently popped through, played happily with the other babies, crawling on the blue, patterned carpet of the Blandor Room, which was full of toys, including building bricks and a xylophone. He did not seem worried about taking some of them for himself either. 'Quite a bruiser,' one onlooker remarked, as George, one of the bigger children, relieved another child of their toys.

Catherine, wearing a Tory Burch dress, occasionally wiped dribble from George's chin, as William chatted to some of the other parents. 'It's madness – there are babies everywhere!' he said. At one point the duchess pulled George to his feet and bounced him up and down. The photographers on the pool position were thrilled. The next day he was dubbed 'Gorgeous George' by the local papers in New Zealand.

Some compared the photographs of George crawling to those taken of William thirty-one years earlier in New Zealand. There was a distinct difference, of course. The pictures of baby William were of him alone, with no interaction with other children. Access was restricted and there was not a member of the public in sight. Sending a clear message, William and Catherine highlighted that George will be a monarch of a very different time.

In Sydney, Australia, George's cameo appearance was at the Taronga Zoo on 20 April, where the royal couple went to unveil a new enclosure named in his honour: the Prince George Bilby Exhibit. He even came up close to the reluctant bilby, a rabbit-like marsupial, which was named after him. Catherine and William warned keeper Paul Davies about their son's iron-like grip when he tried to grab one of the unfortunate creature's ears. Each parent took turns to support George as he stood up and held onto a fence that surrounded the marsupial's pen. He was only interested in the real thing, however, because when Catherine gave him a stuffed-toy replica of a bilby, he threw it to the floor, much to the delight of the crowds.

Local TV networks and commentators could not get enough of the young prince; even the republicans were impressed. Shelly Horton, on Australia's top breakfast show *Sunrise* on the Seven Network, said live on air, 'I think he's a republican slayer. He's just so cute and William and Kate are such a lovely couple.'

The New Zealand and Australian visits gave William a chance to showcase his own brand of royalty, a new style for a new generation. The huge crowds who came out to see the young family were testament to that. The speculation before the visit had been about a comparison with the successful Charles and Diana tour of 1983. Would Catherine live up to Diana and her style? Would the crowds be smaller? As soon as William and Catherine arrived in Sydney, the comparisons just stopped. It was a watershed moment. The crowds were packed with youngsters, enthusiastically greeting this new royal family. A new generation of Australians clearly wanted to keep the monarchy. Figures showed that more than 60 per cent of younger Australians wanted William and Catherine as a future King and Queen.

William, supported by Catherine, showed the world that he had his own way of doing things; a curious hybrid of formality and more populist, photo-led events. He wanted to carve out a unique style that combined his own passions with the traditions of the royal system. The Antipodean tour showed the prince's heartfelt interest in the conservation of endangered species and the planet. His support for the military at home and in Common-wealth realms was also key, as was the couple's endorsement of their own charitable patronages, such as Catherine's for children's hospices.

William chose not to give any TV interviews on this trip, relying solely on rehearsed speeches to express his thanks and views. The formal 'tiara moments' – glamorous events with Catherine decked out in diamonds while meeting the great and the good of a country – were also subtly avoided. The so-called 'Kate effect' in terms of fashion was once again a big winner. She had twenty-three different looks in the eighteen days they were on tour, but she had to find a happy balance, looking cool but elegant in a country where shorts and T-shirts were the norm. Catherine turned to Australian brand Zimmermann, with its bohemian-luxe dresses, using a trip to Manly Beach in Sydney, where the couple visited a children's hospice, to showcase the outfit.

The new royal family inspired the leading Australian television networks to broadcast live coverage for two hours in the afternoon and it was wall-to-wall coverage on the popular morning shows. But if the monarchy was to remain relevant in a modern, vibrant, cosmopolitan country like Australia, the royals would need to be a regular presence, not just a glamorous roadshow every seven or so years.

In June, William and Catherine joined Queen Elizabeth and other members of the Royal Family to mark the 70th anniversary of D-Day in Normandy, France. They sat with the French president François Hollande at the ceremony of remembrance for the 100th anniversary of the outbreak of the First World War. They also met with veterans and Catherine proved a big hit with one of them, Arthur Jones, who asked her, 'Is it OK to kiss a princess?' Laughing, she replied, 'Of course it is.'

They capped off a successful year overseas with a whistlestop visit to New York, where they spent time with the de Blasios, the Clintons and Beyoncé. The royal couple were greeted by crowds of fans and heavy US State Department security at the Carlyle Hotel, where they stayed for the duration of their trip. At a fundraising dinner, they collected $2 million for their foundation, as well as visiting a children's centre in Harlem. On a day trip to Washington, D.C., William also met with President Obama.

Inevitably Catherine was compared to Diana in a country that had afforded iconic status to the late princess. But once again Catherine showed her steely side. She was going to do things her own way and the press soon latched onto that, while initially at least focusing on her fashion.

The American writer and activist Chirlane McCray, also the estranged wife of former New York City mayor Bill de Blasio, said, 'Kate Middleton is great. I mean, what can you say? She's got dignity, she's elegant, and she's engaging. She's just what you want in a public figure.' The former U.S. First Lady and Secretary of State Hillary Clinton went even further: 'I'm a great admirer of hers. I think she carries herself with such dignity and poise in the public spotlight.'[52]

There was no stopping the couple and their growing popularity on the world stage, but as parents in the public eye, William and

Catherine believe there is a clear dividing line between public and private life. Although they appreciate their royal position means they need to allow some access to the media, there were only rare occasions when they would allow the press to photograph their son.

In October, William acted decisively after he accused a paparazzo of 'pursuing' George when he was taken out in public parks with his nanny, Maria Teresa Turrion Borrallo. Kensington Palace said the royal couple had taken legal steps to ask that an individual cease harassing and following both Prince George and his nanny as they went about their ordinary daily lives. William was determined that what had happened to his late mother would never happen to his family. For William and Catherine, their son's safety was a red line they were not prepared to let anyone cross.

On George's birthday, 21 July 2014, they issued two new pictures of him taken by the Press Association's royal photographer John Stillwell. In a statement, the duke and duchess thanked everyone for their 'warm and generous good wishes'.

For an official Christmas photograph, they turned to a member of the Royal Household to take three official photographs of George and of course pass copyright on to them. The pictures, taken by Prince Harry's private secretary Ed Lane Fox, who has also worked as a freelance photographer, were taken in late November in Kensington Palace with the prince sitting on a step. Starved of new pictures of the popular little Prince of Cuteness, the press lapped them up. He bore a striking resemblance to Catherine when she was a child, with delightful chubby cheeks, dark eyes and heavy brows.

The couple sent an important message by issuing these photographs; when it came to their son and his image, they were in control. In the past, famous or trusted royal photographers like Tim

Graham, a favourite with Charles and Diana when their children were young, had been asked to take such intimate royal photographs. But whatever the reasoning behind their choice, it undoubtedly paid off. The photos were relaxed and full of character, reflecting the fact they were taken by someone George already knew.

It was a policy, however, that would backfire spectacularly a decade later in 2024 when it emerged that at least two photographs taken by William and Catherine and issued as official photographs by Kensington Palace had been digitally manipulated by her. Obviously, the row over the doctored Mother's Day photo was blown out of proportion, but the fact that it became headline news around the world shows the power of the Royal Family. In fairness, the couple were simply trying to quell the online noise and take control of the narrative around them. William, shaped by his disdain for the press, a sentiment he has never voiced explicitly but has demonstrated through his actions, wanted to protect his family from the media's invasive gaze during his wife's undisclosed illness.

The constant speculation and intrusion into his life, from his parents' marriage to his own relationship with Catherine, underscores the media's power to shape public perception. William understands the critical role the press plays in maintaining the monarchy's relevance, but it is a delicate balance. Diana, Princess of Wales, was adept at managing the media, using her image and reputation to garner goodwill. But the intense scrutiny also had its many downsides.

On 8 September 2014, on William's instruction, Kensington Palace officials suddenly announced that Catherine was expecting the couple's second child in the spring. Once again, their hand had been forced into releasing a statement. As with her first pregnancy, Catherine had been struck by a severe bout of morning sickness.

William admitted it had been a tricky time, 'but obviously we are basically thrilled'. His ad-lib response came as he left an official engagement in Oxford. As he climbed into a waiting car, he added, 'It's great news but early days. We're hoping things settle down and she feels a bit better. I've got to get back and look after her now.' Catherine had been expected to join William at the engagement at Oxford University on that day, but had to pull out on the advice of her doctor. This meant that she was unable to carry out public engagements planned for the foreseeable future, including a solo overseas visit to Malta due to take place later in September, which the prince carried out in her place.

Six months later, in March 2015, William became an air ambulance helicopter pilot and the first future King of the United Kingdom to receive a PAYE – that is, taxed – salary (outside of military service pay). He took a job with Bond Air Services and contracted to undergo job-specific training before he flew missions. It was something he was desperate to do. The prince made no secret of the fact that he loved flying helicopters and leaving his job as a Royal Air Force search and rescue pilot in September 2013 had been a real wrench.

During his seven years flying Sea Kings, William had carried out more than 150 missions and completed more than 1,300 flying hours. The job had given him a freedom, a sense of normality, and a reason to be other than his predestined duty to reign one day. His new day job would be to pilot the air ambulance to emergencies across Bedfordshire, Cambridgeshire, Norfolk and Suffolk. In his new role, William was paid about £40,000 a year, but decided to donate his after-tax salary to charity. Meanwhile, Catherine based herself at Anmer Hall, situated on the edge of the Sandringham Estate, overseeing the renovation work at their ten-bedroom Georgian country home, given to them by the Queen.

The Palace made it quite clear about the birth of the Cambridges' second child: this time there would be no camping outside the hospital by photographers, reporters and broadcasters. The arrangements would be a more organised affair. There would be accredited spaces, order and most of all, an agreement that the penned-off 'media zone' opposite the famous Lindo Wing door would not become active until after they had announced Catherine had gone into labour, and crucially, that she was inside the hospital.

In exchange for their cooperation, the media would not only be designated, but the Palace would issue reporters with a two-minute warning that Catherine was inside the hospital before it was made public. In addition, the press would get half an hour's warning that she would be coming out with the baby.

Obstetrician Guy Thorpe-Beeston led Catherine's medical team alongside Alan Farthing, the Queen's Surgeon Gynaecologist, who assisted on the birth of George.[53] Catherine, who again used hypnobirthing in her labour, gave birth to a baby girl at 8.34 a.m. on Saturday, 2 May 2015, weighing 8lb 3oz. William gave the press and the public as much media coverage as he was prepared to do, including taking George to the hospital to see his sister in front of the cameras.

The slightly bemused boy melted hearts with his wave to the crowd, earning a kiss from his father on the way in. Dressed all in blue, like his son, William told him, 'Good boy,' as he carried him inside to meet his baby sister. After meeting her, he was taken back to Kensington Palace privately, this time away from the media. Then the real show began with William, Catherine and the little baby appearing on the steps of the hospital. It was an incredible feat for a mother who had given birth only hours earlier.

Catherine proudly showed off the yet unnamed Charlotte to the patient crowd, as the baby slept right through her big moment.

'She's fast asleep,' said the duchess to her husband. William told the waiting press that he and his wife were 'very, very pleased'. 'It's very special having a new little girl,' said Catherine later. 'I feel very, very lucky that George has got a little sister.'

Catherine was revitalised after her hairdresser, Amanda Cook Tucker, had once again snuck into the hospital to give her hair a quick blow dry. As his wife approached the hospital steps, William told her, 'Be careful.' Once she had safely negotiated them, Catherine said, 'This is nice. Lots of people out there. Look up there on the top.' Then, gazing at her daughter, she asked him, 'Do you think she's cold?' William replied, 'No, she's fine, she's good.'

The duchess had undergone an exhausting day, which had started with her admission to hospital at 6 a.m., and the couple were keen to get back to Kensington Palace away from the press. William then strapped the new baby in her car seat, before taking the wheel to drive his family home. He had already sent his brother Harry a snap of the new baby. Queen Elizabeth was one of the first members of the family to meet her, as Catherine let on. 'The Queen was really thrilled that we'd had a little girl, and when we came back here to Kensington, she was one of her first visitors,' she said. Prince Charles was touched by the nod to his name, too.

After the arrival of their second baby, William and Catherine indicated they would switch their main residence to Anmer Hall, Norfolk, as he focused on his family and his new flying career in East Anglia. The house was the perfect place to raise their young children away from prying eyes. It had undergone a £1.5 million refurbishment in preparation for their arrival, paid for from private funds.

Catherine spent time with the Queen at Balmoral during the summer, but was keen to get back to work after her brief maternity leave was up. Sporting a new hairstyle, she carried out her first solo public engagement promoting mental health in children at the Anna Freud Centre in September. In recognition of her service to the Crown, Her Majesty bolstered Catherine's confidence by bestowing the Royal Family order of Queen Elizabeth II, the highest honour she could give to a female member of the family.

Catherine was soon completing up to three engagements a week and simultaneously caring for her two small children. In December, when the duchess was photographed looking a little tired while out shopping, the *Daily Mail* writer Sarah Vine criticised those around her for not supporting Catherine enough. She was 'deep in the baby tunnel'.

She wrote: 'With no fewer than three official engagements, including a formal diplomatic reception at Buckingham Palace, a charity day in the City of London and a visit to an addiction centre in Warminster. Events at which Kate is under the spotlight to a much greater extent than her husband – she is now fully immersed in the juggling act that is resuming royal duties whilst being a hands-on mother. These events are draining enough – all that constant good cheer, all that being introduced to people you're supposed to know but can't for the life of you remember the names of – without having to cope with two small children.[54]

It sparked a backlash, with many criticising the reporter for the snarky tone of the article, saying it perpetuated sexist ideals that made women feel self-conscious.

In reality, Catherine embodies the essence of the contemporary woman, seamlessly blending tradition and modernity. Her life, marked by public duties and private moments, is a testament to the balance that many seek. Yes, she has the support of a household staff, a feature of her royal position, but the way she navigates her roles as a mother and a royal princess with such poise has made her a figure of admiration to many others, enhancing her relatability.

The couple posed as a family for pre-arranged photos after a snowball fight during a ski break in the French Alps, before embarking in April on an ambitious seven-day tour of India and Bhutan. It was their first official tour together for two years and less than twelve months after Charlotte's birth. What unfolded was spectacular, with incredible images of the pair, particularly in the magical Eastern Himalayan kingdom.

Media focus again switched away from what they were doing there to what Catherine looked like and the outfits she was wearing. The middle-market daily newspapers lapped it all up, noting that she wore eighteen different outfits in their six-day visit. She was not the first royal to experience such shallow reporting, and will not be the last, but it began to irritate her. At the outset of the visit, Catherine was dubbed 'Duchess of Style' with the *Hindustan Times* giving her the seal of approval for the fashion fraternity. As the tour went on, however, for the first time she experienced some unjustified negative coverage.

'Princess Diana had her shortcomings, but she always understood perfectly that the public expected glamour and she never let them down, promoting British designers brilliantly. Kate has turned into the Duchess of Drab,' broadcaster and writer Janet Street-Porter wrote in a mean-spirited article.[55] 'But by far, the worst dress on display so far, must be Alexander McQueen. Excuse me – what was that?', novelist and columnist Shobhaa De wrote about Catherine's choice of outfits for the visit, complaining that her clothes looked 'wishy-washy' and 'boring'.

Glamour magazine's writer Sophia Chabbott was having none of it. 'When it comes to fashion, Kate Middleton has a formula – A-lines, jewel tones, smart pumps – and it works like magic. But the Duchess veered from her tried-and-true wardrobe staples on a royal tour of India, and you've *never* seen her like this before. Kate swapped the fit-and-flare dresses that she loves so much in navy for similar silhouettes in riotous prints inspired by the famously bright pink, orange and purple sunsets of India. She echoed the look of saris with draped evening dresses with beading, others with sheer insets.'

Bhutan's Dragon King Jigme Khesar Namgyel Wangchuck and Queen Jetsun Pema were delighted to host the Cambridges and dubbed the couple 'William and Kate of the Orient' during their two-day visit to the last Buddhist kingdom on the planet. Wearing a beautiful, handwoven Bhutanese-inspired outfit, Catherine showed off her prowess at archery, the national sport, as well as throwing a dart while playing the traditional game of Khuru at the Changlimithang Archery Ground.

A tour highlight came when they took part in a ceremony to welcome 'honoured guests', known as a Chipdrel, which was one of the most exotic royal entrances ever seen on any overseas tour. The couple were preceded by dozens of dancers in colourful national dress, along with monks and lay persons bearing musical instruments such as trumpets, cymbals, drums and religious objects, flags and incense. They entered the Thimpu Dzong, the ancient fortress overlooking the capital, to the sounds of Buddhist chanting. The pair were told that the Bhutanese believe the first such ceremony was performed to welcome the Buddha himself when he returned to Earth from heaven on the day that is observed today as the 'Descending Day of Lord Buddha'.

On the route back, the royal couple flew to Agra, India, where they evoked memories of Princess Diana, who had famously sat on a bench alone during a visit to the Taj Mahal, shortly before her marriage breakup in 1992. In a move that was surely not lost on anyone, they sat together on the bench with the greatest monument to love as the backdrop.

The tour had, once again, been a success, but it was significant for being the first time some of the columnists had begun to turn on Catherine. Until then, any criticism had been limited to the odd academic or writer swiping at her for being work-shy.[56] The criticism had irked her, but she kept a dignified silence.

CHAPTER 10

We Five

Family is not just an important thing. It's everything.
CATHERINE, THE PRINCESS OF WALES

In September 2016, for their second official visit to Canada, William and Catherine made a groundbreaking decision to bring their young children along with them, allowing the world to witness their charming family dynamics in action. In PR terms, the move to take George and Charlotte with them was a masterstroke and truly captured the public's imagination. It marked a significant milestone too, as it was the first overseas tour where the entire family of four had made appearances together.

After their arrival in Victoria, British Columbia, the royal couple were a big hit visiting the country's indigenous communities at the Great Bear Rainforest and the Haida Heritage Centre, learning about the rich First Nations cultures and traditions. They enjoyed local food and wines during their visit to the 'Taste of British Columbia' event, showcasing local cuisine, and went kayaking, fishing and on a scenic seaplane ride. They also travelled to the Yukon, where they took part in various outdoor adventures.

Pictorially, the highlight of the visit was a special tea party in the grounds of Government House, the official residence of the Lieutenant Governor of British Columbia, Judith Guichon. She hosted a children's garden party for military personnel and their families, where Prince George and Princess Charlotte were the star attractions. The young royals were photographed playing with children of the Canadian military personnel at a rare joint appearance during an official event.

The residence was transformed into a children's playground that included a petting zoo and miniature ponies. Balloons were clearly the way to the sixteen-month-old princess's heart, as Charlotte's first public utterance was the word 'pop'. William could be heard saying, 'Are we going to go pop?' to his daughter, before asking her, 'Would you like a balloon, Charlotte?' The young girl made everyone laugh when she tried to lift a huge balloon archway that led to the petting zoo.

It was a public relations triumph that bore echoes of history. In the wake of the 1936 abdication crisis, King George VI, along with his wife Queen Elizabeth and their two daughters, Elizabeth and Margaret, often referred to themselves as 'We Four' and photographs of them together were regularly released to the press to increase the popularity of the monarchy. The move helped to reshape the Royal Family's brand and to rebuild public trust. Recognising the importance of the visit, especially as Canada celebrated its 150th anniversary, William and Catherine adopted a similar approach. After all, their children were the living embodiment of the royal future and the photocall helped to connect them with Canadians, strengthening the bonds with royalty.

The *Vancouver Sun* agreed and an editorial on 1 October 2016 described the visit as a 'splendid drop-in', concluding: 'All in all it's been good fun, good-natured and has encouraged the setting aside of differences . . . the departing royals will be welcome again. Probably sooner rather than later.'

Catherine was now ready to sculpt her own path. On 11 October 2016, she took another important step in her royal career by going on her first solo overseas official visit to the Netherlands, five years after marrying William. It proved a brilliant move and she was heralded by the Dutch press as a secret weapon for UK diplomacy.

It was a testament to Queen Elizabeth's burgeoning trust in Catherine as she transitioned from being the glamorous part of a double act so often seen on the world stage. She had of course planned to visit Malta alone in September 2014, but this had been cancelled due to her illness during pregnancy. This time there was no stopping her.

Wearing a pale blue, Catherine Walker pencil skirt and jacket, she set off on her day trip onboard a British Airways flight, only one week after her return from the tour of Canada. First, she paid a courtesy call to King Willem-Alexander at Villa Eikenhorst, his private residence on the De Horsten estate in Wassenaar, close to The Hague. 'Welcome, welcome, very nice to see you,' the King said as the pair posed for photos.

She then travelled to the official residence of Sir Geoffrey Adams, Britain's ambassador to the Netherlands, to convene a round-table discussion on the themes of addiction, intervention, family and mental health. Rutger Engels, the chief executive of the Trimbos Institute, said, 'Still too often children are overlooked when one of their parents has a mental disorder or addiction problem. We are very pleased that the duchess will use her visit to the Netherlands to raise more awareness for the vulnerable position these children are in.'[57]

The highlight as far as the press were concerned was the visit to the Mauritshuis art museum in The Hague to see the exhibition *At*

Home in Holland: Vermeer and His Contemporaries from the British Royal Collection. Catherine, the cultured History of Art graduate, was astute and did not miss a trick. She had studied Johannes Vermeer's seventeenth-century masterpiece *The Girl with the Pearl Earring* and deliberately wore drop pearl earrings for the visit, knowing it would make a good shot. Once the photographers on the press pool saw what she was wearing, they tried valiantly to capture the duchess's earring and the one in the painting in the same frame.[58] Arthur Edwards got the snap, much to his relief.

It was a real highlight for Catherine, too. She had been enthusiastic about art history since she was a child and her royal duties and parental responsibilities limit the time she gets to spend in art galleries or exhibitions. That said, when in London she has been known to head out early in the morning to fulfil that passion with secret visits to art galleries. It is a rare occurrence and she has confided that she really misses getting the fix from that cultural side of her life.

Gallery director Emilie Gordenker was understandably impressed by her and said, 'She was interested in the painting. She asked if it had become a lot more popular since the film came out and I said it had. The Duchess seemed to particularly enjoy seeing *The Goldfinch* by Carel Fabritius.[59] She asked a lot of questions about the presentation of the paintings, because although she is familiar with a lot of the Queen's paintings, she has never seen them in this setting before, which gives them a different context.'

Catherine also hosted a roundtable discussion with two charities that she supports: the Anna Freud Centre, a child mental health research, training and treatment centre in London, and Action on Addiction, a charity that works with people affected by drug and alcohol addiction. Later, she travelled to the neighbouring city of Rotterdam to learn about Bouwkeet, a new community-focused initiative in the centre of a poor district, which provides a creative design and technology workspace. She met with youngsters in woodwork and bike-building classes, and even got the chance to meet a real-life robot, being pictured shaking hands with the machine.

The duchess could have been forgiven for feeling disappointed when she read the British press coverage that followed. After all that hard work in an action-packed day, the press seemed more interested in her mode of transport, flying on a British Airways commercial flight back to London. The scheduled flight at 7.15 p.m. from Rotterdam to London City Airport was full of members of the public, who were somewhat surprised to see her. Catherine was escorted onto the plane by protection officers and sat with her team for the fifty-minute flight. The *MailOnline* bizarrely claimed she 'emulates her "doors to manual" air stewardess mother Carole as she dons a vintage air hostess-style collared suit while joining stunned passengers flying back commercial.'

Nevertheless, Fleet Street editors broadly gave her positive reviews. 'Kate looks brilliant in blue as Duchess visits Holland on first solo trip abroad,' the *Daily Mirror* splashed. Royal reporter Victoria Murphy described Catherine's visit as being a bid to 'beef up' relationships with European Union countries as politicians tried to secure the UK's future outside the EU. The *Daily Mail* said she 'betrayed no hint of nerves' and carried out her duties with aplomb. She had passed the solo test with flying colours.

By Queen Elizabeth II's ninetieth birthday in 2016, she had begun to engage in a seamless transition of the Crown. She was not walking away but started handing over some of her patronages to the younger members of the family, not only to lighten her considerable load, but to inject fresh impetus into those organisations. By the end of that year, she had passed on twenty-five of them.

Catherine was honoured to be the recipient of some plum roles, such as becoming patron of the All England Lawn Tennis and Croquet Club, better known simply as Wimbledon. She was thrilled, as she had long been a keen amateur tennis player, along with her father. She had been a fan since she was a girl and was a regular in the Royal Box even before being handed the role. At the time, she joked, 'Every time Wimbledon is on, I am thinking, yes, I could do the same and get out the racket. Sadly, not the same results.'

Speaking further about the dream role in a 2017 BBC Radio One interview, Catherine talked of her lifelong love for tennis and her memories of watching the Wimbledon championships, saying, 'Being able to go into Wimbledon and be part of an amazing atmosphere is special. It inspires young people, including myself.' Six years later, she revealed to the British US Open winner Emma Raducanu how she used to queue for hours with her father and sister to get tickets. 'I used to do that . . . maybe not overnight, but crack of dawn . . . it meant so much then being able to get the ground passes.'

The duchess was a big hit when she attended the Wimbledon tennis championship in July 2017 with all eyes on her fashion choice, a black-and-white, polka-dot dress by Dolce & Gabbana and a new, shorter hairstyle. Among the players she met there, past and present, was legendary, nine-times singles champion Martina Navratilova. For Catherine it was a dream job, but very high-profile.

At the same time, she was increasing her workload significantly. She took on the royal patronages at Barnardo's, one of the UK's largest and most well-known children's charities; as well as at Save the Children UK, perhaps the most influential child-focused humanitarian organisation globally, and the NSPCC, the National Society for the Prevention of Cruelty to Children, the most prominent child protection charity based in the country.

The duchess was now centre stage more than at any time in her life. The Queen had shown supreme confidence in her and Catherine was determined to repay that trust. She had conquered the nerves she experienced in the early days and was more relaxed when interacting with the public.

Increasingly during this period, the British government saw the Duke and Duchess of Cambridge as the perfect envoys for the post-Brexit era. They brought with them not only a touch of youth and glamour, which helped to rebuild bridges with the UK's nearest neighbours, but a clear message of continued friendship.

It was challenging, but both the British and French did their best to make it work. On 17 March 2017, William and Catherine were greeted in Paris by the French president François Hollande as Britain's exit from the European Union loomed large. It was the prince's first official visit to the city since his mother died in a car accident in the Alma tunnel in August 1997. But this trip was all about diplomacy and winning back hearts and minds. William and Catherine stood on either side of the President and beamed broad smiles for the cameras as he welcomed them on their first visit to the Elysée Palace.

Among the issues discussed were the Syrian conflict and the fight against terrorism, as well as Franco-British relations, according to a French presidential spokesman. William later made a speech at a reception, saying, 'This partnership will continue despite Britain's recent decision to leave the European Union. The depth of our friendship and the breadth of our cooperation will not change.'

In April 2017, as William and Catherine prepared to celebrate their sixth wedding anniversary, they officially started the London Marathon, in support of their Heads Together organisation. Earlier, William had promised that one day he would run a marathon in Kenya. Catherine burst out laughing and said, 'I'll believe it when I see it.' Relaxed in public, she now seemed free to be herself, no longer self-conscious and restricted in how she answered questions. During an appearance on ITV's *Loose Women*, Bryony Gordon asked her if *she* would ever run a marathon, to which Catherine responded, 'Oh no, security and all that.'

If she ever felt the strain of royal life and struggled to cope, which she might well have done, unlike Princess Diana or Meghan Markle, she never complained about her lot publicly. She just got on with it. Her uncle Gary Goldsmith once described her as 'self-sufficient, resourceful, and extremely capable. She comes from a family of doers and fixers. Carole [her mother] has taught her girls to deal with problems with calm capability, not histrionics.'[60]

Kensington Palace officials were keen not to overplay their hand, but the Foreign Office wanted to maximise Catherine's popularity to help bolster Britain's image abroad as part of the 'soft diplomatic' power of the royals. Her visit to Luxembourg in May 2017 was her second solo overseas trip. Wearing a stylish Emilia Wickstead pastel-blue coat, paired with her favourite nude pumps, her first stop was the Musée d'Art Moderne, alongside Princess Stéphanie, Hereditary Grand Duchess of Luxembourg, and the wife of Hereditary Grand Duke Guillaume, heir apparent to the throne of Luxembourg. Catherine took in an 'exhibition of British artists' and attended a cycling-themed festival linked to the 150th anniversary of Luxembourg's 1867 independence.

That summer, William and Catherine took their two children on an official visit to Warsaw and Gdansk in Poland, and Berlin, Heidelberg and Hamburg in Germany. Once again, the duchess won hearts and minds with her modesty.

During a walkabout near Warsaw's Presidential Palace, she chatted to a group of students who had a Facebook group devoted to her style. Magda Mordaka said, 'We love her style and her contact with people. We were waiting for this visit from the very beginning. What would she wear? Would she bring the children?' When another group member told Catherine she was 'beautiful and perfect', she responded humbly, 'It's not true – it's just the make-up.' Both visits proved triumphs, to the delight of the Foreign and Commonwealth Office, who mostly got great response and feedback after the couple's overseas tours.

It was the second time the British government had sent the couple they regarded as their 'super ambassadors' into play while Britain coped with the fallout from quitting the European Union, following their official visit to Paris in March, and they were greeted by large and enthusiastic crowds. Predictably, George and Charlotte stole the show, starting with a series of delightful pictures of them peering through the window of their private jet as they touched down in Warsaw for the first leg of the visit. George, who was just about to start school life at Thomas's independent school in Battersea, looked bored and tired, but he was in better spirits when his dad let him climb into a real helicopter in Hamburg.

While in Warsaw, Catherine made headlines when she was offered a cuddly toy designed to soothe babies at an event for tech start-ups. She joked, 'We will just have to have more babies.' Her words sent the travelling media into a frenzy. Their first engagement was a sombre visit to the site of the Nazi concentration camp at Stutthof-Oranienburg, where more than 65,000 Jewish prisoners were murdered by SS guards. The couple spent more than an hour at the museum and memorial site, which was dedicated to preserving the memory of the victims and educating visitors about the horrors of the Holocaust.

Visibly shaken by the experience, they left a joint message in the visitor's book that read: 'We were intensely moved by our visit to Stutthof, which has been the scene of so much terrible pain, suffering and death. This shattering visit has reminded us of the horrendous murder of six million Jews, drawn from across the whole of Europe, who died in the abominable Holocaust. It is, too, a terrible reminder of the cost of war. And the fact that Poland alone lost millions of its people, who were the victims of a most brutal occupation.'

In private, the royal couple met survivors of the death camp, including two Britons who had returned to the camp for the first time especially for the occasion. They listened to Zigi Shipper and Manfred Goldberg, both eighty-seven, who had become lifelong friends after being detained at the age of fourteen and rescued in 1945, and the couple joined them in a prayer they led.

Later, they visited Gdansk's shipyards, the birthplace of Poland's Solidarity movement, where they joined a street party before going on a tour of the city's Shakespeare Theatre and then heading to Germany, where they had a private meeting with German Chancellor Angela Merkel. The photographic highlight for the media came when Catherine went head-to-head with William in a river race along the Neckar at Heidelberg, in the state of Baden-Württemberg in south-west Germany. Before they set up, she jokingly told her rowing team, 'No pressure, but I do want to beat my husband.' For William and Catherine, who wore nine different outfits in just five days, it was another diplomatic mission accomplished.

The following year, in January 2018, the couple headed to Sweden and Norway for a four-day overseas tour. Again, they were there at the request of the Foreign Office and a series of good photo ops were offered up. They played the popular local sport bandy hockey at an outdoor ice rink, teamed up with Crown Princess Victoria and Crown Prince Daniel, and visited the Nobel Museum. Catherine was a stalwart throughout, undertaking a packed schedule of twenty-two engagements, despite being six months pregnant. In Oslo, they were welcomed by Norway's Crown Prince Haakon and Crown Princess Mette-Marit.

With every overseas visit Catherine was becoming more self-assured and was more relaxed in front of the cameras. In media interviews too, she seemed to have found a new confidence, able to take potentially difficult personal issues in her stride. In an interview with ITV marking the twentieth anniversary of Diana's death in 1997, Catherine discussed the impact of joining the Royal Family and its effect on her life.

'I've learned a lot about myself and the world,' she said. 'It has made me a lot more empathetic.' She spoke too of the darker side of parenting and the impact it can have on anyone's mental health, whoever they are: 'I think as any mother would be, you go through those times where you feel quite low.'[61]

A few seconds into the photocall, Catherine whispered to her husband, 'It's a bit windy, eh? He might get a cold. Let's go now.' William understood immediately and they cut it short. When they finally departed, he joked to well-wishers, saying, 'Thrice the worry now.'

Catherine gave birth to her third child, a son they named Louis, on 23 April 2018, again at the private Lindo Wing of St Mary's Hospital in Paddington. Before introducing him to the world, William had brought the baby's older siblings, George and Charlotte, to meet him. They affectionately called him 'Lou Lou'.

Outside the hospital later, the little prince, weighing a healthy 8lb 7oz at birth, was cradled by Catherine in her arms. The waiting media gave her the affectionate title of 'super mum'. But this time the duchess, who was wearing a striking red dress adorned with a pristine white collar, was feeling fragile and was keen to leave the media circus sooner than on the previous two occasions.

Their baby boy was baptised Louis Arthur Charles at the Chapel Royal at St James's Palace on 9 July 2018. Prince Charles and Camilla attended the christening, along with the Duke and Duchess of Sussex, Prince George and Princess Charlotte, his grandparents Carole and Michael Middleton, Pippa Middleton and her husband James Matthews and James Middleton. Also there were Louis' godparents, all friends and family of his parents: Nicholas van Cutsem, Guy Pelly, Harry Aubrey-Fletcher, Lady Laura Meade, Robert Carter and Lucy Middleton.

The occasion was marked by a series of exquisite portraits taken by Matt Holyoak and Matt Porteous in the morning and garden room of Clarence House, including a stunning picture of Catherine holding Louis in her arms.

With baby Louis, their family was now complete.[62]

CHAPTER 11

Family Feud

My understanding and my experience for the past four years
is that it's nothing like what it looks like.

MEGHAN MARKLE ON HER
RELATIONSHIP WITH CATHERINE

While Prince William and Catherine were earning plaudits working for the Crown at home and abroad, Prince Harry appeared to be drifting. His on-off relationship with Zimbabwean heiress Chelsy Davy had fizzled out in 2010, largely, he claimed, because she found the invasion of her privacy 'terrifying'. His flirtatious nature had led to disagreements too. Whatever the real reason for their split, Chelsy returned to her home in Africa to escape the media circus when the story of their breakup was revealed. They rekindled their love affair for a brief period in 2011, but it ended again without acrimony and with them promising to remain friends.

A few months later, he started dating the beautiful bohemian actress Cressida Bonas. That failed too, because she said she found it 'incredibly frustrating' being 'pigeonholed' as the girlfriend of a royal and she wanted to pursue her career as an actress.[63] When interviewed by the BBC in spring 2016, Harry said he was still single and focused on his work, such as launching the Invictus Games, an international sporting event for wounded, injured or sick armed services personnel and veterans, which he founded in 2014.

At this time, he remained close to his brother and Catherine, with whom he got on well and shared a mutual trust. In 2016, together with William, they had launched the ambitious Heads Together campaign through their Royal Foundation. Catherine had suggested the idea to her husband and from there it gained momentum.

The three of them were united in trying to end the stigma about mental health. William focused on the reluctance of young men to discuss their mental wellbeing, Harry on how it impacted the lives of service personal and veterans, and Catherine on improving the lives of young children. They dovetailed well together and their campaign captured the public imagination. In his autobiography, *Spare*, Harry said that everything had started well. This cosy arrangement would soon change, however, along with Harry's relationship status.

Even before he introduced William and Catherine to Meghan Markle, whom he had secretly started dating, they seemed impressed as the couple were big fans of the Netflix legal drama *Suits*, in which the actress starred. Harry said their 'mouths dropped' when he told them he was dating Meghan, who played paralegal Rachel Zane. His brother turned to him and said, 'F—k off?' His expletive was meant in positive way.

Their secret relationship became public knowledge on 31 October 2016, after journalist Camilla Tominey broke the story in the *Sunday Express*. Furious, Harry released a statement to register his disgust at the 'wave of abuse and harassment' directed at Meghan and demanding it stop. It was an odd stance, given that most of the press had been very positive about their romance.

When asked for her reaction by the press, Catherine smiled and said, 'William and I are thrilled. It's such exciting news. It's a happy time for any couple and we wish them all the best and hope they enjoy this happy moment.' Privately, William was less gushing; in fact he was concerned that his brother's whirlwind romance was rushing towards marriage and he did not really know the divorcée Meghan.

Harry claimed that the goodwill from William and Catherine disappeared long before the build-up to his wedding. William had confided to his brother that he believed it would be better to give Meghan more time to adjust to the royal way of life and suggested he cool the relationship. Harry felt affronted and judged it to be an insult. As a direct result, his relationship with his brother deteriorated fast. According to Harry's book *Spare*, William physically attacked him.[64] Relations between the brothers have never recovered and there is no sign that they ever will, after what Harry regards as a series of public 'betrayals'.

On Christmas Day 2017, when single mother Karen Anvil snapped the four young royals walking arm-in-arm as they walked to St Mary Magdalene Church at Sandringham, she had no idea what she had done. The 'Fab Four' were created as a media concept. In truth, they never really existed.

At the outset, Charles made a concerted effort to form a relationship with Meghan. 'She is so intelligent and so nice,' he remarked. 'She makes Harry happy. We could not like her more.' Harry, however, later claimed that his father, who was Prince of Wales at the time, told him there was 'not enough money to go around' for Meghan, because he was already having to pay for William and Catherine. Harry was furious as he believed that was part of the deal for him and his wife agreeing to serve the Crown. Despite his claims, close sources say that Charles gave Harry a 'substantial sum' and did not financially cut him off.

The Queen had also tried hard to bond with the former actress, as both were dog lovers. During Harry's engagement interview, he claimed that when Meghan took tea with the Queen, the corgis took to her immediately. Yet newspaper columnists like Rachel Johnson, sister of the former prime minister Boris Johnson, spotted cracks in the enforced joint 'foundation' of the Fab Four straight away.

With Meghan on the scene, media stories about Catherine became overtly more positive. Odd headlines were attributed to non-stories such as 'Kate handles fierce wind like a Pro' in the *Sun*,[65] or another in the same tabloid saying, 'Down-to-earth Kate Middleton will be Britain's new Queen of Hearts'.[66] Meanwhile, Meghan faced increasing criticism. 'The Queen bans Meghan Markle from wearing jewellery made famous by Diana – but Kate Middleton IS allowed,' said the *Sun*.[67]

With Meghan on the scene, William and Catherine may have unconsciously raised their game now that there was a new star royal couple. There were whispers of pettiness, even jealousy. While the public largely viewed Meghan as a breath of fresh air, initially at least, there was some 'haughtiness' from courtiers and even family.

Meghan agreed to rise to the challenge and throw herself into her new role, even before she and Harry married. Their whistle-stop tour of the UK, including visits to Edinburgh, Cardiff, Belfast, Lisburn and London, was greeted by enthusiastic crowds wherever they went. As 'the new kids on the block', they were hogging the newspaper headlines.

William, who expected to be treated with deference as he would one day be King, was put out when his brother and future sister-in-law slotted in an engagement in Cardiff on 18 January 2018 that clashed with one of his. William is competitive by nature, even when it comes to media coverage, so he chose to debut his new and dramatic buzz cut as he cheered up patients at a London hospital that same afternoon, knowing the papers would feature him on their news pages too.

Some members of Charles's household were amused that William felt affronted that his younger brother and his American fiancée were not showing him the due deference that came with his royal rank. After all, the prince rarely showed such deference to his father.

Camilla, before she became Queen, handled this cleverly, subtly reminding William that Charles is the royal patriarch whenever she felt he did not show his father enough respect.

One senior source told the author, 'On one occasion when they were leaving Windsor Castle after a joint event, the Duke of Cambridge learned that his father had police outriders from the Special Escort Group for a journey as his royal status warranted. He asked his father if he and Catherine could tag along behind in convoy, making it easier to get through the traffic, and Charles agreed. When Charles was kept waiting several minutes for the couple, Camilla insisted they go without them. As William and Catherine emerged, all they could see were the blue flashing lights of the motorbikes disappearing in the distance.'

Queen Elizabeth then made a significant move. On 29 April 2019, she made Catherine a Dame Grand Cross of the Royal Victorian Order (GCVO), the highest rank in the Order. It is the Queen's personal gift and awarded independently of Downing Street to people who have served her or the monarchy in a personal way. The award was bestowed to Catherine on her eighth wedding anniversary. There was no lengthy citation detailing the reasons for the honour, but the message could not be clearer, as her commitment, loyalty and dedication to her role within the Royal Family was formally recognised.

Harry, whose anger towards the press after the death of Diana had consumed him, now accused the media of societal racism and blamed them for fuelling negative coverage about Meghan, with scant evidence. However, Catherine did seem to be unwittingly set up in competition with Meghan by the press, although she did not invite or encourage such polarising portrayals.

Even at the Royal Foundation Forum on 28 February 2018, there were clear tensions among the so-called Fab Four as they sat before a backdrop with the message 'Making a Difference Together'. William spoke first. Afterwards, a humorous exchange followed. The host, Tina Daheley, asked if they ever had family disagreements. 'Oh, yes,' William said. '[They are] healthy disagreements,' Harry added quickly. When asked for more detail, he added, 'I can't remember, they come so thick and fast.'

Daheley, a BBC journalist, pushed further, asking if the most recent disagreement had been resolved. William said, 'Is it resolved? We don't know.' He went on, 'We've got four different personalities and we've got the same passions to make a difference, but different opinions. I think those opinions work well. Working as a family does have its challenges and the fact that everyone is laughing shows they know exactly what it's like. We're stuck together for the rest of our lives.'

Had he opened a can of worms? In hindsight it certainly seemed so. The phrase 'stuck together' had the ring of truth about it. None of them seemed comfortable with it.

When Meghan's time to speak came, the tension was palpable. 'Women don't need to "find" a voice, women already have a voice,' she said with attitude. What blocked them was that they did not feel 'empowered' to use it. Men, she went on forcefully, had to be 'encouraged' to listen. 'There is no better time to shine a light on women feeling empowered and people really helping to support them,' she said, namechecking the MeToo and Time's Up movements.

Harry was clearly smitten with Meghan. He appeared in awe of her intellect and public speaking skills. William and Catherine, however, appeared unsettled. They shuffled in their seats and looked decidedly uncomfortable. Cracks began to appear from that moment. Meghan, perhaps unintentionally, had ignored the royal hierarchy. She had not so much stepped on royal toes as stamped on them. When Meghan, who had forgotten her lip gloss, asked to borrow Catherine's, the duchess was 'taken aback' but reluctantly handed it to her. According to Harry, she 'grimaced' after Meghan had squeezed some onto her finger and applied it to her lips.

By now pre-wedding spats were in full swing. Catherine was affronted when Meghan, apparently innocently, suggested she had forgotten a small detail about the wedding plans because she had 'baby brain', having just given birth to Louis. There were then tears four days before the wedding about Princess Charlotte's dress. By the time William was confirmed as Harry's best man for the wedding on 19 May, the relationship had worsened. Harry seemed 'petulant and short-tempered' and had even been rude to members of staff.

William, still concerned by the match, even sought assurances from the Queen that his brother's bride-to-be would not wear any jewellery in the collection once worn by Diana, Princess of Wales, even though his wife Catherine had been allowed to wear some, which would be due to her rank.

Nevertheless, the wedding at Windsor was a spectacular success and Harry and Meghan emerged from St George's Chapel as the Duke and Duchess of Sussex after the Queen gave him the title on the day. In public the Royal Family were all smiles, but privately they were metaphorically at daggers drawn.

The two couples tried to patch things up over tea at Kensington Palace after Meghan and Harry returned from honeymoon in Africa. Catherine, according to Harry's memoir *Spare*, confronted Meghan about the 'baby brain' comment and said, 'You talked about my hormones. We are not close enough for you to talk about my hormones.' Meghan was surprised, according to Harry, and said it was the way she spoke to her girlfriends. William stepped in and apparently pointed at Meghan and called her 'rude'. Meghan stood up to him and said, 'Take your finger out of my face.'[68] Things had definitely cooled between them, if not soured.

Meghan's public popularity was holding up after the wedding and it took a more positive turn on 15 October 2018 when the Palace announced they were expecting their first child, just as the couple landed in Sydney, Australia, for the start of their joint royal tour. Their son Archie Harrison Mountbatten-Windsor was born on 6 May 2019. He was seventh in line for the throne and the Queen and Prince Philip's eighth great-grandchild.

The media honeymoon period was short-lived. By July of the same year, negative articles about Meghan outstripped the positive, particularly around the couple's decision to keep details of their baby's birth and baptism private. Many felt that Harry and Meghan wanted to 'have their cake and eat it too'.

The press had already been writing about tensions in the royal brothers' relationship when it emerged publicly that Catherine and Meghan had fallen out too. It was reported that they had clashed over the bridesmaid's outfit worn by Princess Charlotte. In November, the *Daily Telegraph* alleged that Meghan had made Catherine cry at a dress fitting for Charlotte.

Meghan later denied it to TV presenter Oprah Winfrey, saying that 'the reverse happened' and the duchess had made *her* cry. She told Oprah that the confrontation 'really hurt my feelings' and was a 'turning point' in their relationship, adding, 'I don't think it's fair to her to get into the details of that, because she apologised and I've forgiven her. What was hard to get over was being blamed for something not only did I not do, but happened to me.' [69] However, turning on the tears was not difficult for Meghan; she once boasted that as an actress she was very good at it, saying, 'Oh, I can do that so well.'[70]

The Palace, worried about the negative impact of the story, tried to deflect it by arranging for the two women to watch the tennis together at Wimbledon, along with Catherine's sister, Pippa Middleton. Behind the smiles, there was still distrust and a simmering tension. During the Oprah interview, Meghan revealed her feelings about that day. Oprah asked her, 'Did you feel welcomed by everyone? It seemed like you and Kate at the Wimbledon game, where you were going to watch a friend play tennis . . . was it what it looked like?' Meghan replied, 'My understanding and my experience for the past four years is that it's nothing like what it looks like. It's nothing like what it looks like.' Friends they were clearly not.

Kensington Palace announced on 14 March 2019 that William and Harry's households were to separate permanently. Palace spin doctors tried to dress it up as being part of a long-term plan, claiming that work to create the two separate households had been underway since the wedding of Harry and Meghan last May. But the press knew differently. Why then had there been such a fanfare for the joint foundation the previous year?

A possible move next door to William and Catherine's palatial Apartment 1A had been bluntly turned down by the Sussexes too, it emerged later. Courtiers again tried to deflect stories of a feud between the couples, saying it was 'due to timing' and not to the fact that the two brothers did not want to be neighbours. Pretty soon afterwards, even officials realised how daft they sounded.

It is understood that when Meghan and Harry had gone round to have drinks at William and Catherine's apartment, while they were still living at Nottingham Cottage opposite, Meghan had been 'taken aback' at the disparity between the brothers. 'I am not saying Meghan was jealous, but she was really surprised how lavishly Harry's brother was living compared to where they were living,' said a close source. 'It was perhaps the beginning of all the tensions between the two couples.'

Meghan understood that William was above her husband in the royal pecking order as the heir to the throne, but she thought Harry was also a royal prince, so he deserved more materially. She was piqued by the disparity. Soon afterwards, it was announced that the Sussexes were moving to Frogmore Cottage, in the shadow of Windsor Castle. The communications department operation would be split to allow each couple to shape their own media strategies.

The King, who dislikes confrontation, consciously stayed out of the quarrels between his two sons, hoping the hostility between them would ease over time. Sadly, the feud got steadily worse as Harry continued to dish the dirt in public. In an interview with Tom Bradby for ITV, Harry confirmed what the media had already written, that he and his brother were on 'different paths' and their relationship had descended into something that was difficult. William was furious.

'We are certainly on different paths at the moment, but I will always be there for him, and as I know he will always be there for me,' Harry said.[71] The truth, as Bradby later revealed, was they had been arguing for the 'past year and a half'.[72] Meghan also told Bradby, in another interview, that she had struggled mentally throughout her pregnancy and early motherhood amidst all the negative media coverage. She said it was a 'very real thing to be going through behind the scenes' and replied 'Yes' when asked if it had 'really been a struggle' and she was 'not really okay'.

The couples were ensconced in a bitter feud. The Fab Four roadshow was over.

CHAPTER 12

Varying Recollections

*Whilst some recollections may vary, they are taken very
seriously and will be addressed by the family privately.*
STATEMENT FROM BUCKINGHAM PALACE
ON BEHALF OF THE QUEEN, MARCH 2021

Catherine's instinct has always been to resolve problems by talking them through, but the Harry/Meghan feud tested her patience to the limit. She is a solution finder, not somebody who buries her head in the sand or goes out of her way to clash. That is one of the reasons she and the King have such a good relationship. Those close to him say he admires her positivity. Whenever Charles wants to see his grandchildren, he communicates with Catherine, who has also developed a 'warm' relationship with Queen Camilla.

King Charles regards her as the daughter he never had. After all, she acted as a peace broker between Charles and William, and encouraged him to be affectionate to his father. 'I think the prince understands Catherine is a good influence on the entire family. He loves and truly appreciates everything she does.' His eyes light up when he sees her at joint family functions and they always make a beeline for each other.

At first Charles tried to reach out to Meghan and treated her with the same love and affection as he did Catherine. But they are very different characters. He welcomed her with open arms and wanted her to feel part of the family. That is why Harry and Meghan's behaviour has cut him to the quick. Before this all happened, Charles was much closer to his second son than to William. But if there is a positive to be taken from the Sussexes' departure, it is that William and his father are now closer than they were before, perhaps more than they have ever been.

Having Catherine as a loving arbiter has helped William to understand his father better. 'The duchess is somebody who always tries to see both sides of any dispute,' a source said. She has a cool head and is 'emotionally mature'; she can open William's eyes to other points of view like no other. 'She is a stabilising influence.'[73]

Naturally Catherine was loyal to her husband. It led to some soul-searching by the couple, as it took up time in their relationship. On a day trip to Wales during a walkabout, William left the world in no doubt how much he loved his wife. Acknowledging the chilly conditions, he said, 'She [Catherine] has the coldest hands ever. They say cold hands, warm heart!' It was a genuine, loving remark.

In October 2019, Catherine stepped out on overseas duty again and proved a huge hit during the royal visit to Pakistan, where the couple visited a girls' school in Islamabad, met patients at the Shaukat Khanum Memorial Cancer Hospital and went to Badshahi Mosque as well as the SOS Children's Village in Lahore.

Afterwards Catherine spoke to CNN on camera. Relaxed and confident, she told correspondent Max Foster, 'William and I really wanted to come and see an SOS Children's Village like this. There are so many vulnerable women here, but they've really used their positivity and the support that the Village here provides them, really to support and protect the next generation of children in their care and give them the best possible start to their future lives.'

Talking about their five-day visit, she said, 'It's been fantastic. We've seen a lot of Pakistan,' acknowledging the 'huge variety' of engagements they had carried out on the trip. 'It's been amazing seeing some of the geography,' she added, 'but then seeing some of the community activities like this has been really special.' It was the duchess's calm interaction with the press that further increased her standing and royal credentials.

Earlier, the accredited press, travelling with the couple, were invited to the front of the RAF Voyager, where they were to chat about the forthcoming visit. The pair were open and friendly in what was a skilful piece of public relations, especially as it followed the recent disastrous tour – in PR terms – by Harry and Meghan to South Africa.

With the press onside, the coverage of the Pakistan visit was universally positive. Catherine was on top form, delivering speeches using local dialects, and wearing ten different stylish costumes, after completely overhauling her wardrobe for the visit, which gave a respectful nod to local customs and religious expectations. She combined her favoured couturiers such as Catherine Walker with local Pakistani designers to get the right look. The visit was an unmitigated success.

Back home, Charles and Harry had been exchanging correspondence and tense telephone calls for weeks, after he told his father that he and Meghan wanted to step down as front-line senior royals and find a new, semi-attached royal role. Deep down, perhaps Charles hoped if he ignored the situation, it would fizzle out. On 8 January 2020, however, the *Sun* revealed that Harry and Meghan wanted to 'Quit the Royals'.[74] The splash headline writers coined the phrase 'Megxit'. It implied it was all down to Meghan, which it was not.

The couple issued a statement saying they wanted to 'carve out a progressive new role' for themselves within the monarchy, splitting their time between North America and the UK, and be free to earn their own money. They assumed the Queen would back them, but they were wrong. The monarch, Charles, and crucially William were having none of it. On 14 January at Sandringham, the three most senior royals met to decide their response. Later, Harry joined them for the so-called royal summit, but Meghan stayed away, remaining in Canada.

A personal statement released by the Queen read:

Today my family had very constructive discussions on the future of my grandson and his family. My family and I are entirely supportive of Harry and Meghan's desire to create a new life as a young family. Although we would have preferred them to remain full-time working members of the Royal Family, we respect and understand their wish to live a more independent life as a family while remaining a valued part of my family. Harry and Meghan have made clear that they do not want to be reliant on public funds in their new lives. It has therefore been agreed that there will be a period of transition in which the Sussexes will spend time in Canada and the UK. These are complex matters for my family to resolve, and there is some more work to be done, but I have asked for final decisions to be reached in the coming days.

For Queen Elizabeth it was never personal; for her it was all about safeguarding the institution she served. To some commentators, particularly in the US, the handling of Harry and Meghan's departure from the Firm showed just how ruthless the House of Windsor could be when their order is threatened. Even Harry, who was expecting some kickback from his family, was surprised at how unforgiving they were. It would have been easy for him to blame his father and brother, but what happened was the Queen's decision, albeit strongly supported by Charles and William.

She knew instinctively that for the sake of the monarchy's future, there could not be any ambiguity over its role and function or financial structure. As far as she was concerned, you were either working for the Firm fully, or not. There was no halfway house. As a grandmother, Queen Elizabeth undoubtedly loved Harry and the fun-loving side to his character, but as a monarch she saw him as a maverick who had let her down. His departure, she told those close to her, was a 'missed opportunity'. She knew that he and Meghan had much to offer and certainly appealed to the younger generation in a way none of the other royals could. But the idea of the couple earning millions by cashing in on their royal titles and status was abhorrent to her.

She did not object to their decision to leave, but she was adamant that it meant they must be stripped of their patronages and banned from using their HRH titles personally and commercially. Close sources said Harry was shocked and hurt. Yes, it was his decision to go, but it now felt like he was banished. He could not believe the entire Royal Family almost in unison turned their backs on him. Looking to blame anyone other than himself, he went on the offensive. His anger with his father and brother was palpable.

As the negative press coverage continued, William and Catherine headed to Dublin for an important overseas visit. Catherine, with seven different looks in three days, wowed the big and enthusiastic crowds not only in the capital, but in County Meath, County Kildare and Galway, on the first royal visit since the Brexit vote.

Security was tight as they flew in by commercial Aer Lingus jet. After meeting President Michael D. Higgins and his wife Sabina, they met the Taoiseach Leo Varadkar and laid a wreath at the Garden of Remembrance. The couple's short tour focused on the relationship between the two countries and built on the theme of 'remembrance and reconciliation', an official said. There was, sadly, no chance of reconciliation when it came to William and Harry's broken relationship.

A few days after the Cambridges returned to the UK, the Commonwealth service at Westminster Abbey on 9 March 2020 turned out to be the last time all four would be seen together for years. It came just before the COVID-19 pandemic swept the world and enforced lockdowns. Even before the service started, it began awkwardly with the procession of senior royals into the church. Harry and Meghan discovered they had been removed from the line-up without consultation and they were not named in the 2,000 printed orders of service for guests.[75] Instead, only William and Catherine, Charles and Camilla were scheduled to walk with Queen Elizabeth in the procession.

When Harry raised the matter, William and Catherine simply agreed to take their seats at the same time as the Sussexes to avoid accusations of favouritism, or that Harry and Meghan had somehow been snubbed. When it came to being seated, though, they barely acknowledged each other. There had been no thawing of relations; in fact it was the complete opposite.

On 31 March 2020, the Sussexes completed their final official engagements before leaving for a new life in North America. They flew to Canada before later making the inevitable move to California, Meghan's home state. Talk of a private, quiet existence started to unravel almost immediately. In April, details emerged of the couple's new foundation, Archewell, named after their son, which was to replace their Sussex Royal Foundation, the brand name they were forced to abandon because it included the word 'royal'. In September, the couple announced a mega multi-million-dollar deal with Netflix to produce a new docu-series and other future content 'that informs but also gives hope'.

Then on 7 March 2021, nearly fifty million viewers tuned in to watch their much-anticipated TV interview on CBS in the US with Oprah Winfrey.

Meghan claimed that after joining the Royal Family, she had been made to feel suicidal. She also alleged that their son Archie had not been given a princely title after members of the Firm had expressed 'concerns and conversations about how dark his skin might be when he's born.' No names were mentioned, but online trolls soon accused Charles and Camilla of having made the implied racist remarks.

The Palace was forced to issue an unprecedented statement on behalf of the Queen, which said: 'The issues raised, particularly that of race, are concerning. Whilst some recollections may vary, they are taken very seriously and will be addressed by the family privately.'

A paperback edition of Valentine Low's bestseller, *Courtiers: The Hidden Power Behind the Crown*, quoted a source who claimed that the Palace's response had initially been 'a much milder version' of the 'recollections' sentence. The source stated that William and Catherine were both keen for the statement to be 'toughened up'. According to Low, they believed it needed to make clear that the institution did not accept a lot of what had been said in the Oprah interview. The couple reminded those drafting the response that 'history will judge this statement' and it was Catherine who came up with the powerful phrase 'recollections may vary'.[76] The tougher statement was subsequently released, but the racism stain on the Royal Family had already gained traction. It failed to be washed away.

While his father and grandmother decided it would be best to say nothing more about it publicly, the Duke of Cambridge refused to remain silent. He believed his brother and sister-in-law's broadcast was so damaging that when asked publicly, he simply had to respond and challenge their allegations.

As William and Catherine left an engagement at a school in Stratford, East London, on 11 March, their first appearance since the Oprah interview appeared, Sky News reporter Inzamam Rashid shouted from the Press pen, 'Can you just let me know, is the Royal Family a racist family, sir?' Piqued, William, who was wearing a mask due to the Covid regulations in place, turned and replied calmly, 'We are very much not a racist family.' He also said he would be speaking to his brother about it. Catherine, at his side, said nothing. Insiders said William was astonished by his brother and sister-in-law's claims and their total lack of discretion. He was upset too that his wife had been dragged into this ugly row. As far as he was concerned, their behaviour was unforgivable, and they could no longer be trusted.

In December 2023, Omid Scobie's second book, *Endgame*, caused a sensation when in a Dutch edition the author mistakenly named the two royals whom Meghan had allegedly accused of racism as being King Charles and Catherine, now the Princess of Wales. At first it was suggested the 'naming' and 'shaming' was a deliberate publicity stunt cooked up by the publishers, but this was denied by Scobie when put to him during an interview with BBC *Newsnight*.

When pressed, Scobie said he did not know how the Dutch translation of *Endgame* came to include the names of those alleged to have discussed the skin colour of the Sussexes' unborn baby. In the English version of the book, he had claimed there were two people involved and he knew their identities, but legal reasons had prevented him from disclosing their names.

Initially, the Palace said they were 'considering all options'. Once again, both the King and Catherine kept a dignified silence. The idea that either of the accused were racists was preposterous. At worst, if the comments were made at all, they were misinterpreted or taken out of context. After all, during the publicity tour in January 2023 for his book *Spare*, Harry had insisted he did not believe the Royal Family was racist and claimed he and his wife had never said they were. Instead, he predictably blamed the media.

Even without Harry's intervention, the claims of racism against the monarch and Catherine did not stack up, given the body of work both had done in public life. As Prince of Wales, Charles had for years worked hard to promote diversity and interfaith dialogue, and his mission has always been to enhance the lives of people of all backgrounds. Since becoming King, he is also endeavouring to make the Royal Household more diverse and is succeeding.

Catherine said nothing officially, but instead put her best foot forward and walked tall alongside her husband as she arrived at the Royal Variety Performance at the Royal Albert Hall, wearing a stunning £1,288 Talina gown from Safiyaa. Informed sources, however, let it be known that Catherine was 'saddened' that she had been linked to Meghan's fanciful claims and made it clear that she had 'nothing to do with it'. Like William, she has a zero tolerance to racism and believes there is no place for it in society.

Once again, she chose to keep calm and carry on, and to rise above the noise.

CHAPTER 13

Sweet Charity

She gives from her heart and again there is a sense
of sincerity and a sense of love in everything she does.
QUEEN RANIA OF JORDAN ABOUT CATHERINE

After dropping her children off on the school run, even if her public schedule may be empty, Catherine's schedule is relentless, like so many working parents. On a so-called free day, after consulting with her palace team, she will often be making Zoom calls with the executive officers in charge of one of the charities she supports, or spending hours reading up, going through development reports ahead of a public engagement.

'She is totally dedicated to ensuring she is fully briefed on everything she does publicly,' one senior aide told the author. 'Her Royal Highness is a total professional when it comes to her public work and a stickler for the detail; the names, ages and background information of people she is scheduled to meet. Being on top of her brief enables her to put people at their ease when they meet her and makes the engagement she is on run smoother and more productively.' Being well-informed really matters to Catherine as she never wants to let anyone down. She makes sure she knows exactly how a charity operates from the ground up and listening to the feedback from the people doing the day-to-day tasks always helps.

As Queen Rania of Jordan has said, Catherine believes that carrying out her works is a privilege which comes from the heart. Rania, wife of King Prince Abdullah of Jordan, who has met Catherine several times, told CNN in a clip that went viral on TikTok, 'Princess Catherine when she talks about her work, her face lights up. She does it out of sense of duty but more importantly she does it because she absolutely cares. When she talks about her work she says, "I am lucky to be doing this, I have the privilege of doing that." She gives from her heart and again there is a sense of sincerity and a sense of love in everything she does.'[77]

Catherine's primary philanthropic vehicle is still The Royal Foundation, whose board of trustees is now chaired by former Tory Party leader and ex-foreign secretary Lord Hague of Richmond. Established in September 2009 by William and Harry, and later joined by Catherine after her marriage, its purpose is to support various charitable causes and to promote philanthropy and positive social change. Meghan did become involved briefly with The Royal Foundation and joined in its work after her wedding to Prince Harry in May 2018, but within a few months she and Harry decided to go their own way.

On 18 December 2019, an agreement was signed with the Sussexes by which The Royal Foundation intended to grant half of the net future proceeds received by the Diana Fund to their new charitable foundation, Sussex Royal. However, following discussions with the UK government about the use of the word 'royal' in the name, they had agreed not to use it. Instead, the trustees approved the donation of their share of the net income of the Diana Fund to Sentebale, the UK-registered charity of which Prince Harry is a patron.

The Royal Foundation has gone from strength to strength. Official accounts stated that the income stood at £20.4 million in the year to 31 December 2021, up 73 per cent. This was a marked increase on the 2019 figure, which stood at £6.7 million. The increase was largely due to the inaugural Earthshot Prize, the Foundation's environmental award, and income was expected to revert to lower levels when the prize became a separate charity.

This success has enabled Catherine to make a real difference in areas close to her heart. On her instruction the Foundation has invested capital in projects that she believes will really help transform lives. The accounts show that 98 per cent of total income consisted of donations, grants, royalties and legacy income.

With William and Catherine at the helm, The Royal Foundation has been able to reach out and help a wide range of causes causes, including conservation, the environment, early childhood develop-ment, mental health, emergency services and homelessness. It also gives the prince and princess the opportunity to dive deeper into the causes they are supporting. Catherine has made it clear that she is devoted to her patronages for the long term and wants to root out the issues that create problems and address them, as shown by her work with children's early development.

She is not afraid of stepping outside of her comfort zone and is happy to use her voice and celebrity too. In February 2022, she agreed to appear on an episode of the popular CBeebies TV programme, *Bedtime Stories*. It coincided with Children's Mental Health Week and in her composed broadcast, the princess reassured children that it was all right to be scared and they are not alone in their fears. Dressed casually in jeans and a warm sweater, she sat cross-legged on a blanket set against a forest-themed backdrop as she read from *The Owl Who Was Afraid of the Dark*, a book by Jill Tomlinson. It is the story of a young baby barn owl named Plop who fears the dark, but with the support of friends, shows how he learns to face and overcome his fear.

'Hello, my name is Catherine and tonight we're in my bedtime story den,' she began. 'I've chosen a story which I remember reading as a little girl.' The tale resonated with the theme of the week, 'Growing Together'. 'It's an uplifting story,' Catherine went on. 'All of us, like Plop, can be afraid at times. But as the story suggests, understanding our fears with the help of others can make them easier to handle.' After reading the bedtime story to the children watching on television, she signed off by saying, 'Now, it's time for bed. Night, night, and sleep tight.'

Her performance was relaxed and reassuring, and it earned her more praise. Social media lit up with positive reviews. Patricia Hidalgo, director of BBC Children's and Education, said, 'I couldn't be prouder to have the duchess read a CBeebies Bedtime Story to mark the twentieth anniversary of our CBeebies and CBBC channels. It's such a special and relevant tale.'

Ever since she became a Royal Family member, Catherine has gradually developed her interests and built up her charity portfolio. She now has numerous charitable patronages including Action for Children, Action on Addiction, the Anna Freud Centre, East Anglia's Children's Hospices (EACH), Evelina London Children's Hospital, Family Action and the Maternal Mental Health Alliance, which cover a spectrum of interests that are close to her heart.

Passionate about community projects, she invests private time and energy in them, long after the cameras and the press have left. She selects projects where she has a personal interest, such as the 'Nursing Now Challenge', a three-year initiative launched in 2018 to champion the nursing profession, because her grandmother and great-grandmother were both volunteer nurses.

Catherine also has a great love of the arts. Of course, she studied Art History at university and that devotion is reflected in the patronages she has selected to support in her royal career. She has been a great champion of the National Portrait Gallery, as well as its patron since 2012, and is an accomplished amateur photographer too. She has also worked closely with the Royal Photographic Society, where she has been patron since 2019, when the Queen passed down the responsibility to her, as well as an honorary member. 'The Duchess has a longstanding interest in photography, and this patronage will further highlight the beneficial impact that art and creativity can have on emotional well-being, particularly for children and young people,' the Palace press release read on her appointment. Catherine also agreed to become the first-ever royal patron of the Victoria and Albert Museum in 2018.

She has received praise for the official portraits she takes of her children released on their birthdays. Royal photographer Arthur Edwards, a Fellow of the Royal Photographic Society, commented, 'She started off and there was criticism from people about the images not being sharped or cropped properly. Now her stuff is just brilliant; that picture of Louis and the paint is just stunning. The test is when you look at a picture like that. Whether you laugh and smile, you've cracked it, and she does it every time.'[78]

In her first decade as a working royal, Catherine has emphasised the importance of art education for children, visiting schools to promote hands-on creativity among students. She has also spoken about the therapeutic impact on mental health of engaging with art and music. During the COVID-19 pandemic, she became a vocal advocate of using art to manage stress. She urged parents and children to find an outlet for their thoughts and feelings to cope with the pressures of the experience.

In a video to mark Children's Mental Health Week, she said it was important to find creative ways in which to share your thoughts, ideas and feelings. 'Whether that's through photography, through art, through drama, through music or poetry, it's finding those things that make you feel good about yourself,' she said.

A keen sportswoman all her life, Catherine has invested time in promoting active participation in sports. When she backed Sports Aid and the 1851 Trust, she set out to inspire a new generation in sailing, a sport she has enjoyed since her school days. Her influence has made a real difference and given the sport much more publicity. She does not simply turn up to events, she takes an active interest.

In August 2022, while William was supporting the England Women's football team win the European Championship at Wembley, Catherine donned a wetsuit and joined the British racing team on their F50 catamaran in a friendly Commonwealth race against New Zealand alongside her good friend, Olympian Sir Ben Ainslie. When she shared a video of her participation on the Cambridges' Instagram account, she attracted thousands of likes within minutes. 'It was so good to see the Protect our Future programme with @1851trust doing exactly this,' she wrote.

After taking over from the Queen as patron of the All-England Lawn Tennis and Croquet Club in 2016, Catherine made sure that people were aware of her passion for grass-roots tennis and her desire to encourage young people from all backgrounds to get involved in the sport. In September 2021, she went on court with the British teenage US Open winner, Emma Raducanu. Afterwards during an online BBC show, the tennis star was asked if she had more nerves playing the duchess or in the US Open final, and she replied, 'I was actually very nervous playing the duchess – I was like, don't miss, don't miss.'

At the core of everything Catherine does is her desire to stim-ulate conversation and awareness where subjects have previously been taboo: 'We want to end the stigma surrounding mental health that stops people getting the support that they so desperately need. I am a firm believer that it is crucial to confront problems as early as possible, to prevent them from escalating into even greater issues later in life,' she said at a 2016 London awards ceremony.[79]

Through the charities the princess supports, such as Action for Children or Place2Be, which provides school-based mental health support, she uses her celebrity to encourage young people to talk openly or with professionals about their problems. It is, she believes, the first step and often the hardest one to take in the journey to erasing the stigma of talking about mental health.

She nailed her colours to the charity mast in 2015 when she said, 'We need to help young people and their parents understand that it is not a sign of weakness to ask for help. A child's mental health is just as important as their physical health and deserves the same quality of support. No one would feel embarrassed about seeking help for a child if they broke their arm and we really should be equally ready to support a child coping with emotional difficulties.'[80]

The inspiration and driving force behind the Heads Together campaign with William and Harry, the duchess truly believed that with her husband and brother-in-law at her side, they could engage the public to address the often unspoken subject of mental health and end the agony of people suffering in silence.

In 2017, Catherine challenged people to reach out to those who were suffering in silence. 'The question that me, William and Harry have asked ourselves is how can we get more people to start talking? How do we encourage people to take the first step? . . . Fear or reticence, or a sense of not wanting to burden another, means that people suffer in silence, allowing the problem to grow larger and larger unchecked.'[81]

Catherine's biggest fear, according to sources close to her, is that unless direct action is taken now an entire generation of children will have been let down and this could lead to anxiety, depression, addiction and self-harm when they become adults. 'That is why she has made it clear that her mission is to break that cycle of addiction,' explained a source close to her. 'She is driven and determined to break that cycle.'

She has developed an almost encyclopaedic knowledge on the subject. In a speech at Action on Addiction in Manchester, in April 2013, Catherine said, 'Addiction is a hugely complex and destructive disease, and its impact can be simply devastating. All too often, lives and families can be shattered by it. Through my patronage of Action on Addiction, I feel fortunate to have met a wide range of inspirational people who have overcome addiction. It is so encouraging to see that with the right help – like that of Action on Addiction – it can be conquered.'

In 2020, she launched her Royal Foundation Centre for Early Childhood, a 'landmark' survey as a culmination of a decade of research and work, where she had worked to ascertain the significance of a child's earliest years and how their experiences shape who they will become.

In a video message she said, 'Working closely with others, the Centre hopes to raise awareness of why the first five years of life are just so important for our future life outcomes and what we can do as a society to embrace this golden opportunity to create a happier, more mentally healthy, more nurturing society.' She went on, 'By working together, my hope is that we can change the way we think about early childhood and transform lives for generations to come. Because I truly believe big change starts small.'

The research, she said, focused on three key areas: research, collaborations to find solutions and campaigns to raise awareness and inspire action. She is determined to make the science of the early years accessible to wider audiences. To help achieve this, she launched a dedicated website to highlight the importance of early childhood and the work the Centre was doing. It signalled, royal advisors said, 'her lifelong commitment to improving outcomes across society'.

The Royal Foundation has also published the report 'Big Change Starts Small', which brings together research on the early years. Written in collaboration with the Center on the Develop-ing Child at Harvard University and the London School of Economics, the report explores the economic cost of treating problems later in life that might have been avoided through early childhood intervention.

The feedback to her pioneering work has given Catherine renewed vigour and confidence. Undertaking solo engagements is no longer daunting. She has begun to spread her wings and has embarked on more solo overseas visits, albeit relatively short ones, where she can focus on interests close to her heart without distraction. She also appears to be even more confident on her own as the star attraction than when she is accompanied by Prince William, who often takes the lead.

Her two-day visit to Copenhagen in February 2022 was a perfect benchmark. It was not only to honour Queen Elizabeth's Platinum Jubilee year, but to highlight her Early Year Foundation. She wanted to see first-hand the Centre for Early Childhood in Copenhagen, as it has become her passion project. It was a subject in which she felt confident. She was also relaxed meeting her husband's European 'cousins', when she met up with Queen Margrethe and Crown Princess Mary of Denmark.[82]

The duchess came out of herself and thrived. She seemed more relaxed without William, who can famously be a bit fussy when he is on royal duty. Welcomed by the British ambassador to Denmark, Emma Hopkins, Catherine was in buoyant mood. At the airport, she had a spring in her step. She got straight into her busy programme. Her first engagement was at the University of Copenhagen, the country's oldest and largest university, founded in 1479. In a meeting with academics and experts, she discussed the Copenhagen Infant Mental Health Project, whose mission matched hers: the advancement of mental health of infants and their parents. Well briefed, she played an active part in the discussion.

She knew the solo visit was a chance to showcase her work and that photographs of her would be a good hook for any story on the subject, so when the opportunity arose during a visit to the Lego Foundation PlayLab for her to slide down a giant slide inside the building while wearing her high heels, she jumped at it, squealing with delight from top to bottom.

It was part of a partnership between the LEGO Foundation and six Danish universities to stimulate children's creative and experimental approach to learning. One aide explained, 'Catherine has supported her husband magnificently and with real style too. But they are both older now and have their own interests and areas – Catherine is passionate about early childhood development and learning, for example.'

She later visited Stenurten Forest Kindergarten on the outskirts of Copenhagen to better understand the country's approach to early years. The school focuses on teaching children about self-worth and self-esteem. During the trip, the duchess also visited the Copenhagen Infant Mental Health Project to find out more about how the country has promoted infant wellbeing alongside physical health. Other visits included the Children's Museum and the PlayLab at Campus Carlsberg, a creative learning environment for students training to be early years professionals.

The duchess showed how far she had come when she was hosted at Christian IX's Palace by Queen Margrethe II, who was celebrating her Golden Jubilee. She also visited the Mary Foundation with Princess Mary, the Tasmanian-born wife of Frederik, Crown Prince of Denmark, to see the work they are doing there to protect vulnerable women and children from domestic violence. Calm and smiling, she did it all seamlessly.

Catherine's beauty and feminine touch has brought fresh impetus to the Royal Family. As one senior figure put it, 'She is a very good listener and connects with people of all ages. Her warmth and generosity of spirit shines through, she has the likeability factor. Children seem to gravitate towards her, with some dubbing her the children's princess. When people offer advice, she takes it in, but ultimately, she is the one who makes the decision.'

Members of the Royal Family have spoken about her likeability, too. Sophie, now the Duchess of Edinburgh, once remarked that Catherine was 'very easy to get along with' and that 'she's very much the girl next door, if you know what I mean'. [83] Many people have spoken of her as an inspiration, urging them to be the best they can be.

Bianca Nicholas, aged thirty-two from Tonbridge in Kent, who was diagnosed with cystic fibrosis, said in an interview with the *Sun*, 'I was nineteen years old when the charity Starlight Children's Foundation made my dreams come true by allowing me to perform at a glitzy event in front of Prince William and Prince Harry in 2008. Singing has always been my passion and has helped to improve my lung function. She [Catherine] told me she wished she could sing like me. She was naturally down-to-earth and really kind.'[84]

Holocaust survivor Ike Alterman, ninety-three, from Manchester, said that meeting her was 'one of the best days of my life, without doubt.' He said, 'She was delightful. We laughed, she asked questions and she wanted to know the answers.' Meanwhile, Arek Hersh, also ninety-three, said, 'It was very nice. She was very interested. It brought back happy memories of being on the lake.' Both men were 'Windermere children', a group of 300 orphaned Jewish refugees who began new lives in the Lake District in 1945 after they were rescued from Nazi concentration camps. Over time, Catherine has developed a knack of talking openly to people, discussing harrowing topics, but ensuring the person she is with feels good about the conversation.

Her presence also helps to bring in the cash for those in need. Catherine has helped generate a staggering £245,000 of donations for crisis-hit parents and children. Danielle Flecher-Horn, founder of the baby bank AberNecessities, in Aberdeenshire, Scotland, said, 'She has this great ability to make you feel at ease and it was immediately obvious how warm, personable, and interested she was in us as individuals and our organisations.'[85] 'My daughter is now the happy little girl who met Kate, not the girl with blood cancer,' said Lynda Sneddon, from Falkirk in Scotland.

Cat Ross from Sheffield, CEO of Baby Basics UK, said the duchess helped her organisation to support 33,000 families in need, including 2,200 from Afghanistan. Speaking of her involvement to *Hello!* magazine, Ross said that Catherine's help with the initiative was 'amazing' and that donations 'absolutely snowballed' following her hands-on approach to the project. She praised the duchess's 'genuine interest' in the cause.

Meeting ordinary people who are forced to deal with extraordinary problems can be daunting, but Catherine has developed her own coping mechanism when faced with harrowing stories. It has given her a renewed confidence and a stronger and clearer voice. Understandably reserved when she started out as a working royal, her public speaking has improved exponentially. She may look like the picture of poise, but she has candidly admitted that it is one part of royal life she is 'still working out' and confessed it was not her 'natural thing'.

On an engagement in support of the Dame Kelly Holmes Trust at St Katherine's School, Bristol, in May 2023, she sat down for a chat with a group of schoolgirls and spoke candidly when the floor was open to questions, after listening to their own experiences about home and school life. Afterwards, double Olympic champion Dame Kelly said the girls asked Catherine about being a Royal Family member and the princess said it was something 'she had to learn'. Dame Kelly went on, 'She humanised everything to say not everyone's perfect. Doesn't matter what you've got, or what you're perceived to have, as an individual you're still going to have those insecurities.'

With her numerous charities, public appearances and other interests, Catherine is conscious that her busy schedule often eats into the quality time with her husband and children, but she has taken steps to categorise her workload to make time for her loved ones.

'Someone did ask me the other day, what would you want your children to remember about their childhood? And I thought that was a good question, because if you really think about that, is it that I'm sitting down trying to do their maths and spelling homework over the weekend? Or is it the fact that we've gone out and lit a bonfire and sat around trying to cook sausages that hasn't worked because it's too wet? That's what I would want them to remember, those moments with me as a mother, but also the family going to the beach, getting soaking wet, filling our boots full of water, those are what I would want them to remember. Not a stressful household where you're trying to do everything and not really succeeding at one thing.'[86]

So far, at least, she seems to have found the right work/life balance for her.

CHAPTER 14

We'll Meet Again

*These images remind us that, as families, communities and as a
nation, we need each other more than we had ever realised.*

**CATHERINE TALKING ABOUT HER
'HOLD STILL' PROJECT**

By the start of 2020, William and Catherine were established
as confident ambassadors for the country and the British
government capitalised on the positive vibes their visits achieved.
But the couple's overseas visits were quickly put on hold when the
COVID-19 pandemic struck.

In early March, they had just completed a highly successful
post-Brexit three-day visit to Ireland. It was William and
Catherine's first official visit there and was seen as a charm
offensive to highlight the many strong links between the UK and
Ireland. A telling headline in the *Irish Independent* read: 'William
and Kate gear up for post-Brexit charm – and pints of Guinness'.
During the visit, they travelled to Dublin, County Meath, County
Kildare and Galway in what turned out to be their last overseas visit
for a while.

Ironically, during a reception at the Guinness Storehouse in
Dublin, William had asked a paramedic if the coronavirus had

been 'hyped up' by the media. Within weeks, Prime Minister Boris Johnson announced a nationwide lockdown to curb a widening outbreak of COVID-19. The Queen, with Harry and Meghan gone and Andrew also sidelined, would need her star couple to keep up public morale more than ever as everyone's lives were about to change and undergo grief and strain.

The enforced nationwide lockdown that followed led to a wave of public health measures such as social distancing, travel and movement restrictions and closure of non-essential shops. One in three adults in Britain reported that their mental health had deteriorated as a result. Queen Elizabeth, as head of the nation, knew that she and her family had to reassure an anxious country. She defiantly met that challenge head-on, serving as a symbol of national stability when the people needed her most.

The Queen delivered two historic, televised addresses just weeks apart, urging calm but offering the public hope. The virus, she said with conviction, would be overcome. To those who were isolated and alone, she said, 'We will meet again,' while acknowledging the reality that 'we have faced challenges before, this one is different.' She went on, 'I am speaking to you at what I know is an increasingly challenging time. A disruption that has brought grief to some, financial difficulties to many, and enormous changes to the daily lives of us all. Today, once again, many will feel a painful sense of separation from their loved ones, but now, as then, we know deep down that it is the right thing to do.'

It was one of the most powerful interventions by a monarch since her father addressed the nation on the radio on the outbreak of the Second World War. Indeed, the Queen likened Britain's lockdown to the sacrifices people made during the war that she had lived through. Her serene demeanour and experience had authority; her promise of a resolution helped people to have faith.

William and Catherine immediately answered Her Majesty's call. They realised that they had to step up and help in any way they could. The Queen had always said the Royal Family had to be seen to be believed and they knew that despite government restrictions, they had to find a way to be visible. Catherine was one of the first to urge members of the Firm to familiarise themselves with online platforms to reach out to the public in a way that they had never done before. With the prime minister Boris Johnson seriously ill and hospitalised as he battled against the virus, and the Queen isolating in a safety 'bubble' at Windsor, news broke that her son and heir, Prince Charles, had got COVID-19.

When Prince William also contracted the virus in April, while his father was still recovering in isolation and with recorded deaths from the virus in the UK at more than 900 daily and the vaccine roll-out months away, he and Catherine agreed not to announce his diagnosis. He felt there were 'important things going on and I didn't want to worry anyone', so instead he laid low and followed government guidelines by isolating at Anmer Hall, where he was treated by royal doctors.[87]

The Prince later acknowledged how lucky he was to have a country estate where he could isolate with his family, compared to others couped up in small flats. He also provided a touching description of family life at that time, complete with bickering children and scenes of chaos in the kitchen, familiar to millions.

When the schools were closed due to the pandemic in early 2020 and again in 2021, Catherine and William shared that they too, like parents around the world, were home-schooling their children. During an interview with the BBC, they discussed its challenges and its rewards. It was a balancing act, they said, but it was great spending so much time with their young family. 'The children have got such stamina. I don't know how, honestly,' said William. 'You get to the end of the day, and you write a list of all the things you've done in that day. You've pitched a tent, taken the tent down again, cook, bake. You get to the end of the day, and they've had a lovely time. But it's amazing how much you can cram into one day, that's for sure.'[88]

Their youngest son Louis was a little love bug, said Catherine. As she explained, 'Louis doesn't understand social distancing. He goes out wanting to cuddle anything, particularly any babies younger than him.'[89]

In February 2021, William recorded the 'Time to Walk' podcast for Apple Fitness+ and Apple Music 1, and recalled, 'What I've been amazed by is how much my children already have inherited my family's love of music. Most mornings there's a massive fight between Charlotte and George as to what song is played. And I must now basically prioritise that one day someone does this one, and another day it's someone else's turn. So, George gets his go, then Charlotte gets her go. Such is the clamour for the music.'

He went on, 'One of the songs that the children are loving at the moment is Shakira's "Waka Waka". There's a lot of hip movements . . . there's a lot of dressing up. Charlotte, particularly, is running around the kitchen in her dresses and ballet stuff and everything. She goes completely crazy, with Louis following her around, trying to do the same thing. It's a happy moment where the children just enjoy dancing, messing around, and singing.'

It was clear that his children are never far from his mind, nor is his beloved wife. 'We've got hares running across the field over there, fat English partridges going over the hedge just here, with a nice orange tractor up ahead,' he said. 'Louis is obsessed by tractors. It just feels very wild and very peaceful. We spend as much time as we can here . . . and we feel very, very lucky to be out in the countryside. We've got the sheep in the fields. We've got the pond here with the duck and the geese on. It's a fantastic place to be.'

All the working royals were seen on television at their doorways, applauding National Health Service staff, along with numerous celebrities and politicians demonstrating camaraderie with the rest of the country. But as soon as he was well enough, William and Catherine were determined to be as visible to the public as possible and to highlight the work of the courageous emergency services staff, healthcare workers, charity and community workers across the UK. They did what they could within the imposed restriction guidelines to help keep up the nation's spirit.

The couple focused on frontline workers, highlighting their mental wellbeing. They did their best to ensure that those deemed essential workers, who risked their lives daily, also had access to professional support. They made countless Zoom calls to doctors, nurses and emergency services personnel, not only to boost morale, but to call attention to what those people needed. Anmer Hall became their headquarters as well as their home. Whenever they could, they joined in community efforts, delivering food parcels of pasta to nearby families in need.

In-person appearances were replaced by remote meet-ups, with even Queen Elizabeth having to learn her way around a Zoom video call. Catherine soon perfected the art and was lauded for her upbeat appearances. Her positive look for these virtual engagements and her 'down to earth' glamour, sometimes switching outfits between calls to keep her look fresh, was praised too. She wanted the people to whom she spoke to know that they were special and that each call she made and their circumstances mattered to her.

The Kensington Palace communications team was keen for the media to report that the couple were in close contact with their patronages and were still working to support others. 'Self-isolation and social distancing can pose huge challenges to our mental health – in recent weeks the Duke and Duchess of Cambridge have been in regular contact with organisations and patronages to understand the issues they are facing during this difficult time,' their Instagram caption read, with a shot of William and Catherine taking calls from their office.

The pair recorded a special voiceover for Public Health England's *Every Mind Matters* film, which directs people to coronavirus-related mental health support. William and Catherine also spoke about their own lockdown experiences during an interview with the BBC, where they revealed they had been keeping in touch with family via video calls and there had been home-schooling for George and Charlotte.

The duchess took part in a discussion with three parents whose children attend Roe Green Junior School in Kingsbury, North-West London, alongside the head teacher, Melissa Loosemore. In a 'show and tell' exercise during the chat, which was shared on Instagram and the Royal Family's YouTube channel, she directed everyone to answer questions by writing them down on a piece of paper. The first request was to write down 'one word that describes parenting during this pandemic'. Catherine held up the word 'exhausting', while the other parents joined in with similar sentiments, including 'challenging', 'hectic' and 'patience'.

Candidly explaining her feelings, Catherine said, 'I've become a hairdresser this lockdown, much to my children's horror, seeing Mum cutting hair. We've had to become a teacher and I think, personally, I feel pulled in so many different directions and you try your best with everything, but at the end of the day I do feel exhausted.' She added, 'I think as parents you've the day-to-day elements of being a parent, but I suppose during lockdown we have had to take on additional roles that perhaps others in our communities, or in our lives, would have supported us and helped us with.'

She was not afraid to talk about the dynamics of her relationship during the lockdown. When asked who her biggest support throughout the pandemic had been, she replied with one word, 'William.'

Academic Dr Jorie Lagerwey,[90] author of the book *Postfeminist Celebrity and Motherhood: Brand Mom*, believes that 'Brand Mom' has become even more integral to Catherine's public image. Without as many royal engagements, she described her as akin to a world-famous mommy blogger: 'All mommy blogging is about that – you're paying people to create professional photography and content for the successful blog, managing corporate partnerships, and everything that goes with being an influencer. I think she does that, just to the most extreme degree.'

Catherine 'shared pictures of her children's arts and crafts, including an "Instagram vs reality" meme showing the aftermath of her youngest son Prince Louis's finger painting. That [post] is completely harmless – a kid got a bit messy; nothing is serious about that. And so that choice is like, OK, I'm authentic, my kids are messy too.' Her PR team at Kensington Palace posted the results on the Palace social media platforms. They know what makes a good connection, said Dr Lagerwey, but were still doing it in an intensely controlled way.

In truth, what Catherine did and said during the pandemic came from the heart, not as part of a Machiavellian public relations strategy. As far as she was concerned, according to those close to her, she was only ever trying to help others. She wanted to ensure those risking their health felt appreciated.

Every time her face popped up on a computer screen, the call's recipient was met with Catherine's smile, which lit up her face with joy. It undoubtedly helped to lighten the mood. Her words of encouragement gave those frontline workers a sense of being special.

As a source close to the Cambridges said, 'From the moment the government introduced lockdown, both the duke and duchess were the first on the phone asking their team to liaise with the Queen's household and the government to ensure they were doing all they could physically do to help, without breaching guidelines. They felt a profound sense of duty, probably more than at any other time.'

Post-lockdown, the couple was still determined to be seen out and about doing their job. They embarked on an inspiring three-day tour of Britain to pay tribute to frontline workers and thank them for their selfless efforts during the Covid crisis. Senior palace insiders said the pair's ambition for their whistlestop tour of the country was to 'lighten the nation's mood' ahead of Christmas. One senior aide told the *Daily Telegraph*, 'What this year has done has reinforced the value of the Royal Family as natural actors of state. They are not celebrities – they are there, effectively, to thank people on the public's behalf.'[91]

William and Catherine travelled 1,250 miles across the country using the royal train and meeting National Health Service staff, volunteers, care home staff, teachers, schoolchildren and young people to hear first-hand their experiences, sacrifices and the effort they had put in throughout lockdown. Catherine, her aides said, saw it as her duty to highlight these everyday heroes and to pay tribute in person to the work of individuals and organisations who went 'above and beyond' in response to the pandemic crisis. The trip had the full backing of the Queen and Prime Minister Boris Johnson hailed the tour as a 'welcome morale boost'.

Although Catherine is now one of the most famous women in the world, she still does not feel entirely happy when in front of a battery of cameras. But during her decade as a member of the Royal Family she has learned to become more relaxed in front of the lens and her image has adorned countless front pages of glossy magazines, including the coveted cover of British *Vogue* in 2016, marking its 100th anniversary.

The ten-page shoot for its June 2016 issue, by British photographer Josh Olins, was the first she had agreed to and it took several months of talks to nail down. She finally relented when the magazine and the National Portrait Gallery, of which she is patron, agreed to work together on a shoot that would create a new portrait of her for its collection and be a centrepiece in a major exhibition, *Vogue 100: A Century of Style.*

'It's a huge honour and incredibly exciting for us to have HRH The Duchess of Cambridge featuring on the cover of British *Vogue* and as part of our centenary issue,' said *Vogue* editor-in-chief Alexandra Shulman. Catherine liked the idea of being photographed in the Norfolk countryside and she wanted the pictures to reflect an element of her private life, reported Shulman. She was not vain and worried about her appearance either and hardly checked herself in the make-up mirror, arriving in a pair of jeans and a parka jacket, with her hair in big rollers. 'She didn't want to be dressed as a fashion plate and was not keen to be shot in gala gowns and tiaras,' said Shulman. Instead, the clothes reflected her 'off-duty' outfits: jeans, shirts, T-shirts.

Throughout the photo shoot, Catherine showed great interest in the technicalities of the photographer Josh Olin's work and how he composed the photographs. She told Alexandra Shulman, 'The process of the shoot was fascinating to see. It was so much closer to the process of painting a portrait than I had appreciated before, seeing the layers of the setting, make-up, clothes, and light all coming together to form the final image. Seeing everything come together at once made me realise how much work goes into a single image.'[92]

Catherine told Shulman that since becoming a mother she had taken lots of photographs of her children and she noticed the difference between them and herself as a subject. Catherine said, 'From taking photographs of George and Charlotte, I have been struck by the wonderful lack of self-consciousness that you see in photographs of children, without the self-awareness that adults generally feel.'

Catherine's interest in photography was inspired by her paternal grandfather, Peter Middleton, a former RAF pilot who died in November 2010 at the age of ninety. Claudia Acott Williams, the curator of the Historic Royal Palaces, was behind a photography exhibition, 'Life Through a Royal Lens', at Kensington Palace. She told the *Sunday Express*, 'Her grandfather was a very good photographer. When she was a child, he would show her his slides. It was him who taught her how to take photographs.'[93]

In November 2004, Catherine, then a fourth-year History of Art student at St Andrews University, wrote to the Lewis Carroll Society asking for help in looking at Carroll's representations of 'the child' and discovering if his photographs 'support or conflict our notions of childhood'. Carroll was famous, of course, for writing *Alice's Adventures in Wonderland* and its sequel, *Through the Looking Glass*. Acott Williams said the duchess's dissertation on the photographs of children taken by Lewis Carroll, especially of Alice Liddell, would have been an excellent preparation for her method in capturing photos of George, Charlotte and Louis.

Arthur Edwards, who has photographed the Royal Family since the 1970s, highlighted Catherine's ability: 'I was impressed by the photograph she took of Prince William and the three children on the swing that was released to celebrate his thirty-eighth birthday. They are all happy and laughing. Only a mother or a father could get that picture. It is top drawer.'[94] He also praised her for the 2020 project when she photographed survivors of the Nazi Holocaust with their grandchildren. 'She lit it beautifully,' he said.

In a video clip released by ITV News, Camilla shared her experience of Catherine photographing her. 'We had a lot of fun,' she said. 'It was very relaxed. It was very kind the Duchess of Cambridge came with her camera, she's an extremely good photographer.'

Not everyone, however, is a fan of her hobby. Catherine's children, she admits, often tell her to stop. They say, 'Mummy, please stop taking photographs!'[95]

Out of her love of photography came the idea for *Hold Still: A Portrait of Our Nation in 2020*, a photographic book published in 2021 by the National Portrait Gallery. At the height of lockdown, acutely aware of her privilege, Catherine wanted to combine her enthusiasm for photography and her patronage of the National Portrait Gallery in a project that would recognise and reward those who had surpassed themselves to help others during the pandemic lockdown.

Catherine summed it up when she reflected on the lockdown and how it had impacted peoples' lives and mental wellbeing. 'When we look back at the COVID-19 pandemic in decades to come, we will think of the challenges we all faced,' she said. 'But we will also remember the positives: the incredible acts of kindness, the helpers and heroes who emerged from all walks of life and how together we adapted to a new normal.'[96]

Thousands of people submitted photographic portraits, taken in a six-week period during May and June 2020, focused on three core themes, Helpers and Heroes, Your New Normal and Acts of Kindness. Incredibly, the project saw more than 31,000 images submitted, of which judges selected 100 portraits, and the duchess served on the specialist panel that selected the final images used in the digital exhibition. The net proceeds from the sale of the book were split equally to support the work of the National Portrait Gallery and Mind, the mental health charity.

'We've all been struck by some of the incredible images we've seen, which have given us an insight into the experiences and stories of people across the country,' she said in a statement. 'Some desperately sad images showing the human tragedy of this pandemic and other uplifting pictures showing people coming together to support those more vulnerable.'

It was inspired. Through *Hold Still*, Catherine embraced the power of photography and hoped to create a lasting record of our COVID-19 lockdown experiences, good and bad. In one heart-warming telephone call with Niaz Maleknia and her teenage daughter Romy, who featured in the photography project, she thanked Niaz for highlighting the lockdown's impact on young people. In the call, which was shared on the Cambridges' YouTube channel, Catherine was heard cracking up when Romy told her that her mum once went all the way to bribing her with pizza to get her to pose.[97]

Through her project, Catherine had forged a legacy, not merely through the lens, but in the very act of witnessing and honouring our collective ordeal. It was an endeavour that defined her, a testament to the resilience and unity of spirit that she sought to capture. Queen Elizabeth was proud of her. She wrote a message for the *Hold Still* exhibition launch in which she affirmed that 'the photographs have captured the resilience of the British people at such a challenging time.'

CHAPTER 15

The End of an Era

It's a moment that defines something important
and historic for our Royal Family.

BODY LANGUAGE EXPERT JUDI JAMES
ON CATHERINE AT PRINCE PHILIP'S FUNERAL

On 7 March 2021, Harry and Meghan's pre-recorded television interview with Oprah Winfrey was aired in the US. Its content was sensational. Meghan took no prisoners and her onslaught against what she perceived was a hostile Royal Family was relentless. The Royal Family appeared under siege dealing with what was turning into a public relations disaster.

The Queen, however, had more important concerns than her petulant grandson and his wife. While Harry and Meghan were relentlessly attacking his family, Prince Philip was admitted to the world-renowned King Edward VII hospital in London as a 'precautionary measure'. He spent a month in hospital with an infection and heart trouble, and was finally discharged to Windsor Castle, but emerged a different, much frailer and more anxious man. Increasingly deaf, he was never the same again.

Prince Philip, the Duke of Edinburgh, died on 9 April 2021, only twenty-three days after he was discharged from hospital. Shortly before his death, one member of his inner circle spoke to him directly about how amazing it must be to have reached the age of ninety-nine. With his usual quick wit, Philip responded, 'I wouldn't recommend it.'[98]

The funeral of Prince Philip was seen as a turning point for Catherine; a moment when she came of age. As she took her place as one of the most senior Royal Family members, supporting the grieving, frail Queen, she stood tall, exuding poise and calm. The funeral of the family's paterfamilias marked the end of an era, but it also signalled the dawn of the new one, where Catherine will play a central role, just as Philip had done at the start of the Queen's reign.

On the day of the funeral itself, 17 April, much was made in the media of what became an iconic photograph of the duchess. Many commentators said it gave us a window into the future, a glimpse of Catherine as Queen. The picture, by Getty Images' Chris Jackson, encapsulated a moment in history. Catherine, wearing an all-black dress by French fashion designer Roland Mouret, paired with pearl and diamond jewellery and a black netted fascinator hat with a net veil, was no longer at the periphery of the family; she was at its heart. However, it was not what she wore that day, but the way she carried herself. Impeccable, she looked straight down the barrel of the lens and her eyes spoke volumes; she radiated a regal impregnability.

Judi James, a leading body language expert, observed Catherine closely on the day and agreed that the photograph captured an important moment in time. She concluded, 'It's a moment that defines something important and historic for our Royal Family, but it is also a moment that is visually pleasing in terms of style, too.' It was the perfect time for the duchess to look more regal than ever before, as Britons said goodbye to a man who represented a bygone era. Judi James added, 'With Prince

Philip being laid to rest, there was a feeling that an era of royal life was quickly vanishing with him. People were mourning a generation of royals that provided an image of something dashing and glamorous.'[99]

The duchess had real presence. In fact, the way she conducted herself that day was a shining example not only to the public, but to the other royals. She knew the cameras were trained on her but she maintained her sense of compassion. The contrast between her, the elegant, statuesque woman in black, and the frail, grieving Queen could not have been starker. Catherine reached out to Charles too, who was inconsolable at the loss of his father. Through her tenderness and warm interactions with him, she appeared to reassure her father-in-law.

Filmmaker Bidisha Mamata, in a Channel 5 documentary, *The Kate Effect: Kate – Our Queen in Waiting*, noted how Catherine seemed to move effortlessly among the mourners, trying to ease the tension with her generous spirit. 'What I noticed when watching the footage from Prince Philip's funeral was how warm Kate was towards Prince Charles. She seemed to be saying to him it's okay to show we are a family, just like all the other people in the world are families.'

The funeral had come at a time of serious discord in the Royal Family, with William and Harry engaged in a bitter feud that showed no sign of abating. Once again, Catherine showed her innate but subtle diplomacy when dealing with the bad blood between her husband and his brother, as they both mourned Philip in silence on that day.

Ever since they first met, Catherine had always enjoyed a close relationship with her brother-in-law. When William and Catherine announced their engagement, Harry described her as 'the sister I've never had and always wanted'. They had known each other since he was a teenager, and although he later admitted he had worried that she would take his brother away from him, they developed a close bond. When Meghan came into his life, however, the dynamic of that relationship changed. The duchess was said to be 'deeply wounded' by the Sussexes' ongoing media bombshells.

Nevertheless, Harry walked quickly towards Catherine as he left the chapel and the family were processing up the hill. She increased her pace so that the pair of them would catch up with William, who was only a few steps ahead of them. She then fell back, slowing enough to allow the brothers to walk next to each other and at least exchange a few words. It gave the public the impression that they were putting on a united front for their late grandfather, whom they both loved. It was the moment the public had been hoping to see.

Catherine's true class shone through on that historic day. Her modest, but highly effective contribution was seen by commentators as the pinnacle of her royal career to date. She appeared formidable. After a decade as a senior member of the Royal Family, she looked as if she truly belonged. The middle-class girl, some commentators said, looked more royal than the blood royals that day, a pillar of strength and calmness amidst the emotional swirl.

A few days later, on 29 April, William and Catherine celebrated their tenth wedding anniversary. Acknowledging the TikTok generation, the royal couple offered up a brief glimpse into their private life. In the video they thanked their followers for their messages of support. The charming video montage by filmmaker Will Warr was shared on their official @KensingtonRoyal Instagram handle, accompanied by a heartfelt note that read, 'Thank you to everyone for the kind messages on our wedding anniversary. We are enormously grateful for the 10 years of support we have received in our lives as a family. W & C.'

It featured Catherine, William and their three children immersing themselves in nature. All wearing matching casual outfits, they are seen scaling the sandy dunes of Norfolk's beaches, gathering around a countryside campfire to roast marshmallows and playing in the gardens of Anmer Hall, their Norfolk home. It presented a warm and loving picture of a truly happy family.

On 20 March 2022, William and Catherine landed in Belize for a week-long tour of the Caribbean to mark the Queen's Platinum Jubilee. It was their first joint overseas trip since the pandemic and they would also visit Jamaica and the Bahamas. Before setting off, the duke and duchess had held high hopes and were determined to meet as many people as possible. It was soon clear, however, that their officials and the British Foreign and Commonwealth Office had totally misjudged the mood of the host nations. Inexplicably, they did not expect such a hostile reception or predict the wave of negative headlines that followed. One critic even described their controversial three-country tour as 'offensively tone-deaf'.[100]

In fairness, the visits were largely organised by the governments of the host nations, as they were realms. It started badly and got progressively worse. First, their opening official event was scrapped after residents protested them. They were then slammed when they were photographed dancing with the Garifuna people, of mixed African and indigenous American ancestry, and Catherine was filmed shaking maracas. The couple then visited ancient Mayan ruins before heading to Jamaica, for the worst flak they had ever received as royals.

From the moment they touched down, they faced hostility. Jamaican leaders immediately rejected the royal visit to the island, instead using it to demand reparations from the UK for slavery. Here, the protests were louder, more organised, and more meaningful. The political kickback against the couple was certainly more forceful.

Even at the official welcome, Jamaican Prime Minister Andrew Holness ambushed the royals for his own political benefit. In what was supposed to be a 'meet and greet', he was filmed telling them they were unlikely to ever be King and Queen of his country. 'There are issues here which are, as you would know, unresolved,' he said. 'Your presence gives an opportunity for those issues to be placed in context, put front and centre, and to be addressed as best as we can.'

It was excruciating to watch. As the cameras rolled, the royal couple stood awkwardly next to Mr Holness. He knew William could not react given he was representing the Queen, then the constitutional monarch of Jamaica. Yet the republican politician knew his words would make headlines and win over voters.

Among the public, initially at least, it seemed the royal pair got an enthusiastic welcome. They were mobbed in Trench Town, the birthplace of reggae music and home to the late Bob Marley, one of the pioneers of the genre. But it soon went badly wrong when a photograph went viral of them shaking hands with children through a wire-mesh fence at a football match.

The Cambridges were strongly criticised and accused of 'white-saviour parody'. Author Malorie Blackman slammed them and their team on social media. She shared the image of Catherine greeting people through the pitch-side fence on social media and wrote, 'Do Prince William and Kate employ even one person of colour in their PR depts and run the optics of such images below by them first?'

Even when William and Catherine met the Jamaican bobsleigh team and everyone was pictured smiled broadly as they sat inside it, they still faced criticism, despite the reaction from those on the ground being undoubtedly positive. It seemed everything they did backfired. William and Catherine rode standing in an open-top 1953 Land Rover during the Commissioning Parade in Jamaica, something the local organisers had wanted, but again this was deemed controversial by critics, who claimed it echoed Britain's colonial past.

There were some lighter moments. On the third leg of their tour in the Bahamas, they made an unscheduled stop at a fish fry. Catherine, wearing a pretty pink RIXO dress, was in playful mood. When locals told her that a dish called conch pistol had the same effect as Viagra, the medication used to treat erectile dysfunction, her eyes lit up. She then held up the strip of flesh, which comes from the inside of the conch and is said to be the conch's male genitalia, before putting it in her mouth to rousing applause from the crowds.

She then teased her husband, saying, 'I'm a little bit more adventurous than William is,' which drew more laughter and applause. She added that she had already tried conch fritters, but had yet to try conch salad. Catherine then got hold of a knife and helped Jade 'Kow' Adderley, owner of the Kow Conch Stall. As the pair joked around, William hit back, saying, 'I can handle it.'

This encounter showed just how far Catherine had come from the shy woman who first stepped out on her royal journey. It also demonstrated how confident she was in her marriage. Jade Adderley said afterwards, 'She was a good helper. I'd like her to stay and help me at the stall.' William then made an impromptu stop at a bar. He slapped his hand on the bar top and said, 'This is *my* stop!' He was offered a Gullywash, which is coconut juice with condensed milk, and seemed to enjoy it, joking, 'You guys talk amongst yourself, I'm staying here.'

The BBC's royal correspondent Jonny Dymond was uncompromising in his assessment of the tour. He was spot on when he wrote:

Quite how defeat was plucked from the jaws of victory in Trench Town, Kingston, may one day become the stuff of public relations legend. Palace staff must be wondering how the defining image of the Cambridges' trip to the Caribbean was not the explosion of joy and pleasure that greeted the couple in downtown Kingston. But instead, what looked to many as some sort of white-saviour parody, with Kate and William fleetingly making contact with the outstretched fingers of Jamaican children, pushing through a wire fence. It was a bad misstep for a couple who are surprisingly media-savvy. And it was not the only one on this curiously disorganised trip. Times have changed. The Royal Family have in the past been pretty good at changing with them. But not on this tour. And second chances are these days few and far between.[101]

As William prepared to make a speech going as far as he could to apologise for Britain's dark history in profiting on slavery, dozens gathered outside the British High Commission in Kingston, singing traditional Rastafarian songs and holding banners with the phrase 'Seh yuh sorry' – a local patois phrase that urged Britain to apologise.

The Duke of Cambridge went on to publicly condemn Britain's role in slavery, calling the slave trade 'abhorrent' and expressing his 'profound sorrow', but he did not have the government authority to address the elephant in the room: the multi-millions the Jamaican government had been demanding in reparations. The evening was 'deeply embarrassing'.

Left: Catherine Middleton on the day she graduated with an Upper Second-Class MA in History of Art from the University of St Andrews, Scotland, on 23 June 2005.

Below: William celebrating his twenty-sixth birthday after an eventful twelve months that had seen him earn his RAF wings, rekindle his relationship with Catherine Middleton and take a more prominent role in public life.

Catherine watches as her then boyfriend Prince William passes out at Sandhurst Military Academy on 15 December 2006 and was commissioned into the Blues and Royals with his Commander-in-Chief and grandmother, Queen Elizabeth II, looking on. Catherine was seated away from the royal party, next to William's friend Thomas van Straubenzee and her parents Michael and Carole Middleton.

Prince William and Catherine celebrate their engagement on 16 November 2010 and are later photographed together in the State Rooms at St James's Palace, London.

Above: The new Duke and Duchess of Cambridge sent the crowds into raptures when they kissed on their wedding day on the Buckingham Palace balcony with (L-R) Eliza Lopes, Prince Charles and Camilla, Lady Louise Windsor, Grace van Cutsem, Lady Margarita Armstrong-Jones, Tom Pettifer and William Lowther-Pinkerton, after their wedding in Westminster Abbey on 19 April 2011.

Below left: The Royal Wedding of Prince William to Catherine Middleton as they left Westminster Abbey.

Below right: Catherine, the Duchess of Cambridge with Prince William, the Duke of Cambridge, and Prince George outside the Lindo Wing of St Mary's Hospital, Paddington, on 22 July 2013.

The Duchess of Cambridge steers a dragon boat as her husband Prince William paddles in another boat on Dalvay Lake on 4 July 2011, on their first joint tour of Canada.

The Duchess of Cambridge with pupils from Vauxhall Primary School interacting with sheep and lambs, thanks to the Gloucester charity Farms for City Children established by children's author Michael Morpurgo and his wife Clare.

Catherine takes part in a drumming music therapy session as she attends the Anna Freud Centre family school Christmas party in north London, on 15 December 2015.

The Duchess of Cambridge greets children as she arrives at Roe Green Junior School in Brent, London, on 23 January 2018. She was there to launch a mental health programme for schools through the Heads Together campaign and she participated in a lesson designed to help support a child's mental health and wellbeing.

Top left: Catherine encourages members of the team Heads Together before officially starting the 2017 London Marathon on 23 April 2017.

Top right: The Duke and Duchess of Cambridge arriving at the Earthshot Prize Awards Ceremony, Alexandra Palace, London, on 17 October 2021.

Centre: Queen Elizabeth II and the Duchess of Cambridge during a visit to Leicester. Catherine joined her grandmother-in-law for the start of the Diamond Jubilee tour in March 2012.

Left: The Duchess of Cambridge delivers a speech on 15 November 2019, when she officially opened the Nook, East Anglia's Children's Hospices' new hospice in Framingham Earl, Norfolk.

Prince William, now the Prince of Wales, with Prince George, Princess Charlotte and Catherine, the Princess of Wales, as they watch the coffin of Queen Elizabeth II being placed into the hearse following the state funeral service in Westminster Abbey on 19 September 2022.

The Prince and Princess of Wales with their children and Mia Tindall, daughter of Zara Tindall, arriving at the Church of St Mary Magdalene, Sandringham, on Christmas Day 2023.

Catherine, the Duchess of Cambridge, with Prince William, the Duke of Cambridge, Meghan, the Duchess of Sussex, and Prince Harry, the Duke of Sussex, during the RAF Centenary service at Westminster Abbey on 10 July 2018.

Prince Harry, Meghan Markle, and the Duchess and Duke of Cambridge during the first Royal Foundation Forum in central London on 28 February 2018.

A picture showing the front pages of some of the UK's national newspapers on 23 March 2024, dominated by stories about Catherine announcing her cancer diagnosis.

A view of breaking news on television on 22 March 2024, as the Princess of Wales announced that she was undergoing preventative chemotherapy after being diagnosed with cancer.

'It wasn't a royal failure, but I wouldn't quite deem it a regal success either,' said Tyrone Reid, an associate editor at the national newspaper, the *Jamaica Gleaner*.[102] He added that before William and Catherine's arrival, the local press had highlighted demands by Jamaicans for the British monarch and British state to apologise for and accept its role in the abhorrent slave trade of years ago. 'The man on the street is demanding reparations as well, it's not just at the intellectual level. That's when you know something is really gathering momentum, when it's spreading across a broad section of society,' Reid told the *Guardian*.

Some critics went so far as to claim the Cambridges' ill-fated tour had accelerated moves to ditch the late Queen Elizabeth II as the head of state. It was a false impression, as all three countries, along with others in the region, had been pushing to become republics and were a long way along that road to constitutional reform well before William and Catherine had even set foot in the Caribbean.

The Palace had failed to see the bear traps and totally misjudged the mood. The programme appeared dated and patronising and harked back to the colonial days, glossing over the social and economic divisions that reinforced the dark days of white supremacy. It was also taking place as the Black Lives Matter movement – which had not only captured the imagination across America, but in the Caribbean and the West Indies – was reaching its zenith.

The couple's advisers and the Foreign Office were described as 'incompetent' for not seeing how the visit would be received. William was accused of being 'tone-deaf' for his failure to apologise for slavery and address the issue of reparations. Indeed, critics claimed the visit was actively paying homage to Britain's colonial past. Inevitably, given the reception they received, a series of inexcusable PR blunders followed.

The vitriolic backlash stung the Cambridges. It proved a wake-up call for the couple and their team. The informal 'meet-the-press' chat at the back of the royal plane en route to RAF Brize Norton was ostensibly to thank the media for covering the visit. This time, unlike on so many of the previous overseas visits by William and Catherine, they had not received positive feedback or coverage and wanted to address it.

William was quick to appreciate that age-old platitudes would not be enough on this occasion. In post-tour debriefings with he and Catherine and senior officials, both insisted there must be no more slip-ups going forward. Everyone agreed that even if the intentions were well-meaning, the optics were all wrong. The pair allowed their senior courtiers to brief the media that going forward, there would be a new 'Cambridge way' for future royal overseas tours.

They would ditch the decades-old 'never complain, never explain' mantra favoured by Queen Elizabeth and her courtiers. The couple, senior officials said, would adopt a more pro-active approach and present a different image, more in tune with modern times. They got to work on their plans straight away.

On their return, William and Catherine conducted a root and branches review of the tour to identify the serious errors made and to find workable solutions to what went wrong, and why. William and Catherine's ability to embrace and acknowledge failures is a big plus. 'They are not the type of people who bury their heads in the sand. Refreshingly, they both acknowledge they are not immune to mistakes and are prepared to act on it,' said a source close to them. It is a glimpse into what the modern monarchy may look like under King William V, should he use his first name when he accedes to the throne, with Queen Catherine at his side.

The Jamaican government has since announced plans to hold a referendum in 2024 to become a republic.

The rift within the Royal Family became the media focus ahead of the Queen's Platinum Jubilee celebrations. How could there possibly be a rapprochement after what had been alleged by Harry and Meghan? The Sussexes nonetheless flew to the UK and met with Charles and Camilla and the late Queen in separate meetings at Windsor. Despite high hopes, very little was achieved. Nobody was ready to take responsibility, least of all Harry, it seemed.

Harry and Meghan's presence threatened to dominate the media coverage in what was supposed to be the final public thank-you to Queen Elizabeth II during her lifetime. As it transpired, the couple became an insignificant sideshow in what was a huge outpouring of love for the record-breaking service by the monarch. They were even booed by the crowd as they arrived at the National Service of Thanksgiving at St Paul's Cathedral, which the Queen did not attend. Inside, Catherine looked visibly upset at being in the same space as Harry and Meghan. William, who was clearly uncomfortable too, gave his wife a consoling look.

The Sussexes were photographed watching Trooping the Colour shortly before the working royals including Charles, Camilla, Catherine and William took to the Palace balcony. But once again it was William, Catherine and their children who were the star attractions alongside the Queen. Catherine's parenting skills were tested when Louis stretched his mother's patience by blowing raspberries and thumbing his nose at her in the front row of the royal box during the Jubilee pageant. She urged him to take a break from his naughty behaviour, but he persisted.

Viewers watching later wrote on social media how they felt sorry for the duchess, but commentators praised her patience as she tried to calm her youngest son down. Eventually, he broke free from Catherine and William asked his father to intervene. Charles happily bounced his grandson on his knee and Louis was finally content.

The death of her beloved Philip had hit the Queen very hard. She also lost several close friends who died in quick succession around the same time and as a result, felt increasingly isolated. She had taken to inviting ex-members of her staff to come and visit her in her private apartments to talk about the old times. One revealed later, 'She told me she didn't know anybody [her staff and servants] anymore.'

Behind the scenes, Queen Elizabeth had been feeling terribly frail. Her team of doctors had advised her to rest, but she felt she had to put her people first and as Head of the Nation she was determined not to disappoint them. When Charles urged her, for the sake of history, to acknowledge the crowds in The Mall with a wave from the Buckingham Palace balcony as the finale to the Platinum Jubilee, she agreed.

The final appearance took real courage. Her late Majesty was suffering constant pain, as she had a form of myeloma, a bone marrow cancer, which explained her tiredness and dramatic weight loss in the final years of her life.[103] Bravely clutching her walking stick, the Queen stood on the balcony with her close family and acknowledged the enthusiastic mass of loyal supporters in front of the Palace for the last time.

Her health deteriorated rapidly over the next three months. She struggled terribly with her eyesight and had low vision. She even had difficulty lifting a full teapot to pour into her cup. 'Her Majesty could hardly see and just didn't have the strength,' a source close to the Queen said. 'She would get terribly frustrated as she hated causing a mess, pouring it over the tray. She asked for a smaller pot and would get frustrated when the staff forgot and brought the big one.'

Queen Elizabeth knew she was dying, but even towards the end she was worried that her passing at Balmoral in Scotland would make things more 'difficult', Princess Anne has disclosed. She was told her concerns 'should not be part of the decision-making process'.[104] Her late Majesty passed away peacefully at 3.10 p.m. at her beloved Balmoral on 8 September 2022, three hours and twenty minutes before it was publicly announced. Sir Edward Young, the Queen's private secretary, described in a memo how the monarch 'wouldn't have been aware of anything' and suffered 'no pain' when she died.[105] She had been on the throne for seventy years and 214 days, the longest-reigning monarch in British history.

The Princess Royal had been at her mother's bedside when she died, but other senior members of her immediate family did not make it to Balmoral in time, including Charles, who had been picking mushrooms at nearby Birkhall to clear his head after seeing his mother earlier in the day. As he was driving back to Balmoral he took a phone call, prompting him to pull over when he was addressed for the first time as 'Your Majesty'.

Her sons, Prince Andrew and Prince Edward, together with Edward's wife, Sophie, Countess of Wessex, and Prince William, boarded an RAF Dassault Falcon flight from RAF Northolt at 2.39 p.m. as the Queen's life was slowly ebbing away. They landed at Aberdeen airport at 3.50 p.m., by which time it was too late. Catherine, who as a future Queen might have expected to join her husband, stayed with her children, a decision that may have been influenced by Harry's petulance. She later revealed when meeting grieving royal supporters, 'My little Louis is just so sweet. He said, "Mummy don't worry, she's now with Great Grandpa.""

Prince Harry had decided to travel separately from his brother and the other senior Royal Family members. He took a private jet to Scotland, not getting there until just before 8 p.m. Close sources said he had elected not to fly with his brother and uncles after a disagreement over Meghan not being allowed to join him. It emerged that when he insisted that his wife accompany him to Balmoral during a phone call with his father, Charles told him she could not come.

King Charles III acceded to the throne aged seventy-three years and 298 days. The following day at 6 p.m., he paid a heartfelt tribute to his late mother in a pre-recorded television address from the Blue Drawing Room at Buckingham Palace. In the same broadcast, he also confirmed that William and Catherine would become Prince and Princess of Wales and William would also take on his Scottish titles. Charles was proclaimed King before the Accession Council in a televised ceremony in the red-carpeted Throne Room at St James's Palace two days later.

The King and the wider family were disappointed by Harry's self-absorbed behaviour. Amidst all the grieving, on 10 September, William, now Prince of Wales and heir to the throne, took decisive action. He called for a truce with his brother, personally telephoning him and suggesting they and their wives put on a show of unity for the sake of their late grandmother. He invited Harry and Meghan to join him and Catherine to view the floral tributes at Windsor Castle and Harry accepted.

The Duke and Duchess of Sussex held hands together before all four of them walked forward to greet the crowds. For a moment and for the cameras, at least, it was as if they had slipped straight back into the Fab Four routine. Sadly, nothing could be further from the truth, as close sources have confirmed. Catherine later admitted privately to a member of the Royal Family that it was one of the hardest things she had ever had to do, given the extent of the ill feeling between the two couples.[106]

CHAPTER 16

Tough Act to Follow

Being a princess isn't all it's cracked up to be.
DIANA, PRINCESS OF WALES

I t was a moment etched in Princess Diana's memory. Despite her physical discomfort, caused by her squeezing into a tightly fitted, black taffeta strapless dress, Lady Diana Spencer could not wait to attend a VVIP reception. It was her chance to meet Princess Grace of Monaco, the one-time iconic Hollywood actress. On the night, the two women bonded instantly as they chatted while the champagne flowed at the soirée before a musical recital at Goldsmiths' Hall on 9 March 1981.

The nineteen-year-old English aristocrat, who had accom-panied her fiancé Charles, Prince of Wales to the event, soon found herself swapping stories and then sharing her fears about her impending royal life, despite hardly knowing the woman in whom she was confiding. As they chatted in the privacy of the bathroom, perhaps more than anyone, Grace instantly understood the traumatic life experiences Diana was facing.

Lady Diana was captivated by Grace Kelly and her life story that took her from Hollywood to become a global figure as Princess

Grace of Monaco after turning her back on her movie career to wed Prince Rainier III. Despite her glamorous lifestyle in the tax haven in the South of France, Diana sensed that Grace, who was fifty when they met, had faced hidden struggles in what became a tempestuous marriage. 'I recall Princess Grace in all her tranquillity and grace, but beneath that serene surface, I sensed turbulence,' Diana said later.[107]

The lives of both women were indeed marred by adultery and lies, and ultimately ended tragically. Grace died in a car accident on 13 September 1982 about two miles outside of La Turbie. She was driving when she missed a particularly sharp turn. 'I can't stop. The brakes don't work,' were the last words her daughter Stephanie, a passenger in the car, heard her say. Stephanie escaped with minor injuries, but her mother Grace never regained consciousness, and died aged fifty-two.

Princess Diana suffered a similar fate. She died on 31 August 1997 at Pitié-Salpêtrière University Hospital, Paris, from fatal injuries received in a car crash in the Alma tunnel. Both accidents became the subject of media speculation and conspiracy theories. In the popular imagination the two women, both restless souls, arguably remain the most famous princesses of recent times, certainly of the twentieth century.

According to Princess Diana, who attended Grace's funeral eighteen months after their one and only meeting, the last thing the princess said to her resonated deeply. Grace laid a comforting hand on Diana's cheek and told her, 'Don't worry, dear, it'll only get worse.'

Sadly, and prophetically, she was right.

For those who lived through the so-called 'Diana era' – the fifteen years in the 1980s and 1990s when she was the darling of the media – it is hard to imagine anyone else styled as or even being called HRH The Princess of Wales. From the moment she burst on the scene as the shy 'Lady Di', she captivated people around the world. She was a media darling who regularly appeared on the covers of glossy magazines and newspapers during her lifetime, beloved for her kindness and selfless humanitarian work. The press could not get enough of her and her life became public property, because editors and publishers knew a cover shot of Diana could dramatically increase circulation. But such fame came at a cost. She was overwhelmed and afflicted by the eating disorder bulimia nervosa, her marriage failed and she suffered from low self-esteem.

She would go on to become the most famous woman of her generation, a global icon. Millions of people who had never met her mourned Diana when she died in the car accident aged only thirty-six. In her all-too-short life, she captured the hearts of a nation. As the British Prime Minister Tony Blair declared at the time of her death, she was the 'People's Princess', destined never to be crowned Britain's Queen.

Unlike Catherine, Lady Diana Spencer was an aristocrat, the daughter of British nobleman John, the 8th Earl Spencer. After she wed Prince Charles on 29 July 1981 at St Paul's Cathedral, she regularly topped the polls as the world's favourite royal and the most-photographed woman.

People who had never met the princess somehow felt they knew Diana; they could relate to her. They would turn out in their thousands for official engagements, lining the streets just to catch a glimpse of her. She in turn would ensure she gave them time, making an extra effort to engage with people on unscheduled walkabouts. As her life began to unravel, they empathised with her even more.

Following her divorce from Charles on 28 August 1996,

Queen Elizabeth II ruled that Princess Diana – then HRH The Princess of Wales – should be stripped of her royal title and status. The Palace announced that from then on she would be styled Diana, Princess of Wales until she remarried. She never did, of course, and it remained her title until her tragic death in Paris the following year. Many felt the removal of her HRH was petty, even vindictive, especially as Diana still had an important role to play as the mother of the future king, her eldest son Prince William.

As Diana's brother Earl Spencer put it so passionately in his eulogy at Westminster Abbey, she was someone 'with a natural nobility who was classless and who proved in the last year that she needed no royal title to continue to generate her particular brand of magic.'

When Charles finally married his mistress, Camilla Parker Bowles, in 2005, she chose to be known as HRH The Duchess of Cornwall and decided not to use the title Princess of Wales. Many felt this was a wise move designed to avoid a backlash from the army of Diana fans. Camilla, rightly, felt that most people would not accept her as the Princess of Wales because of the title's strong association with Diana and the fact that the princess had publicly blamed Camilla for wrecking her marriage, saying she was the third person in it. Instead, Camilla was styled as a royal duchess until Charles's accession, when she became Queen Consort.

Catherine, who became HRH The Duchess of Cambridge on her marriage to William, accepted the new title as being part of her duty as William's wife. When King Charles III announced his eldest son and daughter-in-law would become the Prince and Princess of Wales in his television address the day after his accession, it was a *fait accompli*. If Catherine was daunted by the decision, she was given little time to reflect on it. Those close to her say she now regards the title as an honour, in recognition of her husband's royal rank; something that she acknowledged when she entered the family, saying she would take time to forge her own career. It was not always the case.

Catherine knows her own mind and even established some fundamental life rules that she would stick to when she joined the Firm. Her 'terms' were in fact presented to Queen Elizabeth and Prince Charles in early 2015, at the time when she was pregnant with Charlotte, not in some formal document but by Prince William. On her behalf, he explained that she wanted space to grow into her role and said she needed more time to adapt to the peculiarities of royal life. She was clear from the outset that she would not be pigeon-holed into carrying out particular duties and insisted on having her full quota of maternity leave, away from the glare of the media and public. Her priority, she emphasised, would always be her family.

She also found media and household comparison to Princess Diana stressful. At the time it was even understood that when the moment came, just as Camilla had done, she might not want to adopt the title HRH The Princess of Wales because Diana had been such an iconic figure and she would find it too much to live up to. When that time did come, however, she accepted the title with good grace out of respect for her husband and for the King.

During their engagement interview on 16 November 2010, ITV news presenter Tom Bradby asked Catherine directly, 'William's mother was this massive iconic figure. The most famous figure of our age, is that worrying? Is that intimidating? Do you think about that a lot, both of you, you particularly, Kate, obviously?'

It was a punchy question. Catherine paused briefly to consider her answer, before replying, 'Obviously I would have loved to have met her and she's obviously an inspirational woman to look up to. Obviously on this day and you know going forward and things, you know it is a wonderful family, the members who I've met have achieved a lot and you know very inspirational and so, yes, I do.'

It was the first time most people had heard her speak publicly and she was understandably self-conscious. Her answers were breathy and a little nervous, her accent perhaps overly posh, even compared to William's. Afterwards even members of her own family gently ribbed her about how high-class it sounded. Over time her accent has become less clipped and more natural.

Back then, understandably, William was perhaps overly protective of his fiancée and even stepped in to answer some of the quickfire questions put by Bradby and, on occasion, he corrected her. 'There's no pressure though. There's no pressure,' he said. 'Like Kate said,[108] it is about carving your own future. No one is going to try to fill my mother's shoes, what she did was fantastic. It's about making your own future and your own destiny and Kate will do a very good job of that.'

He was right. Diana was a completely different character to Catherine. Diana was an archetypal free spirit, a royal rebel, dramatic and instinctive, who used her fame to raise awareness for difficult causes from leprosy to AIDS, homelessness and the clearing of landmines. She used public life, it seemed to many, to drag the Royal Family consciously and single-handedly into a modern age, making the House of Windsor more in touch and more relevant to the people than ever before.

Diana's tragic death in 1997, and the public's tsunami of grief and angry reaction to it that followed, genuinely rocked Queen Elizabeth II and her family. But the fallout and high emotion also shook many people's faith in the institution of monarchy itself.

People began to question their loyalty to the Crown. Front-page headlines like 'Show Us You Care' in the *Daily Express* genuinely alarmed the mandarins at the Palace, indeed the monarch herself. The writer and educator Christopher Hitchens noted that in the week after Diana's death Britain became a 'one-party state', such was the coercive nature of the public reaction, and attacked the 'tear-stained hordes' for their overreaction.

Even before her passing, Diana's impact on the Royal Family and its people was seismic. When she and Charles separated, she knew that she would never be Queen, but she did not make his path to kingship any easier, saying she did not think he would 'adapt' to the top job. She remains to many 'The Queen of People's Hearts', perhaps the only title by which she ever wanted to be known by, as she claimed in her BBC *Panorama* interview. But she was wrong about Charles's desire and ability to be king.[109]

Today, Diana's legacy lives on through her sons and the work and causes they champion. William and Harry are both very proud of what she achieved in her all-too-brief lifetime. Despite his involvement with AIDS charities and landmine clearance, Harry is not the only one who has continued her work.

William, whom Diana took to homeless shelters when he was an impressionable boy, has spent years working to eradicate homelessness, like his mother. In 2005, he became patron of Centrepoint, a leading youth homelessness charity, taking on a role that his mother held for the last few years of her life. In June 2023, he announced an ambitious five-year initiative called 'Homewards' to test ideas and models to end homelessness in six locations in the UK. 'This is about creating a programme that is truly sustainable and that will create systemic change in the homelessness system. This isn't just his legacy; it's his mother's legacy and he is committed to this,' said his official Palace spokesman.

Diana was always going to be a tough act to follow, but from the outset Catherine has never tried to do so. She has not sought comparisons with her late mother-in-law in any way. Perhaps more importantly, say sources close to her, nor has she felt the need to. While fashion writers and media commentators persist in trying, such articles are not something to which Catherine pays much attention. Yet, given the type of clothes that royal women are expected to wear for official and formal occasions, style comparisons between the two are inevitable.

Catherine, through her charity work, as well as her natural warmth and empathy, has connected with the public in much the same way as the trailblazer Diana did. Indeed, in many ways she has set the template for interaction with the public that all young royals today follow, crouching down to talk to children at their level being a must. Catherine may have fewer royal patronages than Diana, but this is a deliberate move, according to sources, because it allows her to dig much deeper into the causes that she is lending her support.

She is now a royal princess due to her marriage, styled Her Royal Highness too. Her seamless rise is testament to her grace, elegance and strength of character – a remarkable journey that will echo through generations.

The memory and legacy of Diana is ever-present for Prince William and his family. Catherine, who normally maintains silence regarding Diana, gave a rare window into her feelings about her late mother-in-law while chatting to a well-wisher in Wales on an official engagement to Dowlais Rugby Club in Merthyr Tydfil.

When asked about her engagement ring, which used to be Diana's, Catherine confirmed it was the 'same ring'. She also revealed that she had not needed to have it adjusted to fit her when William presented it to her when he proposed in 2010. 'It was the same size; it is very special. What an honour to be able to wear it,' she said. She added that Diana would have been a 'brilliant grandmother' and that the family 'miss her every day'.

'But sadly, I never got to meet her,' she added poignantly.

CHAPTER 17

No Place Like Home

If we don't act now, we will permanently destabilise our planet
and we will rob our children of the future they deserve.

CATHERINE, THE PRINCESS OF WALES

Sitting on a bench on the pier overlooking the harbour, a loving couple shared their haddock and chip supper wrapped in paper bought for £7.85 from the Anstruther Fish Bar on Shore Street. The award-winning fish and chip shop, twenty miles east of Fife, used to be a favourite of theirs back in their student days, so this pit stop was a nostalgic trip down memory lane. Totally relaxed in each other's company, after polishing off the meal and disposing of the rubbish, they strolled along the seafront of the Scottish coastal town, which has the North Sea as its backdrop. They then headed back to the Brattesani ice cream parlour for dessert, his in a cup and hers in a cone.

There were no official cameras around to record the stop in May 2021. It was, royal aides explained later, just an impromptu break. Once again, consciously or not, it showed William and Catherine's normalcy. They chatted happily to locals as they walked through the town and did not seem to mind when some people took photographs of them on their mobile phones. Inevitably, the charming story and snap found their way into the *Sun*.[110]

The chip-shop owner Alison Smith told the *Sun* royal correspondent Matt Wilkinson, 'They were customers of ours almost twenty years ago when they were at university. We were honoured to serve them fish and chips back in the day. We haven't seen them since, so we got the surprise of our life.' Somebody went in the shop to get fish and chips for them. 'We were unaware until a customer said the Duke and Duchess were sitting out on a bench. It was a beautiful scene,' she said.

Ever since she married into the Royal Family and began royal engagements, Catherine's natural empathy has enabled her to connect with people. She may have been a little shy at the start of her royal career, who would not be? But she has learned to really listen to the people to whom she speaks and is now often seen lagging some distance behind her husband William during public walkabouts, something she says she is teased about by him and other members of the family. It is precisely this instinctive behaviour, chatting freely with strangers in the crowd who have sometimes waited hours to see her, that makes Catherine our most relatable royal today.

Before the stop at the chip shop on a visit to Scotland in May 2021, the couple had carried out several engagements linked to their charity work and their commitment to the local communities. Among them was a visit to the social care charity Turning Point, which supports those affected by homelessness, drug use and mental health issues. The royal couple also spent time in the Orkney Islands and met with local fishermen and their families to discuss the extreme challenges facing the fishing industry and their communities.

Their week in Scotland culminated in them returning to the place where they met and fell in love, St Andrews University. It was a chance to reminisce. They also helped to finish painting some socially distanced hearts on the university's St Salvator's Lawn, introduced by the 'Can Do' scheme to encourage students to spend more time safely outdoors in small groups. They met and chatted with undergraduates and discussed how the COVID-19 pandemic had affected them. Afterwards they planted the first tree for the St Andrews Forest, one of the key initiatives in the university's action plan to become carbon neutral by 2035.

Before the visit to St Andrews, William had given an emotional address in his role as the new Lord High Commissioner to the General Assembly of the Church of Scotland, when he reflected on his time at St Andrews. 'It was here in Scotland twenty years ago this year that I first met Catherine . . . the town where you meet your future wife holds a very special place in your heart.'

It clearly did to him.

Catherine loves being in the thick of family mayhem, chaos in the kitchen and the rough and tumble over what music should be played over breakfast. It is part of the buzz of being a hands-on parent. Those who know the royal couple well say their children and family life are the heart and soul of their world. Watching their children just dancing, messing around and singing brings them real contentment. Those who organise their public life know too that they will always put their family first.

That is not to say that they neglect their public duties. The Court Circular – the official record of royal engagements – shows that over the past twelve months up to December 2023, the Prince of Wales completed 173 engagements, with the Princess of Wales undertaking 128. While this is considerably less than the King on 425 and Princess Anne, the hardest-working royal last year, carrying out 457 engagements, it does not show the behind-the-scenes and preparation work they do for major projects like Earthshot or Shaping Up.[111]

After all, they are parents to a young family and have made it clear that they will always prioritise their children. To both, that means preparing George for his future role as heir to the throne, and ultimately King, as well as making sure all their children's individual family needs are met. George and Charlotte thoroughly enjoyed their experience at Thomas's, the independent day school in Battersea, London. The school mantra of 'Be Kind' resonated with the Cambridges' own core beliefs, as did the friendly informality of the school. Mostly, they liked the fact that they were able to remain an active part of their children's daily lives, with each of them doing their best to do the school run.

Catherine always stressed she would take a direct role in the way their children would be raised, something that has endeared her to parents across the country. The way she lives her life shows that being a hands-on mother is her main priority, giving her children the stability and warmth that has not always been present in the Royal Family. Like Princess Diana, who fought hard for her sons, Catherine has led from the heart. But with Diana, perhaps because of her unhappiness, came drama and volatility, while with Catherine, there is an overriding sense of calm.

William has admitted that on occasion he felt embarrassed by his mother's behaviour as she lurched out of control. He asked Diana to stop saying negative things about his father to him because he did not want to take sides. One day the writer Bel Mooney and her daughter Kitty were invited, along with others, to have dinner with William and his father. Charles began to chat about his love of the Goons, the comedy radio series of his youth, and Bel burst into a popular song from the show called the 'Ying Tong Song'. When

Kitty turned to William and pointed out how embarrassing parents could be, his response was telling. 'Papa doesn't embarrass me,' he said, 'Mama does.'

Catherine wants her children to enjoy the same loving, safe environment that she herself experienced growing up. Spelling this out, she said, 'My parents taught me about the importance of qualities like kindness, respect and honesty, and I realise how central values like these have been to me throughout my life. That is why William and I want to teach our little children just how important these things are as they grow up. In my view, it is just as important as excelling at maths or sport.'

Catherine admitted being a parent today is 'tough'. When she spoke about the difficulties of being a modern parent with the UK radio host Roman Kemp, in February 2023, she said, 'The environment in which you bring up a child is as important as the experiences you engage them with.' She went on, 'It's not about the number of toys they've got or the number or sort of trips that you go on with them. It's just making sure that they've got the right emotional support around them and that comes from the adults in their lives.'[112]

Like Diana, who was never afraid of showing emotion in public, Catherine makes sure she is very affectionate with her husband and her three children, and that they know the importance of showing love too. On a 2018 visit to England's Basildon Sporting Centre, she echoed Diana when she revealed, 'Hugs are very important. That's what I tell my children.'

In August 2022, the new school for their children was finally announced. Kensington Palace issued a statement saying that all three, George, Charlotte and Louis, would be attending Lambrook School in Winkfield Row, near Ascot, an independent preparatory school for 560 boys and girls, aged three to thirteen, with nearly

190 staff. Founded in 1860, it is set in fifty-two acres of beautiful countryside, with a croquet lawn and old tyres hanging from the trees for pupils to swing in.

William and Catherine were keen for the school for their children to be co-educational. But it is expensive, charging around £21,000 a year, more if they want to use the flexi-boarding system. They know the royal children will be in good hands, with many of its leavers heading off to prestigious secondary schools such as Eton College, William's alma mater, or Catherine's, Marlborough College.

The royal couple praised George and Charlotte's old school, Thomas's Battersea, saying they were 'hugely grateful' that their two eldest children had such a happy start to their education. They added that they were pleased to have found a school for all three of their children that shared a similar ethos and values to Thomas's.

In a press notice, Ben Thomas, Principal of Thomas's London Day Schools, said: 'We would like to thank George, Charlotte, and all our leaving pupils for upholding the school's values and for their many contributions to school life throughout their time at Thomas's. We wish them every happiness and success at their next schools and beyond.'

The royal children's new headmaster, Jonathan Perry, said, 'We are delighted that Prince George, Princess Charlotte and Prince Louis will be joining us this coming September and very much look forward to welcoming the family, as well as all of our new pupils, to our school community.'

Since boyhood William has craved normalcy, even though others – such as his nannies and some of his relatives – insisted on him being aware that he was special. Diana did her best to free him from that feeling of being in a gilded royal cage. Along with Prince Harry, she took him to theme parks and burger bars and even on a London bus, because she wanted him to see the other side of life. Charles was not keen on these outings, especially trips to fast food restaurants such as McDonald's, but Diana insisted.

She also took William to meet the homeless in shelters, because she wanted him to appreciate how lucky he was, but also how other people can be forced to live. 'He promised himself he would always remain grounded,' a senior royal source said. Having experienced the heartache of his parents' divorce, William also wanted the woman he married to be his best friend.

Now, after two decades together, the last of that as a married couple, they are truly at one with each other. They enjoy the simple things, such as chilling out on the sofa at home in comfy clothes, watching box sets like *Homeland* and *Game of Thrones* when 'the kiddies are in bed'. They would love to go to Glastonbury Festival and recalled one of the favourite concerts they attended was seeing the British rock band Coldplay, fronted by Chris Martin, at Wembley Stadium.[113] Even after all this time together, they still make each other laugh.

The busy couple make the most of their private time together with their children. That is why their move to the four-bedroom Adelaide Cottage on the Windsor Estate, a relatively modest home in royal terms, was so important to them. Although their offices and staff remain at Kensington Palace, the move from London suits the lifestyle of their growing family. They love the outdoor life, long walks and bike rides together. For longer holidays they also have their large country home, Anmer Hall, on the Sandringham Estate in Norfolk. The late Queen Elizabeth, however, privately voiced her concern to William over him flying his entire family for breaks there by helicopter. She regarded it as an unnecessary risk.

Their low-key life at Adelaide Cottage works for them. It is ideally located close to Windsor Castle, the royal headquarters, while

Buckingham Palace is undergoing a major restoration. Another reason they moved to the semi-rural cottage, which has been in the Royal Family since 1831, is the privacy it gives them and their children. Situated on the 4,800-acre Windsor Great Park, privately managed by the Crown Estate, it offers the children the chance to explore, with its resident red deer herd and long-horn cattle roaming around the native oaks. 'This house gives them the opportunity to enjoy that lifestyle without being too far from central London. It is comfortable and homely, and, in all honesty, they are content living there,' a senior source said.

The house was once the home of the late Princess Margaret's lover and the man she longed to marry, the Battle of Britain fighter pilot Group Captain Peter Townsend, George VI's equerry. At that time in the early 1950s she was in her early twenties and Townsend was sixteen years her senior, and divorced from his wife, Rosemary. Margaret was later forced to choose between love and duty, because if she had married Townsend, it would have meant giving up her position and all the money and her royal privileges that went with it.

The Grade-II listed property was also offered by Queen Elizabeth to Harry and Meghan before they married, but they decided on Frogmore Cottage instead, before vacating it after they quit the UK entirely. It has been beautifully renovated with French windows, multiple fireplaces, a covered veranda and large covered entrance, and gingerbread trim. When they moved in, there was also a nautical-inspired theme with unique features such as golden dolphins and ceiling rope decorations recycled from a nineteenth-century royal yacht. William and Catherine funded all the further interior renovations privately.

Through senior aides, briefing the accredited media, the couple have made it known that they will each take turns at the fifteen-minute morning school run to Lambrook School.[114] The couple had set their hearts on the highly regarded Berkshire school to help replicate their own happy childhoods. This long-term plan was accelerated by the pandemic and the death of Prince Philip, which left the Queen isolated for the last seventeen months of her life. The move did not cost the taxpayer either as the couple pay the rent privately and due to the location within Windsor Home Park, there was no need for extra security.

Catherine understood that for William, as a future king, it was important for him to be geographically closer to the late Queen in her final months, when he was required to support both her and his father. It made a real difference. They were in regular contact, seeing each other in person and speaking on the phone several times a week, bringing them even closer. 'The relocation to Windsor was accelerated, primarily so that the prince could spend as much time as possible with Her late Majesty. He knew his time with his grandmother was precious and he is delighted they, as a couple, made that decision,' one aide explained.

Some commentators have praised William and Catherine for putting their family first. Others, including the influential *Daily Mail* editor-in-chief and royal writer, Richard Kay, questioned the wisdom of the move – which meant they now had three homes – at a time when families across Britain were facing a cost-of-living crisis with rising inflation and soaring energy bills. He wrote that it appeared 'clumsily insensitive'.[115] Former BBC royal correspondent Peter Hunt also waded into the argument when he noted, 'A fourth home for the Cambridges is a reminder the royals don't suffer from the cost-of-living crisis and a looming recession in the same way as the rest of us.'[116]

There has been talk that William and Catherine might move into Royal Lodge, the thirty-room mansion in Windsor Great Park occupied by Prince Andrew. But at the time of going to print, there is every sign he will continue living in his home of three decades, even though the King wants him to vacate the property so that the Wales's can move in. Andrew, who informally shares the sprawling Grade II-listed royal mansion with his ex-wife Sarah, Duchess of York, is in no mood to leave Royal Lodge, as he paid £1 million for a 75-year lease on the Queen Mother's former residence in 2003 and has since spent more than £7.5 million on extensive renovation work. What's more, in a private meeting with his older brother, he reminded him that their late mother Queen Elizabeth had promised him he could stay there.

What is clear is that William and Catherine are prepared to make the most of situations. When it comes to making uncomfortable and possibly unpopular decisions, they will always put their family first. If they believe it is for the benefit of their children, they will do so.

For William being a hands-on dad in his children's formative years is extremely important. He is happy to spend quality time with his eldest son George, one on one. He also seems to want to show their close bond to the world too. George, who insists on dressing like his father when he accompanies him, is even beginning to copy his father's mannerisms. William keeps a watchful eye on his son, and if George appears awkward or overwhelmed, his dad is always close by to put a protective hand on his shoulder. He has a more tactile parenting style than his father and wants his three children to look back on their childhoods with a feeling of being wrapped in love.

Sadly, William feels he did not experience that same sense of devotion from his own father growing up, particularly after his mother died. 'In recent years they have become much closer and now they enjoy a good relationship,' said a senior source. 'He also respects his father and his devotion to service, but he feels the fact his father put work first had a detrimental impact on him when he was growing up and didn't help their father/son relationship.'[117]

Diana was devoted to both her sons and was often pictured hugging them or stroking their hair. But the heartache of William's parents' broken marriage and the divorce meant his memories were of a fraught childhood. His father could be distant and perhaps his emotional mother leaned on him too much when he was far too young to understand what was going on. He was largely playing the role of her 'emotional crutch', sources close to the prince have said. William does not blame either parent, but feels that his father retreated into the safe house of his work, putting duty before being a parent, with the result that both his sons felt a little lost and alone during their childhoods.

William knows that his time with his children is precious. If anything, as a source close to the couple explained, 'The duke sees his most important roles in life as just being a loving husband and a loving dad. He knows he has a lifetime of royal duty ahead of him, and he will never eschew that responsibility; he is a dedicated servant of the Crown, in the same way as the King. He has a very clear sense of what is right and wrong, more importantly of what is right for him. Before Her late Majesty passed away, William made it clear to both the Queen and his father that his priority will always be his family.'

For Catherine, life at Adelaide cottage has evoked memories of a very happy childhood being raised in a quiet Berkshire village, surrounded by her mum and dad and siblings. Her parents, Carole and Michael Middleton, whom Catherine has described as being 'hugely dedicated',[118] have always played an important role in their grandchildren's lives. William has made it clear that he would not always be available for his family and he had another family that is important to him and his children, the Middletons.

Catherine's mother and father are hands-on grandparents too. So it is no surprise that the move to Berkshire has seen them spending more time with their grandchildren, especially as they live only about forty miles away, down the M4 motorway. The location of the royal children's new school, which is even nearer, also means Catherine can call on Carole if needed. The Middletons are known to love taking them on outdoor adventures.

When they returned to school in September 2023, the three royal children were listed on the school register as George, Charlotte and Louis 'Wales' in consideration of their parents' new titles, the Prince and Princess of Wales. Walking together holding hands on the first day of school, they started the new chapter of their lives. For little Louis, proudly sporting his summer uniform, it was his very first day at school, his older siblings having previously attended Thomas's Battersea. On what was called the settling-in day, William referred to his children as 'all the gang' as he ushered them up the steps and into their new school.

Headmaster Jonathan Perry was on hand to greet the young royals, looking them in the eyes and shaking each of them firmly by the hand. 'It's lovely to have you with us,' he said. When he asked if they were excited, all three replied, 'Yes'. 'They are all looking forward to it,' William said. 'We've had lots of questions.' None of them looked nervous as they strode in the sunshine with their parents. They could be heard laughing as they went inside.

All three children have enquiring minds. Giving the public a sense of what their children are good at, William and Catherine revealed in September 2022 that all three are puzzle solvers. In the foreword to a children's book called *Puzzles for Spies* by Puffin Books, they wrote that they would be looking at the puzzles themselves with the help of George, Charlotte and Louis. They are all interested in the environment too, like their father, and George has a particular passion for earth science, being fascinated by fossils and volcanoes. Charlotte is a keen dancer and makes the most of the dedicated dance studio at the school.

They all admire Sir David Attenborough's environmental documentaries such as *A Planet for Us All*. During a visit to Kensington Palace, the biologist gave Prince George a shark's tooth. William and Catherine posted on Instagram: 'Sir David found the tooth on a family holiday to Malta in the late 1960s, embedded in the island's soft yellow limestone, which was laid down during the Miocene period some 23 million years ago.'

Catherine is also a big fan of Sir David Attenborough, whom she has met several times, most recently at the naming ceremony of the RRS *Sir David Attenborough*, a polar research ship. During a call with Casterton Primary Academy in 2020 during the lockdown, the children asked her who was the best famous person she had met. Anita Ghidotti, chief executive of the Pendle Trust, recalled, 'The Duchess said that George has been watching lots of David Attenborough, *Blue Planet* and the like, so that [he] would probably be her [choice].'[119]

When the children visit their grandparents at seven-bedroom Bucklebury Manor, the £5 million home in Berkshire where they have lived since 2012, Carole encourages them to take part in activities such as putting up the Christmas decorations ahead of the festive break. She is a great motivator and whips them up to join her and help in the garden. She said, 'It's important for children to grow up appreciating nature and part of that is allowing them to grow.'

As early as her engagement interview in 2010, Catherine spoke of how 'dear' her family were to her. Proud of her family and her roots, she said, 'They've been great over the years, helping me with difficult times. We see a lot of each other and they are very, very dear to me.'

CHAPTER 18

Shaping Up

We are all responsible for building a more compassionate
world in which our children can grow, learn and live.
CATHERINE, THE PRINCESS OF WALES

Hands tucked into the pockets of her olive-coloured jacket and dressed casually in black jeans, she was anonymous amidst the sea of sad faces. For the briefest moment, the young woman stopped to read the handwritten notes attached to the scores of floral tributes left at Clapham Common's Victorian bandstand in memory of Sarah Everard. She laid some daffodils of her own, picked from her garden, and then with a quiet dignity she turned away, her head slightly bowed. Most of the women there were oblivious to her presence; yet, hidden behind the veil of the everyday, was one of the world's most recognisable women, Catherine, the Duchess of Cambridge.

On Saturday, 13 March 2021, she had joined the ranks of hundreds of defiant women across the UK's capital city, participating in a vigil held in memory of the victim, 33-year-old marketing executive Sarah Everard, whose life had been brutally cut short by Police constable Wayne Couzens as she walked home to Brixton Hill. The off-duty officer had kidnapped and raped her, before murdering her. It was a heinous crime that united the nation in horror. It also reignited the national debate about the ever-present fear faced by millions of women when walking the streets alone at night.[120]

The duchess had arrived without fanfare. She was a solitary figure trailing behind a small group. 'She looked quite emotional,' said one fellow attendee, who recognised her among the crowd. 'She was just on her own. About ten metres behind her there were two people following her. It wasn't obvious she had security with her.' In fact, her plain clothes Scotland Yard personal protection officer was watching from a discreet distance, poised to react, if necessary, but not wanting to draw attention to the situation.

At first glance, when the story broke on online news platforms, some blinkered media cynics wrongly dismissed Catherine's appearance as a publicity stunt, made during turbulent times for the Royal Family. With accusations flying about cruelty and racism levelled at the royals by Prince Harry and Meghan Markle still fresh, some commentators wrote that the duchess's presence at the vigil could be seen as opportunistic. Perhaps it could, but it should not have been.

It was a seminal moment for the Duchess of Cambridge. After all, she had defiantly disregarded one of the fundamental royal rules: that of avoiding entering the political fray. For her appearance at the vigil was undeniably political, an unequivocal kickback against power and authority. Her very presence there that day meant she had also consciously broken the 'lockdown' laws, breaching restrictions laid down by the government and enforced by the police during the COVID-19 pandemic. But the duchess judged this to be irrelevant as this was her personal acknowledgement of the shared fear and danger faced by all women.

A vigil had initially been called by members of a social justice movement known as 'Reclaim These Streets', but they pulled out after the police intervened and told them it would be regarded as an illegal gathering under the lockdown regulations in place and threatened them with £10,000 fines. But Catherine never wavered, despite her decision being scrutinised by Palace courtiers, her personal protection officers, even senior Royal Family members. She had the courage of her convictions and went anyway.

Later, around 6.20 p.m., the vigil turned ugly when senior police, fearing that it was fast becoming an out-of-control, 1,000-strong anti-police protest, rushed towards the bandstand trampling flower beds on their way as they tried to stop those leading the chants. Some in the crowd started booing and there were cries of 'Let her speak!' and 'Shame on you!' Becky Gardiner, a lecturer at Goldsmiths College, University of London, even accused the police of 'effectively whipping the crowd up'[121] when dozens of overzealous police officers descended on the bandstand to intervene. They were filmed pinning women to the ground to handcuff them and afterwards the police faced intense media and political criticism for the gross mishandling of the event.

When asked if the police had been aware of the duchess's visit, Metropolitan Police Commissioner Cressida Dick replied, 'Absolutely.' She added that her visit had been legal as the duchess had been 'working', totally contradicting what Palace aides had advised off the record. They had been very clear that the visit was private. The backlash did not worry Catherine. Just for a short time she was not a royal figure, but a symbol of sisterhood and solidarity.

As she bowed her head in quiet reflection at the bandstand, she must have been remembering who she had been before entering the gilded cage of royalty. She would have recalled what it was like as a woman to walk London streets at night, alone and vulnerable. She only wanted to pay her respects to the tragic victim Sarah and to her grieving family.

For that briefest of moments, she was Kate Middleton again, a young woman with mettle, who acted for no reason other than it was right to do so.

The two women had been chatting enthusiastically for so long that the cup of English breakfast tea Catherine had been served was now stone-cold. She had been so engrossed in the conversation with author Giovanna Fletcher that when she went to take a sip, she burst out laughing, before going on to drink it anyway. It could have been easy to forget that every word was being recorded for Giovanna's hugely successful podcast, *Happy Mum, Happy Baby* in February 2020.

'What a complete career high. Just two mums nattering away,' Giovanna said later, when she appeared on the hit ITV reality television show *I'm A Celebrity … Get Me Out of Here!*, which she went on to win in December 2020. 'In true mum fashion, we were nattering so much that by the end we were drinking cold tea!'

It certainly was a great coup. If anyone had not heard of the podcast before the interview with the duchess, they certainly had afterwards as it received blanket coverage in the media. The actress, television presenter and writer's podcast with the most famous mum in the world as a guest inevitably boosted the numbers even further.

What was even more surprising about the interview was how candid Catherine was about deeply personal aspects of her life, considering her supposedly reserved nature. When the transcript was released to the press, they lapped it up. It seemed every minute of the podcast produced another headline as Catherine's candid remarks, possibly for the first time, gave the public real insight into the enigmatic duchess.

Catherine shared her experiences with challenging pregnancies and openly expressed her occasional 'mum guilt' when forced to leave her children behind to be cared by their nanny, so she could carry out official duties. Such willingness to discuss her frailties and anxiety about her parenting skills made it one of the most intimate royal interviews.

Talking about her feelings of guilt, she said, 'Anyone who doesn't [feel guilty] as a mother is lying. Even this morning, how could you possibly not be dropping us off at school this morning? It's a constant challenge.' Catherine, who has employed a nanny since 2014 to support her, maintained she is still a hands-on mother.

'There's such a pull,' she began, her voice tinged with both determination and vulnerability, 'but I am such a hands-on mum, and whatever you're doing, you want to make sure you're doing the uttermost best job you can for your children.'

The conversation turned to the severe morning sickness she had experienced with each pregnancy, known as *hyperemesis gravidarum*. 'I got very bad morning sickness,' she revealed, her tone betraying the weight of this ordeal. 'So, I'm not the happiest of pregnant people. I've had it every time. Lots of people have it far worse, but it was a challenge. Not just for you, but for those around you.'

She also shared her apprehension when facing the press and public with her first baby in her arms. 'It was slightly terrifying, not going to lie,' she admitted. 'I was keen to come home as all my memories of being in hospital were from being sick, so I didn't want to hang around and was desperate to come home and get back to normality.'

William, understanding the weight of public scrutiny, had encouraged her to speak freely on the podcast. To be fair, he also knew that the Kensington Palace communications team had secured a deal giving them the final say on the edit, so there was nothing to worry about. The recorded interview had been scheduled to last forty-five minutes, but the two women ended up 'nattering' for double the allotted time.

'I might have fallen in love. A girl crush,' Giovanna told her fellow contestant, Shane Richie, star of the BBC's *EastEnders*, when they both appeared on *I'm a Celebrity*. Catherine was 'divine' and 'absolutely elegant and self-deprecating' throughout the interview, she told the actor.

Catherine had agreed to appear on Giovanna's podcast to coincide with the launch of her ambitious initiative, '5 Big Questions on the Under Fives'. She believed it would encourage British parents to get involved in her project and to spread the word. The landmark public survey gathered the responses of parents, carers, teachers, kindergarten workers and families across Britain as part of an extensive body of research commissioned by the Royal Foundation and conducted by Ipsos Mori.

This was the first time that the UK public had been asked its views on the topic of early childhood in an open survey and the huge take-up showed the country's appetite for talking about the issue. It also got to the heart of Catherine's work as a senior royal. Between 22 January and 21 February, she conducted a nationwide tour, visiting Cardiff, Birmingham, Woking, London, Belfast and Aberdeen to speak to people about their experiences and opinions.

Passionate about the formative years of children, Catherine declared, 'We must do all we can to tackle these issues and to elevate the importance of the early years so that together we can build a more nurturing society,' before delving into the study's key findings.[122]

'Firstly, if parents are struggling to prioritise their own wellbeing, how can we better support them? Secondly, what is at the root of why parents feel so judged? Thirdly, how can we address parental loneliness, which has dramatically increased during the pandemic, particularly in the most deprived areas?' Her words weighted with concern, she added, 'And finally, if less than a quarter of us understand the unique importance of a child's first five years, what can we do to make this better known?'

'I think ultimately if you look at who's caring and nurturing children in the most vital period from pregnancy all the way to the age of five, you know parents and carers are right at the heart of that, and families are right at the heart of that,' she asserted. 'And although I've spoken to the scientists and the service providers, it's so important to listen to families. What is it that they aspire to? What are their challenges?'

Both mothers of three, the bond between Catherine and Giovanna deepened through the shared journey of motherhood. Reflecting on their own childhoods, they expressed a desire to impart similar experiences to their children and others. 'One thing that stands out is the quality of connections we make, the moments spent with those around us. It's etched in my memories from my own youth,' Catherine reflected.

'I had an amazing granny [Valerie Glassborow, who died in 2006],' she explained, 'who devoted a lot of time to us, playing with us, doing arts and crafts and going to the greenhouse to do gardening, and cooking with us. And I try and incorporate a lot of the experiences that she gave us at the time into the experiences that I give my children now.'[123]

She also emphasised the necessity of creating secure havens where children could thrive, explore the outdoors and flourish within happy family environments. 'As children, we thrived in the great outdoors and it's a passion I hold dear,' she affirmed. 'It's the key to physical and mental wellbeing and the bedrock of development. It's a serene haven for nurturing genuine relationships, devoid of the distractions of daily chores. It's simplicity at its finest.'

What would she like her children to remember about their childhood? she was asked. Catherine paused for a moment, before responding, 'I think, would I want them to remember me trying to do maths and spelling homework? Or that we've tried to cook sausages on a bonfire, but it didn't work as it's too wet,' she said. 'That's what I want them to remember and as a family, us going to the beach, filling our boots full of water and getting soaking wet. Not a stressful household where we're trying to do everything.'

Before the interview, the pair had spent time in a London nursery school, where they interacted with the staff and served breakfast to the young ones. It was a day that left Catherine brimming with ideas, reassured that she was on the right path. This project, after all, was something she held close to her heart and she had been the relentless driving force behind the entire endeavour.

Giovanna later recalled one cute moment between Catherine and one of her youngest fans. 'My highlight was possibly one little girl telling us her name was Peppa and that her mate was George . . . she then told us the duchess was called Daddy Pig, leaving me to be Mummy Pig. I laughed a lot,' Giovanna wrote on her Instagram account. 'It was clear how passionate she is about the Early Years.' Summarising her time with the duchess, she said, 'It was then beyond wonderful to sit and talk further about the survey, her work – for which she has so much knowledge – and her own experiences of being a mother.'

Giovanna said later, in an interview with *Hello!* magazine, 'I don't think I'd ever heard her speak so much before on anything else, so it was a proper insight into her and who she is.' She went on, 'And I feel that weird sense of pride every time I see her do stuff now. I just think she's amazing. I can't wait to see what she does for Early Years and the work that she continues to do, because there's so much passion there. She's so aware of things that are going on and only good things can come from that.'[124]

Perhaps it was taking part in the podcast interview that sparked something deeper inside the duchess. She soon realised that she wanted to delve far deeper into this subject and embarked on a course of intellectual discovery about early childhood. Joining the dots, she realised that helping people to understand and embrace their early years could make a significant difference not only to the lives of the under-fives, but enable a whole generation of people to become happier, more balanced adults.

When the Prince and Princess of Wales touched down at Boston's Logan Airport in November 2022, for their first visit to the US in eight years, they knew there was a lot more riding on it than supporting Prince William's Earthshot Prize initiative.[125] It was also their first overseas visit since Queen Elizabeth's death and both Palace and Foreign Office mandarins saw it as an exercise in restoring the Royal Family's somewhat tarnished image within the US, after Harry and Meghan's PR media onslaught against the family and the institution.

If they were fazed by the size of the task ahead of them over the next three days, neither William nor Catherine showed any signs of letting on. They focused on the main objective: to get the royal brand back on the front foot in America.

Catherine looked stunning in a green tartan dress from Burberry as she stood alongside William, trying to shelter from the torrential rain outside Boston City Hall. After a warm greeting by Boston's mayor, Michelle Wu, the prince delivered a confident speech.

'On this, our first overseas visit since the death of my grandmother, I would like to thank the people of Massachusetts and particularly of Boston for their many tributes paid to the late Queen,' he said. 'My grandmother was one of life's optimists. And so am I. That is why last year we launched the Earthshot Prize with the ambition to create a truly global platform to inspire hope and urgent optimism as we look to save the future of our planet.' He concluded, 'To the people of Boston, thank you. I'm so grateful to you for allowing us to host the second year of the Earthshot Prize in your great city. Catherine and I can't wait to meet many of you in the days ahead.'

William had not only paid homage to his late grandmother, but to Boston's most famous son, President John F. Kennedy. His Earthshot Prize, which had partnered with the John F. Kennedy Foundation to bring the prize to the city, was after all a play on the late president's 1962 'Moonshot' pledge that America would put a man on the Moon within the decade 'not because it is easy, but because it is hard'. NASA fulfilled that pledge in 1969 when astronauts Neil Armstrong and Buzz Aldrin walked on the Moon's surface. Now it was William's turn to echo that pledge. Invoking that JFK-like faith, he urged humankind to repair the planet. 'Earth holds such splendour and gives us many things,' he said, 'beauty, curiosity, joy, and most importantly, Earth gives us life.'

Catherine backs William wholeheartedly in his passion project and was at his side for the Boston visit. It came at a decisive moment for the Royal Family. The trailer for Harry and Meghan's upcoming Netflix series had threatened to derail the trip, but the royal couple ensured it did not.

The Prince of Wales met with Caroline Bouvier Kennedy, daughter of President Kennedy and US Ambassador to Australia, hours before he met with President Joe Biden. Meanwhile, Catherine pulled out all the stops and brought her own brand of star quality to the 2022 awards ceremony, where she wowed the crowds in a neon-green rented dress from Solace, to promote a more sustainable, and affordable, way of dressing. At the MGM Music Hall at Fenway, Boston, they mingled with stars like David Beckham, Annie Lennox, US singer Chloe Bailey and actor Rami Malek, as well as powerful politicians such as the Massachusetts Governor-elect Maura Healey and Mitt Romney.

Just before William and Catherine's entrance, Reverend Mariama White-Hammond, Boston's Chief of Environment, Energy, and Open Space, addressed the audience on 'the legacy of colonialism and racism' regarding its impact on climate change. As they waited to go on stage, Reverend Hammond said, 'On this day, I invite us all to consider the legacy of colonialism and racism. The ways it has impacted people across the world and its connection, its deep connection to the degradation of land and our planet that we are all seeking to reverse. The stories lost, the species made extinct, but also the persistence of people in the face of oppression and the fundamental dignity of all our relations.'

Nobody mentioned the elephant in the room, the racism row engulfing William's godmother, Lady Susan Hussey, who had been effectively forced to resign as a Lady of the Household following her comments to a Black woman at a Buckingham Palace reception. The media pounced on it, connecting the controversy with the Reverend's speech. Her comments came months after William and Catherine's controversial overseas tour to the Caribbean, which had been widely criticised for elements that smacked of colonialism.

Problems arose when it emerged that Lady Susan had questioned Ngozi Fulani, founder of the charity Sistah Space, about her background and repeatedly asked her where she 'really came from'.

Accusations of racism at the Palace followed. It was another perfect storm for William and Catherine to ride.

The couple carried on regardless and William gave a bold speech. 'When I founded this prize in 2020, it was with the ambition to harness the same spirit of ingenuity that inspired President John F. Kennedy to challenge the American people to put a person on the Moon within a decade,' he said to cheers from the crowd.

When Catherine took to the stage to present the final award of the evening in the Clean Our Air category to Mukuru Clean Stoves, a Kenyan company that creates safer, cleaner cookstoves, she looked a little apprehensive, fiddling with her emerald choker and constantly flipping her hair. She still finds making speeches nerve-racking, but when the moment came, she nailed it.

'Nature is vital to us all,' she said. 'A thriving natural world regulates our climate, nurtures our physical and mental health, and helps feed our families. But for too long we've neglected our wild spaces and now we're facing several tipping points.' She continued, 'If we don't act now, we will permanently destabilise our planet and we will rob our children of the future they deserve. Our Earthshot Prize Finalists show us however that we can, by 2030, see the natural world growing, not shrinking, for the first time in centuries.'

She looked a little relieved when she finished and smiled and clapped after a short video told the inspiring story of the company's founder, Charlot Magayi. It was another job well done. The US visit had achieved a lot, but it was not a runaway success. Television news presenters were quick to criticise the couple, claiming that the Boston visit had been overshadowed by a barrage of bad news.

Sky News correspondent Laura Bundock went further, saying that William and Catherine's 'star quality' was not enough to quell the fallout from the latest Palace racism row involving Lady Susan Hussey. Again, an overseas visit by the couple, which had been expected to shine a positive light on the Royal Family, began to unravel. It was not supposed to remind Americans of Meghan's accusations of racism against them.

The New York Times reported on the lukewarm reception, saying it was unsurprising: 'Boston doesn't care for the royals, Ya don't say.' Other US media outlets reported that the visit was 'floundering' after Harry and Meghan had dropped their Netflix series teaser on Day 2. *Boston Globe* columnist Kevin Cullen drew on the latest racism row at the Palace when writing that William's effort to showcase a new Royal Family in Boston had been distracted by 'the old one back in London'. Even the BBC agreed. 'The Prince and Princess of Wales have visited Boston as part of a tour of the US that has been overshadowed by a row over racism in the UK.'

Prince William's spokesperson Lee Thompson addressed a room of journalists ahead of the royal arrival in Boston. Speaking as William's 'office', he said, 'Racism has no place in our society.' He went on, 'These comments were unacceptable, and it's right that the individual has stepped aside with immediate effect.'

Lady Susan later apologised in a face-to-face meeting with Ngozi Fulani, but the 'racism and the royals' story was not going away.

CHAPTER 19

Dissenting Voices

*The British monarchy has worked its usual magic, turning a
vibrant commoner into an underweight thirty-something with
no pizazz.*

JANET STREET-PORTER, WRITER AND BROADCASTER

The hot chilli-red Alexander McQueen £1,980 tailored power
suit radiated authority. Matched with accessories including a
beautiful £640 red suede bag by Miu Miu and Florence earrings in
gold by the brand Chalk, it was clear Catherine meant business as
she stepped out to a pre-campaign launch event at BAFTA in central
London in January 2023. After years in the public eye, she had now
fully grasped the unwritten rules: every stitch of fabric and flash of
colour delivered a powerful visual message to complement what she
was going to say in her keynote speech. She understood that her
image as well as her words really mattered.

After a decade-long immersion in royal duties, Catherine had
seen the darker side of life too. Through her charitable roles she
had witnessed first-hand how the roots of adult problems often start
off in childhood. Mental health and addiction, she discovered, were
invariably deeply anchored in a person's early years. 'From the cradle
to the grave, our infancy imprints upon us,' she said. 'It steers the

course of our relationships and our professional successes.' With this bold assertion, she launched her passion project, the 'Shaping Up' campaign at the BAFTA event hosted by the Royal Foundation Centre for Early Childhood.

Her speech was eloquent and well-researched, and it came from the heart. The event was backed up by the brilliant work of some of the finest minds in the field that she had convened for her campaign. She emphasised the paramount significance of early childhood on all of us, earning a nod of agreement from her husband, the Prince of Wales, who was present for moral support.

It was not new ground for her. In November 2020, at the launch of the findings of the '5 Big Questions on the Under Fives' survey conducted by the Royal Foundation, Catherine had delivered a powerful statement. She said, 'The early years are not simply about the wellbeing of our children. They are about the foundations of our society. By focusing on the early years, we might just be able to take a big step forward in solving some of our greatest societal challenges.'

That project had sparked her ambition to do more, much more. Now she had instructed aides that she wanted to find solutions that could transform society for the better. She had won over many top scientists, social workers, academics, child psychologists, paediatricians and health experts, as well as celebrities, who were in the audience to support her as she unveiled her pioneering work. There was a cinema screening of a 90-second Claymation film, which showed how a little girl named Layla developed from pregnancy to age five and the way she was shaped by her interactions, thus spelling out the delicate process of how the environment moulds a child's growth and early development.

Catherine then got to her feet and underlined just how crucial early childhood is in the formation of adults, laying the groundwork for life. Through the Royal Foundation Centre for

Early Childhood, she said she had introduced this long-term project to stress the pivotal role of early years and the onus was now on us to unite to create the next generation of well-adjusted adults. She got a standing ovation.

An assortment of celebrity supporters turned out to support her and the cause, including the captain of the England women's football team, Leah Williamson. Afterwards Williamson praised the project as an excellent initiative for societal transformation. 'I think it's an amazing thing to start raising awareness,' she said, 'because we won't see the fruits of this tomorrow or next year, but in years to come and how we look at our society. I hope that we are in a better position because of things like this.'

The timing of the launch was unfortunate as it coincided with the release of Prince Harry's tell-all book *Spare*, which raised questions about the societal contributions of the royals. Critics turned on Catherine, saying they found the campaign lacking in ambition. They said it focused too heavily on awareness rather than concrete action to solve future problems. Despite the criticism, she remained committed to using her voice and celebrity to highlight important issues and inspire open conversations about them. Comparisons with *Spare* were inevitable, and a little cheap, but Catherine's focus lay elsewhere.

For her, the campaign was about using her influence to draw attention to an issue close to her heart, in a manner that fitted with her role as part of the Royal Family. Where Harry and Meghan had bolted to do things 'their way', Catherine wanted to develop her role and the causes she supports by embracing them. Whether or not the project appealed to everyone, her tenacity in sparking change was evident. This work could result in a lasting impact on early childhood development, which might eventually influence real changes in policy. To do this directly, she knows, is beyond her royal remit, but raising the bar so that such an important issue can be discussed and addressed is no mean feat.

Although she received an impressive 16,000 likes on Twitter, now X, the responses on social media to Catherine leading this campaign were polarising. Some challenged her qualifications, with one critical post that garnered 4,000 likes asking the question: 'What certifies this woman, who has never worked and whose degree lies in the History of Art, to make such decisions?' Many wondered what concrete solutions she was advocating. Others dismissed her as 'all talk'.

They had misunderstood her intent. The research, which they were dismissing for reasons best known to themselves, came from the foundation for developing effective solutions. Critics overlooked the immense convening power that she had and the fact that the pioneering work was supported by some of the most brilliant minds in medicine, who exclusively focused on early childhood, particularly before the age of five.

Some critics, while praising her good intentions and accepting that early childhood is important, felt she had not gone far enough. Dr Mine Conkbayir, a member of the Practitioners of the Early Years Sector, told *Sky News*, 'But nothing is done. The time has long passed for awareness. We need action, long-term investment and funding in the early years.' Others highlighted the fact that the programmes necessary to make children happy and healthy adults had been closed by government and funding to others had been slashed. Dr Conkbayir added, 'Childcare providers are having to turn to food charities to provide nutritious meals for children . . . The paltry government funding of early years that is provided does not cover the provision of any food.'

But Catherine was not put off. She countered by writing a thought-provoking op-ed urging more support for parents and children, especially during their formative early years. The article was published in the *Daily Telegraph* to coincide with the launch of her campaign. She disclosed that she had consulted with leading experts over the past ten years on issues ranging from mental health to physical challenges.

'One thing has become increasingly clear: if we aspire to cultivate a healthier and happier society for future generations, we must start by understanding and acknowledging the profound importance of the first five years of life. Early childhood, from gestation to five years of age, deeply affects our entire lives, shaping the fundamental frameworks that allow us to thrive as individuals, within our communities, and as a society.'

Catherine may not have had solutions to the many issues, but she knew it was an 'incredible opportunity' for experts to at least start to make a 'huge difference' to future generations. She continued, 'I am determined to continue to shine a light on this issue and to do everything I can to secure much greater focus on those first crucial few years for the youngest members of our society – they are, after all, our future.'

It would be wrong to suggest that Catherine has had an easy ride. Even before her marriage, she faced light-hearted but nonetheless cruel banter from some in William's circle for being middle-class. The fact that her mother, Carole, a self-made entrepreneur, once worked as cabin crew for British Airways also led to some pathetic jibes. When they went out partying, some of William's upper-class friends would call her 'doors to manual'. She has faced unfair criticism and personal attacks from the media too, but has remained resilient, focused on her role.

Oddly, Catherine can divide opinion even now. Most people see her as a positive influence, but she still has some detractors, particularly after the so-called 'Megxit'[126] debacle, which polarised opinions. She first attracted public attention when the media identified her as William's girlfriend on a ski trip to Klosters in 2004. Back then she was seen as little more than a distraction. Most royal commentators, given the fact that William was only twenty-two at the time, doubted Catherine would last the course and expected her to be the first serious girlfriend in a long line of attractive females that would be linked to the prince.

Indeed, when she had still not received a marriage proposal after a year or two, some snarky media commentators dubbed her 'Waity Katie'. More unfair jibes followed. Others described her as 'an incorrigible frump'[127] and a 'plastic princess' as well as labelling her 'the anti-professional'.[128]

The double Booker Prize-winning author, the late Hilary Mantel, for some inexplicable reason, went completely over the top, describing her as a 'jointed doll on which certain rags are hung'. She added to her personal attack, saying, 'Kate seems to have been selected for her role of princess because she was irreproachable: as painfully thin as anyone could wish, without quirks, without oddities, without the risk of the emergence of character.'[129]

Quite why the author of such literary gems as *Wolf Hall* and the sequel *Bring Up the Bodies* felt the need to unleash such a malicious personal attack remains unclear. This spiteful criticism led to a public slanging match that reached the highest levels, which Catherine was powerless to do anything about. The British Prime Minister David Cameron even jumped to the duchess's defence, saying that while Mantel was a 'good writer', he found her comments were 'hurtful' and 'completely wrong'.

The row escalated further and when pressed to explain herself during a radio interview with journalist and presenter Anne McElvoy on BBC Radio Three's *Night Waves*, Dame Hilary became flustered and pushed back against her detractors. 'I have absolutely no regrets – what I said was crystal clear. I have absolutely nothing to apologise for,' she insisted. Mantel claimed her comments that Catherine was a 'shop-window mannequin', whose only purpose was to breed, had in her opinion been completely taken out of context by the tabloid press.

In fairness, Mantel's lecture had been addressing a perception of Catherine that she said had been created by the media. Hurtful as it was to Catherine and her family, the Palace remained silent, as it was felt best to let others argue it out, with the majority siding with Catherine, not Mantel.

Complete strangers also attacked Catherine, without knowing her. Why was she wasting her expensive education? Why was she not pursuing a career while she was dating William? For somebody who was not technically a public figure, it was inordinate fault-finding. Curiously, most of these attacks came from women writers, whose censure was relentless.

Joan Smith, a heavy-hitter in the feminist arena, was particularly vehement when she wrote in her book, *The Public Woman*, 'By the age of thirty, Catherine had done little career-wise since leaving university except play a supporting role to her boyfriend, marry him with great pomp and ceremony, and get pregnant. She had never really enjoyed an independent identity or income, even her clothes were paid for by her father-in-law, and didn't seem to aspire to either.'

Novelist Wendy Holden was even more barbed about Catherine in an article for the *Independent*. She wrote, 'Kate did a great job marrying up, but bagging a rich man is now seen by many as a serious career move, which can't be right. What happened to having a fulfilling job and your own money? I can't stand educated women who don't work.'[130] Katrina Onstad, another writer, chipped in further when she wrote disdainfully, 'If I lived in London, I'd ride by her window on my bicycle and shout, "Get a job!"'

Even after all these years in her public role, Catherine, so often praised for her poise and sense of style in public, still faces some nit-picking criticism from fashionistas. In July 2023, she was attacked for dumbing down her jewellery by former *Vogue International* editor, Suzy Menkes, in her podcast *Creative Conversations*, saying, 'The Princess of Wales is a bit of a disappointment about jewellery. She gives the impression that she only puts it on when she absolutely has to. I imagine her looking beautiful in one of those gowns behind the scenes and then pulling a face as if to say, "Do I have to wear this?" She doesn't give any sense of adoring jewellery and being pleased to put it on.'

Perhaps it is precisely this normalcy and Catherine's attainability with ordinary people, who like the fact that she sometimes wears high street affordable earrings, which so irritates some of the commentators in the media elite. Her everydayness appeals to the public, who have always warmed to her and can relate to her. She is stable, undramatic, empathetic and genuine.

Catherine, of course, now has access to millions of pounds via her marriage. The profits from her husband's Duchy of Cornwall Trust generate around £23 million annually to fund his family and running his household. Even before that she was wealthy enough to buy an exquisite £5,000 golden gown with flowing train by couturier Jenny Packham, which wowed the crowds at the James Bond premiere *No Time to Die* in 2021. It was an extra-special event and she would not have made such a fashion statement unless the occasion warranted it. Her choice certainly caught the eye, prompting James Bond actor Daniel Craig to tell Catherine when he met her in the line-up that she looked 'jolly lovely'.

With her model's figure and 5' 9" height, five inches taller than the average British woman, as well as being a British size 6 (American size 2), Catherine has the perfect ectomorph body type that makes her couture outfits look chic. But she does not need high-end fashion to look good, she appears flawless in affordable high street labels too. She knows precisely when she must put on the style with high-end fashion and when not. Perhaps that is part of her appeal; she always seems to get it just right.

Dame Anna Wintour, former editor-in-chief of American *Vogue*, is a big fan of how Catherine presents herself, observing, 'The Duchess of Cambridge always looks impeccable. I think right now when you are thinking very much about styles that are a little bit more classic and have a heritage feeling, when you look at what she wears when she goes to church, could be a Catherine Walker dark red princess coat, or when she has to go out at night with her husband something a little more glamorous like a McQueen, but she always looks absolutely impeccable.' In another interview, with the *Daily Telegraph*, Wintour said, 'I think everyone admires the fact she's not changing due to her new position. She's very much an individual.'

She even inspired the phrase, the 'Kate effect', for the economic influence she delivers, which in recent years has been estimated to give a staggering £1 billion annual boost to the UK fashion industry and economy.[131] Even before she married William, Catherine had caught the eye of big names in fashion such as the Italian designer Giorgio Armani, who spoke of his admiration of her sense of style in 2011. He noted that she is 'highly aware of fashion trends'.

Chanel's creative director, Karl Lagerfeld, who died aged eighty-five in 2019, was known for his many biting quips. He was also complimentary about Catherine, but less so about her sister, Pippa. Of Catherine, he said, 'Kate Middleton has a nice silhouette, and she is the right girl for that boy [Prince William]. I like that kind of woman; I like romantic beauties. On the other hand, her sister [Pippa] struggles.'[132] Therefore, as a princess Catherine is acutely aware that what she wears matters. She knows the clothes she selects and the designers she chooses to wear on overseas tours or high-profile events can sell out within minutes and set fashion trends.

She is also mindful that what she wears carries a message. Her 'diplomatic dressing' – wearing the colours of the host nation when on overseas royal tours while representing the Crown – demon-strates her thoughtful approach to fashion. At home she prefers shades of red, white and blue, according to Carly Whitewood, who runs 'Kate Middleton's Style Blog', and one recent study found that 67 per cent of Catherine's outfits fall within these three colours.

With a style that exudes elegance, Catherine has found her own path. In March 2023, when she took part in a military exercise, she was praised for the way she looked so good while out facing extreme weather conditions. She was photographed taking part in a casualty drill in snow on Salisbury Plain and looked effortlessly elegant as she helped administer first aid to a wounded soldier as part of a mocked-up exercise. But she had prepped for the job. She appeared in a khaki outfit, but made sure she had practical walking shoes, her hair was pulled back into a French braid and she wore many layers under the uniform.

Again, it was her preparedness that gave her the edge. A senior Palace source said, 'She knew it was not only about looking the part, but making sure her clothes were practical and above all, kept her warm.'

In December 2021, Catherine mesmerised viewers with her virtuoso piano performance of 'For Those Who Can't Be Here' at her Westminster Abbey Carol Concert alongside singer-songwriter Tom Walker. Despite some ridiculous claims that her performance was fake, she won widespread praise for her talent and courage.

Catherine, who had gained her Grade 3 Piano and Grade 5 Theory at school, also made a surprise appearance at the Eurovision Song Contest in Liverpool in May 2022 showing support for Ukraine with a performance by the previous year's Ukrainian winners, Kalush Orchestra. With such impromptu public appearances, Catherine has helped revitalise interest in the Royal Family at a critical time.

Many from today's younger generation, particularly in the 18–24 age group, have begun to tire of the institution of monarchy, questioning its relevance and legitimacy in a democratic society. They no longer rely solely on newspapers or television for information; personalised online feeds and mobile phone access provide them with alternative sources, a chance to listen to wider voices with an anti-establishment bent. Younger individuals are less exposed to the traditional representation of the monarchy presented by organisations such as the BBC or even pro-establishment newspapers. When they do engage with royal stories, they often encounter sensationalised gossip.

At the time of King Charles' Coronation, 38 per cent of those aged 18–24 supported an elected head of state, while only 32 per cent were supportive of the monarchy, according to a YouGov poll commissioned by BBC *Panorama* in April 2023. A survey by the National Centre for Social Research taken just ahead of the Coronation in May 2023 also showed public support for the monarchy had fallen to an historic low. 45 per cent of respondents said either it should be abolished, was not at all important or not very important. Only three in ten Britons thought the monarchy was 'very important', the lowest proportion on record.

Support for a UK elected republic is rising too, as the public become increasingly apathetic to what many see as an outdated system. People are sceptical about how much money the Royal

Family receives, according to an exclusive *Sky News*/Ipsos opinion poll. William, Catherine and Princess Anne all had 47 per cent net favourability ratings, significantly ahead of the King on 31 per cent, Harry (-22 per cent), Meghan (-27 per cent) and Andrew (-55 per cent). This undoubtedly heaps pressure on the prince and princess as the institution's very survival is now on their shoulders. They must be seen as relevant and in touch.

Catherine is not the monarchy's 'last shiny thing for many years to come' or a 'Stepford-like royal wife', as author Omid Scobie scathingly describes her in his book *Endgame*, but a woman with passion and a voice, prepared to fight for what she believes in while respecting the institution she serves. As she has stepped up to her role as the Princess of Wales, she is determined to continue her groundbreaking work shaping the development and mental health of young children. It is her legacy project. In the coming years it will be at the heart of her public role and something she will continue to highlight even when she becomes Queen Consort.

In this age of digital scrutiny, when public figures face relentless online monitoring, Catherine has shown there is strength in silence too. She has not had it easy, as the Princess Royal herself has acknowledged. As a youngster, Anne had a poor relationship with the press and was branded 'bad-tempered', but she feels that royal life has been tougher for the younger royals like Catherine due to the advent of social media. 'The pressure that is applied to the younger members of the family, it's always worse,' she has said. 'That's what the media is interested in. That's hard sometimes to deal with. But there was no social media in my day, and it's probably made it more difficult.'[133]

Sadly, Catherine and William have been subjected to many vicious and unjust attacks and false accusations, particularly from the so-called Sussex Squad, who are supporters of Meghan Markle.

In some instances, it has led to wholly false rumours circulating online, like the one suggesting a feud between Catherine and her friend Rose Hanbury, the Marchioness of Cholmondeley, because of her alleged relationship with Prince William.

Such slanderous tales failed to gain any traction not only because of their lack of veracity, but due to Catherine's dignified silence. In August 2023, the princess attended a dinner hosted by Rose Hanbury at the Houghton Festival. There, she enjoyed both the company and the festival, thus debunking the misconceptions about her. Catherine is not a shrinking violet nor a prig, but a self-assured woman who knows her worth. Her friends insist she is not a jealous person. Today, she has transcended any malicious commentary and instead chooses to rise above inane chatter to focus on her family and duty.

Catherine accepts her role within the Royal Family, where others have kicked against theirs. She understands it is an honour to serve and she embraces her duties, carrying them out with the minimum of fuss, epitomised by her hosting of the Christmas Carol Concert at Westminster Abbey, which will now become an annual event. Like King Charles, her leadership style is to convene people who can join her to make a difference and affect change for the greater good.

Catherine enjoys a solid and loving marriage with the man she fell for two decades ago. The ever-watchful cameras often capture William looking at her when she is not aware, with a deep love in his eyes. He never misses an opportunity to praise her. In a video taken on an awayday to Birmingham in April 2023, a woman in the crowd told Catherine that her outfit, a burgundy wrap dress by Karen Millen, looked amazing. Without thinking and with a loving glance at his wife, William said, 'She always looks stunning.' The video went viral with royal enthusiasts leaving positive comments.

'There's a man who truly loves his wife,' said one, while another stated simply, 'He's not wrong!'

Since the death of Queen Elizabeth, they have both stepped up and appear to be more in sync than ever. She is respected as a hands-on mother to her three children and for the way she has embraced her role as Princess of Wales, one of the most senior Royal Family members. As the years pass, she will become the embodiment of all things British, a symbol but with a voice and purpose. Catherine has found her place in the world. She has gained increasing confidence with the passing of time and continues to forge her own path. The princess celebrated her forty-second birthday in January 2024 with a low-key, quiet family gathering at Windsor.

There was no fanfare. There was no drama either, unlike the previous year when the celebrations were overshadowed by the launch of Harry's memoir *Spare*, in which he wrote of her 'coldness' towards Meghan. King Charles wished her a happy birthday on the official Royal Family social media account by publishing a stunning previously unseen picture taken by photographer Chris Jackson of the princess on the day of the Coronation. It showed Catherine looking upon the recently crowned Charles and the close connection between them, with the caption reading, 'Wishing the Princess of Wales a very happy birthday today!'

Catherine has emerged as the vibrant core of the Royal Family during a time of transition. With her beauty, glamour and tireless dedication, to many she is perceived as the contemporary embodiment of monarchy. Instinctively, she has adapted to her role as the Princess of Wales, playing the long game with an eye towards the future.

CHAPTER 20

The Royal Labyrinth

A labyrinth, when it is big enough, is just the world.

CATHERYNNE M. VALENTE, *THE GIRL WHO FELL
BENEATH FAIRYLAND AND LED THE REVELS THERE*

Unlike other senior royals past and present, Catherine and William's embrace of modern media and communications shows their commitment to staying relevant and effective in their roles. After the Coronation of King Charles in 2023, they released a slick five-minute-long online video showing what went on in their home behind the scenes.

The footage provided a rare window into their family dynamic during the historic weekend on their official YouTube account and captured the joyful mood as they greeted the excited crowds outside the Palace. It also showed how they prepared for the event at Kensington Palace along with Charlotte and Louis. With a new broom, such changes were inevitable. But it did not go unnoticed that, once again, this media-savvy pair wanted to handle their own narrative.

Perhaps after the way their 2022 tour of the Caribbean was reported and seen to have backfired for being out of step, they knew that the way they presented themselves needed a revamp, with a new direction and even new leadership. They reached out to the top media executive and PR high-flyer Lee Thompson, Vice President, International Communications, Marketing & Strategic Partnerships with broadcaster CNBC, who had previously worked at the leading public relations agency Freuds. It was one of those roles that could not be turned down. His appointment was part of a long-term strategy to ensure that their core messages reached their target audience.

In March 2022, the prince and princess also announced the appointment of Amanda Berry OBE as the Chief Executive Officer for their charity, The Royal Foundation. As the former CEO of BAFTA for twenty-three years, it was widely seen as an inspired move given that Berry had turned the arts charity around during her long stewardship. The following year, in a bid to shake things up even further, Catherine hired public relations guru Alison Corfield, who had previously worked for the popular TV chef Jamie Oliver among others, as her new private secretary after Hannah Cockburn-Logie stepped down.

In September 2023, the royal couple 'showed they mean business' by advertising for a new role of CEO to run their household of about sixty staff.[134] The move gave an insight into how William may approach his reign, running the institution like a corporation rather than an outmoded government department. The emphasis will be on fresh thinking.

At the time of publication, the CEO role has not been filled, but in February 2024, William announced the appointment of his new private secretary, diplomat Ian Patrick MBE. Patrick previously worked for former Liberal Democrat leader Lord Paddy Ashdown when he was in Bosnia from 2002 to 2006 before joining the Foreign, Commonwealth and Development Office. He is also a trustee for Crohn's & Colitis UK, a charity for the two main forms of inflammatory bowel disease.

The late Queen Elizabeth II, like King Charles, was immensely proud of what William and Catherine had achieved and the wholesome image they portrayed. Quietly behind the scenes, Her Majesty was a huge help to Catherine and helped to guide her over what was expected of her at court and in public. 'She's been very generous in not being forceful at all and in any of her views,' Catherine said about her relationship with the late Queen, 'but I feel she's been there, a gentle guidance really for me.' It is knowing she has always been fully supported by the Firm that has perhaps given Catherine the inherent confidence to carry out her duties as she sees fit.

William respects his wife's advice, but what matters more is that he is very much in love with Catherine and she with him. They share a similar sense of humour and she also knows when to step in if he is nervous or unsure of himself. 'Obviously we both have a very fun time together,' he has said. '[We] both have a very good sense of humour about things, we're down to earth, we take the mickey out of each other a lot, and she's got plenty of habits that make me laugh that I tease her about.'

Their three children keep the couple well-grounded too and for that, William has never been shy in acknowledging his wife for reminding him what really matters in life. 'Catherine has been doing an amazing job as a mother and I'm very proud of her,' he said.

Unlike her husband and her children, Catherine was not born with a royal title, so she is the only one in their family group who truly appreciates what it is like to be a member of the bourgeoisie. Her conventional upbringing has enabled her to ensure this new Royal Family has a down-to-earth appeal. Unlike Charles or even William, their children George, Charlotte and Louis are not surrounded by servants. Their home at Adelaide Cottage fits the bill because it is a four-bedroom home and they do not need any more space as they have no live-in staff.

On the RAF Voyager return flight from the Bahamas at the end of the royal tour of the Caribbean in April 2022, Catherine told reporters that her children were always on her mind. In a candid moment while chatting to some of the accredited press at the back of the plane, she admitted that on top of her official duties she had been busy ensuring her children had everything they needed while she was away, including arranging Princess Charlotte's ballet classes.[135]

Of course, they have the support of their steadfast family nanny Maria Teresa Turrion Borrallo, but Catherine revealed that even while jet-lagged after an eleven-hour flight from RAF Brise Norton to Belize, she busied herself going through the stream of WhatsApp parents' messages about playdates that popped up in the middle of the night, local time. Once again, with a few carefully chosen words, she became just another caring mother, which makes her much more relatable. Above all it is perhaps Catherine's ability to rise above the noise with silent dignity, along with her relatability and genuine nature, that is the key to her popularity.

Over the years, Catherine and William have given several candid interviews, but they prefer to be in an environment where they feel confident and in control. Podcasts with people they know well and trust have been the best vehicle for them to be more open and divulge interesting snippets about their lives. Just ahead of the Rugby World Cup in September 2023, the prince and princess joined Princess Anne and her son-in-law Mike Tindall on his podcast, *The Good, The Bad and the Rugby*.

Tindall, who is the husband of William's cousin Zara, is affectionately nicknamed 'Shrek' by Royal Family members including the King, after the children's movie cartoon character.

With fellow presenters Alex Payne and James Haskell, he recorded a special royal episode of his podcast at Windsor Castle and it was a big hit. The podcast showed the fun-loving side of Catherine, in which she displayed her sense of humour and let slip details of her secret fitness regime.

Tindall said he seen her play beer pong – a drinking game where players try to land ping-pong balls into cups of beer and force the loser to drink – and she was 'uber competitive'. Catherine agreed and said that she and William were still very competitive even after twelve years of marriage. She added, 'I don't think we've managed to finish a game of tennis, the two of us. It becomes a mental challenge between the two of us.' William agreed that they try to 'out mental' each other.

Catherine also revealed that she loves cold-water swimming, which bolsters cardiovascular health by increasing blood flow and decreasing blood pressure. 'Cold swimming – the colder, the better. I absolutely love it. Slightly to the point where William's [saying], "You're crazy," and it's dark and it's raining. I will go and seek out cold water. I love it.' Despite her passion for cold-water swimming, the princess admitted that she did not share a similar love for ice baths.

Catherine also revealed that she and William had taken part in races on school sports days. On one occasion, the school called a last-minute parents' race and the prince revealed he finished second. He said, 'I started off just running and joining in, and then looked around and I was so far out in front. There was this Italian dad up in front and I thought, I'm going to catch him. A friend of mine, who tried catching up with me, pulled a hamstring.' Catherine, who ran barefoot, could not remember where she finished.

When asked whether George, Charlotte and Louis were picking up their parents' sporty traits, Anne shared her thoughts, chiming in, 'Just a little bit, I think.' She said, 'They're all of different temperaments and as they're growing and trying out different sports, it's going to be interesting to see how that grows and develops.'

Catherine said she had experienced plenty of ups and downs through her love of sport and always enjoyed attending live events. 'I was absolutely gutted to have missed Andy Murray's game when he won his gold medal event [at the 2012 Olympics],' she disclosed. Both agreed they would encourage their children to be sporty. 'Being able to come together, fight adversity together, win or lose, cold and wet, damp, whatever kind of days you're playing in; get a few knocks or bruises, it's an important part of growing up,' said William. When he told the group, which included rugby legend James Haskell and Mike Tindall, how he had enjoyed playing the game at school, his wife playfully responded with a mocking smile, 'Did you? Did you?'

For Catherine, being active as a young person was character building. When taking part in a social media Q&A session to promote her Early Learning programme, she revealed her own stand-out memories from childhood. 'I actually get asked this question a lot. I think people assume because I am a parent, that's why I've taken an interest in the Early Years. I think this really is bigger than that. This isn't about happy healthy children, this is about the society I hope we could and can become. Right from the early days, meeting lots of people who are suffering with addiction or poor mental health, and hearing time and time again that their troubles now in adulthood stem right back from early childhood experience.'

As a mother of three, the duchess laughed when posed a question about how to handle temper tantrums. She replied, 'Yes, that's a hard one. I'd also like to ask the experts myself!'

To cope with this labyrinth of royal life and all its complexity, Catherine not only leans on her husband's family, but relies on her own family too. Her parents, Carole and Michael, understandably brim with pride over the way she has gracefully embraced her role and the vicissitudes of public life, but they help to keep her grounded. Her siblings, Pippa and James, are also essential pillars of support.

Her brother James Middleton offered a glimpse of this familial bond during an interview with Kate Garraway on ITV's *Good Morning Britain*. He praised the Prince and Princess of Wales for their unwavering backing in his battle with clinical depression. 'I am extremely proud and I am always taken aback by how much she does and that does continue to sit in the forefront of my mind,' he said. 'But actually, to be honest, she is my sister, so I know all of her quirks and everything and actually to see her blossoming in that role . . . I am very proud of her.'[136] His sentiment is shared widely.

The King cherishes his relationship with Catherine. He often refers to her as his 'beloved daughter-in-law' in public and says she is the daughter he never had. He always greets her with a loving kiss and her unique strength is not lost on him. They share a close bond and are often photographed together sharing a laugh and a joke. Privately she addresses him affectionately as 'Grandpa', a moniker she used during a reception at the G7 summit in Cornwall in June 2021, even when the children were not with them.

When tensions have arisen between William and Charles, it is Catherine who has smoothed the way to a more genial relationship. As one courtier explained, 'The King's relationship with both his sons has been difficult over the years. Even now he is king, with the Prince of Wales, there can be differences of opinion and tensions.'

Such simmering tensions are nothing new. 'Of course, they love each other but they clash and sometimes William needs handling with kid gloves,' said the senior source. 'You have to check first which way the wind is blowing with the prince,' another courtier explained. 'They don't see eye to eye on several issues, but why should they? His moment in the top job will come. Perhaps he would do well to remember it is not yet, this is His Majesty's time.'

'William felt the images of the Duke and Duchess of York walking to church at Christmas [in 2023] with the rest of the royals sent out the wrong messages,' the senior household figure continued. 'Perhaps the King is subliminally trying to show William that forgiving one's brother and giving him a second chance is a strength not a weakness. But Prince William disagrees and as for his own brother, as far as he is concerned there is no way back.[137]

Navigating such tricky flare-ups between her husband and her father-in-law has put the princess in an invidious position over the years. She has learned to tread carefully on occasion and let time heal. She is always loyal to her husband, but the King knows that in Catherine he has a pragmatic ally on whom he can rely. At times William is a bit of a shouter when he loses it. It is fair to say they give as good as they get if their disagreement results in raised voices, but they know each other so well, it usually blows over quickly and the princess is, overall, a calming influence on her emotionally charged husband, those close to the couple say.

Catherine first became William's friend and confidante when they were both undergraduates at the University of St Andrews in Scotland. Before their relationship blossomed, she was one of his trusted confidantes. Even today, William always consults his wife, as well as his chief advisers, before making big decisions. They operate as a true partnership, knowing that what one does impacts on the other. He clearly values her opinion, candour and honest guidance.

In public she is often seen subtly encouraging him before he delivers a speech with a loving smile or a gentle touch on the arm. They are without doubt a *tour de force* in royal teamwork and present themselves as such in public.

As a solo performer Catherine is impressive too. She has the courage of her convictions and, those close to her say a singularity of purpose that surprises many when they first meet her. In December 2022, on day three of their royal visit to Boston, she visited the Center on the Developing Child at Harvard University, where she interacted with several acclaimed academics, intellectuals and researchers in the field. Throughout the meeting she contributed as well as listened and took notes. Afterwards, Jack Shonkoff, director of the Center, described her visit as a 'wonderful opportunity for shared learning as part of a global effort to improve life outcomes for young children'.

However, she was not there simply to adorn the proceedings, but to get involved and help make a difference. The academics and experts present went away very impressed by the depth of her knowledge. One senior figure who knows the princess well, and has also mixed in academic and government circles, said, 'I have never met anyone who is more on her "A Game" than the princess.' She is focused and undeniably committed to the causes she cares deeply about.

The princess prides herself on knowing her subject inside out. She is not only widely read on her core subjects, but on a whole range of broader issues. Academically sharp, Catherine has a keen intellect and according to those who have worked alongside her, she is able to grasp concepts very quickly. She appreciates that her royal rank gives her great convening power. When it comes to issues such as early years and the under-fives project, she is totally across her brief and able to engage with academics in the room on the same level. 'She truly appreciates the power of knowledge. It matters to her,' a former aide said.

Committed as they are to the Crown and helping the less fortunate through their charitable foundation, William has made it clear to the King, as he did to the late Queen and the army of courtiers, that he and Catherine are determined to achieve a healthy work/life balance. The royal couple will of course carry out their fair share of duties, but they both believe that being good parents is their most important role.

'Preparing Prince George to embrace and appreciate his future role as the next Prince of Wales, and ultimately as monarch, is of course high on their priority list. They are determined he understands his position and responsibilities, but don't want the pressure of expectation to weigh too heavily on his young shoulders,' said a senior palace figure.[138] They want their eldest son to slowly become a well-adjusted and balanced adult first, so he has the tools in place to cope when his time comes.

Another senior palace figure, a former member of the Household, told the author, 'The princess sees her primary role as a supportive wife to William and as a mother. Her public duties and core charities really matter, of course they do, but raising her children and preparing them for what is next will be her focus. Some might see this as very traditional, but the princess believes her duty first and foremost is to support her husband in his public work and, if you like, to shine the light on him, as well as of course support the current king.'

Some have wrongly dismissed this notion as being twee or overly sentimental, but that is to misjudge the woman and the importance she places on family life and the family unit. To Catherine, it comes 'first, second and third'. A close source added, 'The princess believes it is so important to do the little things and do them consistently.

Wherever possible she will do the school run and drop; she makes a point of being there for the school plays and sports days too.'

Why? It is simple: she remembers how her parents were always there for her when she was growing up and the secure feeling that their attendance generated within her. 'She wants her children to experience that same level of security that she experienced as a child,' a senior source added.

CHAPTER 21

A Cause for Concern

The Princess of Wales appreciates the interest this statement
will generate. She hopes that the public will understand her
wish that her personal medical information remains private.
KENSINGTON PALACE STATEMENT ON THE
PRINCESS OF WALES' HEALTH, 17 JANUARY 2024

I t came like a bolt out the blue, a moment that reminded everyone that serious health challenges can affect anyone at any time, regardless of their apparent fitness. With her slender frame and lush hair, Catherine radiates good health. A youthful-looking mother, she is celebrated for the vibrancy and energy she radiates. She is often spotted running in Windsor Great Park and is an enthusiastic tennis player when she can find the time. Rugby World Cup winner Mike Tindall even gave her the nickname 'Engine' because of her impressive levels of physical fitness. 'She can run all day,' he said on his popular podcast *The Good, The Bad & The Rugby.*

It therefore struck a profound chord when the Palace issued the significant news on 17 January 2024 that the Princess of Wales was recuperating in a London hospital, having undergone abdominal surgery. The Palace statement said that she was expected to stay at the London Clinic for ten to fourteen days. With Queen Elizabeth's sad decline and death still fresh in the public consciousness, the announcement about Catherine sent a collective shiver through royal admirers worldwide.

Hardly had the news settled of the princess's hospitalisation when Buckingham Palace issued a statement revealing that King Charles, at seventy-five, was due to be admitted to hospital for treatment for an enlarged prostate. A double dose of such serious medical bulletins involving two of the most senior royals was unprecedented.

Benign prostatic hyperplasia affects about 50 per cent of men between the ages of fifty-one to sixty and up to 90 per cent of men older than eighty, so the initial reaction to the King's treatment was relaxed. Catherine, however, defies her age at forty-two and her hospitalisation was not to be expected. Kensington Palace, while not giving specific details of her surgery, guided that it was 'abdominal surgery' and that her condition, thankfully, was not cancerous.

'Based on the current medical advice, she is unlikely to return to public duties until after Easter [2024],' the statement read. 'The Princess of Wales appreciates the interest this statement will generate. She hopes that the public will understand her desire to maintain as much normality for her children as possible, and her wish that her personal medical information remains private.' It was the least she could ask. Obviously, it led to a wave of speculation, with people wanting to know what she had been treated for.

The news also ignited a heated debate on X, formerly Twitter, when a person purporting to be an NHS doctor claimed without knowing Catherine's condition, which had not been officially divulged, that she would have been discharged from an NHS hospital within a day. It prompted a flurry of critical responses condemning the comments, given the lack of knowledge about the princess's treatment and care needs.

Online trolls even attacked the princess as she recuperated in hospital. I will not dignify their bile by repeating it but suffice to say it was so offensive that it beggars belief that these laptop warriors, who are invariably hiding behind pseudonyms, are allowed to get away with spewing such vile hatred. Fortunately, recent legislative changes in the UK have emphasised the need to focus on psychological harm in online communication, as well as content that is simply offensive, in a bid to quell such absurd hostility.

Most people were warm and sympathetic, however, and wished the princess well. Celebrities sent messages too, including her podcasting friend, the actress Giovanna Fletcher, who simply said, 'Sending love' on her Instagram account. TV presenter Fearne Cotton, who had shared the stage with the princess during a symposium on childhood the previous November, posted two crimson heart emojis, while John Torode, the Australian-born celebrity chef, messaged, 'Wishing her Royal Highness a speedy and comfortable recovery.' Prince Harry, though, was accused of disrespect for failing to wish the King and Catherine well during his acceptance speech at the Living Legends of Aviation Awards in Beverly Hills.

Apart from debilitating bouts of morning sickness and, of course, stays in the Lindo Wing at St Mary's Hospital to deliver her babies, Catherine has fortunately avoided hospital for most of her life. As a teenager, however, when at Marlborough College she discovered a lump on the left side of her head, just under her hairline. The school notified her parents immediately and her mother Carole took her to hospital, where she had surgery to remove it. The three-inch scar was first noticed by the public in 2011, when she was attending her first solo royal engagement at Clarence House. The Palace issued a statement saying simply, 'The scar is related to a childhood operation,' but that the details would remain a private matter.

Meanwhile, in California, Harry and Meghan's LA-based public relations team used the opportunity to garner some goodwill, claiming they had 'reached out' to both the King and Catherine to wish them well. That does not mean, of course, that there was any one-to-one contact. In fact, there was none. At that stage, the King did not wish to engage. 'Perhaps he wanted to apologise for all the heartache he has caused,' one senior courtier said acerbically. Another Royal Household member was more cynical about this apparent gesture of goodwill, particularly as it coincided with Harry losing his High Court battle against the *Mail on Sunday*, and now faced having to pay up to £750,000 in legal costs for both parties. The 'Harry problem', as it is known among Palace officials, remains something that plagues the King. 'What worries His Majesty, and his top team, is what is going to happen when all the money runs out.'

Perhaps mindful of the fake news that swirled around whenever his parents went into hospital, and in a bid to quell unwanted speculation, the King took the unprecedented step of confirming the specific details of the procedure to treat a benign enlarged prostate. He was lauded for doing so, with commentators saying he had ushered in a new era of transparency in matters of health and the Royal Family. It was something his medical team had been monitoring for some time. Charles had even considered going in for treatment in September 2022, close sources confirmed, but put it on hold due to the death of his mother.

Queen Camilla had initially been against disclosing his condition, but the King overruled her as he felt it was a chance to take a lead and in doing so to encourage men experiencing similar symptoms to seek timely medical attention. There was a significant increase in searches related to enlarged prostate on the National Health Service website following the monarch's revelation. The

NHS England page on benign prostate enlargement had more than 26,000 visits in the forty-eight hours after the announcement, compared to a daily average of just 1,400.[139] This openness contrasted with past practices, where even minor health concerns of Royal Family members were cloaked in secrecy, often fuelling baseless rumours.

The King rested initially at Balmoral before returning to stay at Sandringham. Early on 26 January, he went back into the London Clinic, the same hospital where Catherine was recuperating, and visited his daughter-in-law before going in for his procedure and what was expected to be a two-night stayover. In fact, he spent three nights there, which raised eyebrows. He was accompanied by the Queen when he was admitted and again at the departure, a break from the past as the late Queen and Prince Philip would always go and leave alone.

Kensington Palace made it clear that as a loving husband and father, William would have to scale back his royal duties to care for their three young children and for Catherine after she left hospital for her long period of recovery. He had the back-up of the couple's trusted nanny, Maria, and support staff, and relied on Catherine's parents, Michael and Carole, for support. Michael, however, had his own health issues and was convalescing after undergoing surgery himself,[140] so Pippa and James both rallied round to support their sister. Even with all this assistance, William knew that balancing his royal duties, especially with his father laid up too, was going to be difficult.

With the King, Catherine and to a lesser extent William out of action, the Sussex-shaped void in the Royal Family now loomed large. Not that long before, Charles had two sons in public life to whom he could turn to help him shoulder the burden of kingship. Harry's decision to quit the Firm had exposed the King's plan for a slimmed-down monarchy. Even before he wore the crown, Charles had grasped the urgency of reforming the institution, not only by trimming the Royal Family's budget, but making the monarchy a more efficient and transparent operation. He had already started reorganising the top-heavy Royal Household staff.

Amidst these royal health revelations, the *Daily Mail* high-lighted the seriousness of having two of the most senior royals so stricken with the front-page headline, 'Let's Pray They're Both OK'. It may have been a tad melodramatic, but it emphasised the point that two pillars of our modern monarchy both faced serious medical challenges that would keep them out of action, in Catherine's case for months.

A few days later, the *Sun* featured a photograph of the King at the wheel of his car on the Sandringham Estate with a banner headline: 'Slow Down'. It had nothing to do with him driving too fast, but the fact that Camilla had urged her 'workaholic' husband to work less ahead of his operation.[141] His advisers had also suggested he should pace himself. In the past, however, he had always turned a deaf ear to such requests.

Catherine, while willing for people to know she was in hospital, wanted to keep the specific reasons for her operation private. Her thoughts were with her husband and children. In the statement issued by Kensington Palace, the princess said that while she appreciated the interest the news of her hospitalisation would generate, she hoped that the public would understand her desire to maintain 'as much normality for her children as possible, and her wish that her personal medical information remains private'. It went on:

> Kensington Palace will, therefore, only provide updates on Her Royal Highness's progress when there is significant new information to share. The Princess of Wales wishes to apologise

to all those concerned for the fact that she has to postpone her upcoming engagements. She looks forward to reinstating as many as possible, as soon as possible.

It meant that planned overseas visits to Latvia and a short overseas tour to Rome and the Vatican both set for early 2024 were postponed.

The double royal health crisis had revealed a crack in the King's long-term strategy for a streamlined monarchy. It became apparent that not everyone within the family endorsed this plan. When questioned about such proposals, Princess Anne, known for her frankness, expressed scepticism. She was not convinced it was a prudent decision, citing the already diminished number of active royals. She told *CBC News* in January 2022, 'From where I'm standing, it doesn't sound like a good idea, I must say.' Not for the first time she hit the nail on the head.

Catherine, much like the Princess Royal, is regarded as the jewel in our crown. Yet even the brightest gem has its limits. In the wake of Harry and Meghan's departure, she significantly ramped up her official engagements, demonstrating her dedication to the Firm. The void left by Prince Andrew's retreat from public life following the Epstein scandal has also heightened the demand for working royals. Edward and Sophie, now the Duke and Duchess of Edinburgh, have risen to the occasion, alongside Princess Anne.

In December 2023, at the King's request, Edward and Anne became Counsellors of State, ready to step in if duty calls, after MPs passed a new law. They joined the Prince of Wales, Queen Camilla and Princess Beatrice on the list. Princes Andrew and Harry remain as stand-ins, despite standing down as working royals, but are now unlikely ever to be needed. The other working royals, given their respective ages, can no longer be expected to carry the heavy load of engagements. They are first cousins to the late Queen Elizabeth, 87-year-old Prince Edward, the Duke of Kent and Prince Richard, the 78-year-old Duke of Gloucester.

With fewer senior royals available, the burden of official responsibilities has shifted. Catherine's delayed return to royal duties until after Easter 2024 has underscored not only the Royal Family's reliance on her and her husband, but also the wider public's recognition of her value to the institution. Her unwavering presence and radiant spirit serve as a beacon of hope and stability in uncertain times.

After thirteen nights in hospital following abdominal surgery, Catherine was finally discharged from hospital on 29 January without being photographed and returned home to Windsor. The Kensington Palace statement emphasised that her return to public engagements would depend on medical advice closer to the time and William would only return to public engagements once she was settled. The King, who was pictured smiling as he left the London Clinic with Queen Camilla at his side, left hospital the same day. Both royals, the Palaces said, would have an extended period of recuperation.

The unfolding story then took a dramatic turn on 5 February, with a statement from the Palace that the King had been diagnosed with 'a form of cancer' that would prevent him carrying out face-to-face public duties and he was already being treated for it. The exact nature of the cancer remained a closely guarded secret, but it was understood to be in the pelvic and bladder region. All Palace officials would divulge was that it was not prostate cancer, but this had been an unexpected discovery amidst the treatment for the enlarged prostate, something no one could have foreseen.

The King faced this new chapter in his life with a stoic resolve. His treatment would involve regular journeys to the London Clinic and had already started before the official announcement commenced. Amidst the uncertainty, those close to him said he was positive and felt blessed that it had been caught early.

When Charles contacted his son Harry in America to tell him of his diagnosis, before going public, the Duke of Sussex then flew to be by his side unbidden. Once his 'darling boy', the events of the past two years have left their relationship fractured and Harry's impetuous decision caused some disquiet. Put bluntly, the King was unhappy about what amounted to a *fait accompli* served up by an emotional but well-meaning son at a time when he needed peace and quiet.

The official narrative was that the King was 'touched' by the gesture, though the truth was more complex. Indeed, the unscheduled visit disrupted Charles's plans for tranquillity with Camilla at Sandringham. Instead, they idled at Clarence House, awaiting his youngest son's arrival. Thirty minutes. That's all they shared. Clearly not nearly enough to mend the shattered bridges, not after all the disparagement and misrepresentations echoing from Montecito. After a brief embrace and short conversation, they said their goodbyes before the King and Queen were driven away to Buckingham Palace to board the monarch's helicopter bound for Norfolk.

The Duke of Sussex, living so far away in his own familial bubble, had perhaps not grasped that his public betrayal of his father and family has left far deeper wounds than he anticipated. Familial trust, too, lies in tatters. His gesture, well-intentioned as it was, served as a stark reminder of discord between father and son, a weight that Charles could ill afford in his fragile state. The next day, Harry headed back to Los Angeles and his wife and family. The unfounded accusations of racism against Charles and Catherine have cut deep, especially for a man like the King, who has devoted his working life to promoting dialogue and diversity. Yet, amidst the turmoil, Harry's visit led to glimmers of hope in the media.

As the King retreated from public life to recuperate, while continuing his formal constitutional responsibilities, Catherine unexpectedly became the centre of a media storm of her own making. Her absence from the public stage and Kensington Palace's silence had fuelled frenzied internet conspiracies theories. So, in a bid to dampen down the rumours, the couple shared a family photo to mark Mother's Day in mid-March, which Catherine edited using Photoshop to enhance its appeal.

The doctored photo, however, sparked a furore when respected wire agencies, including the Associated Press, Reuters, AFP and eventually the Press Association, all rejected the doctored image, saying it had been manipulated and the source could not be trusted. They refused to distribute it. Kensington Palace faltered in its response and the global fallout was huge.

The unfortunate episode was dubbed by the media as 'Kategate' or 'Sleevegate' and not only left an already fragile Catherine saddened and deeply embarrassed, but seriously damaged Kensington Palace's credibility and the royal brand. The mistake had been innocent enough. Naively, Catherine had edited the best shot taken by William at least three times using Photoshop to make the family look better before passing it to the Kensington Palace communications team, who then posted it on their Instagram account and released it to the media as an official photograph. As soon as it was issued, people noticed that something was wrong with Princess Charlotte's sleeve.

Criticism came swiftly, not only from the press but from international figures too, highlighting a breach of expected transparency. Even the White House press secretary mocked the royal couple, giving their press corps assurances that no images by them would ever be doctored. Holland's King Willem-Alexander also seemed to poke fun at the controversy surrounding the princess during an engagement in Zutphen. When a child in the crowd mentioned a photo of the King with his family, he replied, 'At least I didn't Photoshop it!'

Kensington Palace was even compared to North Korea and Iran by a foreign news agency. Agence France-Presse (AFP) said the fiasco was a 'big deal'. 'The previous kills [of photographs] have been from the North Korean news agency or the Iranian news agency, just to give you some background and context,' said global news director Phil Chetwynd. Asked by the BBC if Kensington Palace was still one of AFP's trusted sources, he replied, 'No, absolutely not.' Cartoons published in world media mocked the princess. The *Washington Post* depicted Catherine as a cut-out, with William as the puppet master.

The international condemnation was so fierce the British tabloids moved to defend the princess. The *Sun* published a front page under the banner headline, 'Lay Off Kate' and its editor, Victoria Newton, said that it was time to give the princess a break. 'I spoke to Kensington Palace that morning,' she told Times Radio. 'They said she's really upset and sad that she's caused all this trouble.'

It amplified the debate over the Royal Family's communication strategy and the expectations placed upon them. Despite demands, the Palace refused to release the original photo, which only deepened the intrigue, particularly when the notable absence of Catherine's wedding and engagement rings sparked fevered speculation. Explained away as a post-surgery oversight, the lack of clarity did little to satisfy public curiosity.

It was a moment of misstep, but it also speaks to the evolving dynamics of royal communication in an age where the line between personal and public, authenticity and perception, is ever more scrutinised. It may have been an innocent mistake, but the incident highlighted the modern monarchy's challenges in managing its image. PR expert Mark Borkowski told the *London Evening Standard* that releasing the original photo might restore some trust, but close sources said that Prince William refused to budge.

It is understood that William's PR team suggested that he issue a joint statement from Kensington Palace to help deflect the blame from his recuperating wife. At first a statement was prepared using the words 'we' and 'our', but the prince opted not to release it. After all, it was Catherine who had manipulated the snap and it had been nothing to do with him. When the statement was finally issued, she owned it.

Making light of the situation during a royal visit a few days later, William raised eyebrows when he joked, 'My wife is the arty one,' as he participated in a children's activity, highlighting his own and his children's lesser artistic skills.

Catherine stepped back into the limelight on 16 March with a visit to her favourite farm shop, a stone's throw from Adelaide Cottage in Windsor. Those who saw her described a woman at ease, her improved health apparent in her smile. The following day, she and William were spotted watching George, Charlotte and Louis compete at Windsor Tennis Club. Such appearances began to quell the storm of scurrilous rumours that had swept through social media, but even then conspiracy theories abounded.

Some attention seekers cashed in, wearing 'Free Kate' T-shirts, echoing the 'Free Britney' movement in the US when long-time fans of the singer Britney Spears fans displayed their dissatisfaction at the star continuing to be under a conservatorship at the age of thirty-eight. It was tasteless and baseless.

The *Sun* finally cut through the fog of conspiracy on 18 March with a clear video of the princess on their news website. There, in broad daylight, was Catherine, casual in a hoodie and leggings, as she walked through the farm shop's car park carrying groceries, with William by her side. Both seemed totally at ease, the weight of the world lifted for a moment. It was not some shameless set-up, the kind that certain celebrities engage in. Nelson Silva, aged forty, was only there to buy steak and found himself an accidental witness to this normal behaviour, catching the royal couple in the mundane act of choosing bread. His footage, which surfaced hours after revelations of Catherine's weekend outings, stood as a silent rebuke to the darker corners of speculation.

For weeks, unfounded stories had festered online, bullying the princess from the shadows. Yet even now, in the face of undeniable public sightings, some eyes remained closed to the truth. Catherine was still the only story in town and the doubters continued with more fanciful claims, alleging that the noticeably thinner woman in the video was not her.

The next day it emerged that the London Clinic, where Catherine and the King had been treated, was at the centre of an investigation following claims that three staff members had illicitly attempted to access Catherine's private medical records. The King's notes were not compromised. The Information Commissioner's Officer (ICO), the UK's data protection authority, acknowledged receipt of a report concerning the breach. The *Daily Mirror* revealed that Kensington Palace had been told about the 'significant security lapse' and pledged to undertake a thorough investigation.

And then came Catherine's deeply shocking video announce-ment that she had cancer and had started preventative che-motherapy.

CHAPTER 22

The Heart of the Family

She is a real role model. I like her. I think she is wonderful.
**FORMER U.S. FIRST LADY MICHELLE OBAMA, INTERVIEWED
IN *GOOD HOUSEKEEPING* MAGAZINE**

The King's declaration of pride in Catherine's courage resounded deeply. In a statement issued moments after the princess's televised cancer revelation, His Majesty said he was 'so proud of the princess for her courage in speaking as she did' and he remained in the 'closest contact with his beloved daughter-in-law.' The King and Queen said they 'will continue to offer their love and support to the whole family through this difficult time.'

His Majesty and the princess had met for a private lunch on Thursday, 21 March 2024 at Windsor Castle, underscoring the gravity of her impending cancer. Catherine, facing the spectre of the disease, had chosen to share her journey with a candour in a video message and he bowed to her courage, remaining steadfast by her side.

Harry and Meghan extended their support, a whisper of reconciliation hinting at mended rifts. 'We wish health and healing for Kate and the family, and hope they are able to do so privately and in peace,' they said via a spokesperson. Catherine's brother

James Middleton, invoking shared childhood conquests, pledged his solidarity. He posted a photo of the pair as children donning backpacks on Instagram, accompanied by the words: 'Over the years, we have climbed many mountains together. As a family, we will climb this one with you too.'

With King Charles already being treated for the disease, it became clear that the Royal Family was facing possibly its gravest crisis since the 1936 Abdication. Stripped of its stars, with the King out of public action and now the beautiful and compassionate Catherine sidelined too, serious concerns began to be raised about the House of Windsor's resilience.

Following the disclosure that she was undergoing treatment for cancer, many of those who had been making jokes about Catherine or mocking her on social media now rushed to apologise. Journalist Julie Burchill wrote an article in the *Daily Mail* titled, 'Why I spread rumours about Kate – and I'm so ashamed of it'.[142] Hollywood actress Blake Lively expressed her remorse on Instagram, saying, 'I made a silly post around the "photoshop fails" frenzy, and oh man, that post has me mortified today. I'm sorry.' The political commentator Owen Jones wrote on X, formerly Twitter, 'As someone who speculated on this without considering it could be a serious health condition, I'm very ashamed to be honest, and all the very best to her.'

It transpired later that Catherine had continued her usual routine of driving George, Charlotte and Louis on the school run, but she took the precaution of wearing a face mask. Several parents had noticed, without realising that the mask was to prevent her from picking up an infection while having her chemotherapy treatment.

As this book goes to press in 2024, these are unstable times for the monarchy, yet history has shown that the institution has overcome the direst obstacles, having survived revolution, civil war and dark threats. Since the death of Queen Elizabeth, so dignified and constant, it has been shaken, made threadbare by scandals and the Harry and Meghan saga. The monarchy's adaptability and its openness, especially Catherine's cancer statement, countered the wild rumours and deserved support.

In her powerful video message, Catherine said she had found not only a partner in William but a fortress against the trials ahead, their union a testament to enduring love and shared resolve. She was determined to face the future not with resignation but with an embrace of life in all its fullness. Now, more than ever, William needed his strength, all of it. The blows had never come so hard, so fast, for the Prince of Wales. First, his father, now his wife.

Those close to the prince know he has never shied from a challenge, he has always faced adversity head-on. As when he was fifteen, under the world's gaze after the sudden death of his mother Diana. Yet, the crisis faced by his wife would be a trial as grave as his mother's loss, perhaps more so. As parents, William and Catherine's thoughts were first and foremost for their children's welfare. They are a team, valuing each other's opinion above all; no decision made without consulting the other, since before their marriage. The prince knows that Catherine has practical solutions, even to complex problems.

On 18 April, William returned to his public duties after spending the Easter holiday with Catherine and the children. He spent the day with groups that make a real difference in their communities, focusing on food waste and hunger.

His first visit was to Surplus to Supper in Sunbury-on-Thames, Surrey, a charity that takes excess food from large entities and delivers it to smaller community groups within a five-mile stretch. While assisting in the sorting and packaging, the prince pointed at a tin and said, 'That's spaghetti hoops.' Surprised, volunteer Rachel Candappa asked him, 'How do you know about spaghetti hoops?'

He replied. 'I've got children!' Rachel also handed him two get well soon cards addressed to the King and Catherine. William looked visibly moved and said, 'Thank you, you are very kind.' When she told him to take care of Kate, he put his left hand on her shoulder and promised, 'I will do, I will.'

King Charles resumed his official public-facing duties on 30 April. With Queen Camilla by his side, he visited University College Hospital Macmillan Cancer Centre, where he lent his support to both the patients and medical staff. Four days earlier Buckingham Palace officials had announced that his physicians were encouraged by his recovery thus far, although the specifics of his cancer remained private.

The King shared a moment of personal connection with patients during his visit to the chemotherapy day unit. Among them was Lesley Woodbridge, who was receiving her treatment in a room filled with others fighting similar battles. The King revealed his own vulnerability when he mentioned, 'I've got to have my treatment this afternoon as well.' When asked about his health by another patient, Asha Millen, who is battling bone marrow cancer, Charles responded with a stoic and reassuring, 'I'm well, thank you very much, not too bad.' This underscored the positive strides he had made after nearly three months of outpatient cancer care.[143]

While fate may have brought Catherine and William together through love, she has evolved into the person she always aspired to be. Her success in life has been shaped by her unflinching character for behind that sparkling public smile is a strong-willed woman with a sharp intellect and a tenacious resolve. Someday, this middle-class Berkshire girl will be King William V's consort, arguably becoming the first true Queen of the People, from the people.

Her health concerns, hospitalisation, cancer diagnosis and long period of recuperation out of the public eye, coming simultaneously with the King's diagnosis of cancer, have helped focus attention on just how important Catherine is to the nation and the Royal Family. Before his own cancer treatment, the King knew that he could always count on his beloved daughter-in-law. Their shared experience has brought him and the princess even closer together.

His Majesty and Queen Camilla trust and admire the princess for being a team-player and supporting William. Indeed, her leadership style is not unlike the King's. She leads by example, convenes people and is an excellent listener. It is understood that Charles is poised to mark her dedicated service by appointing her as a Royal Lady of the Order of the Garter, the ancient and prestigious Order of Chivalry, dating back to the reign of Edward III in the fourteenth century. In doing so, he will not only be recognising her loyalty and dedication to the monarchy, but her seniority of rank within the Royal Family.[144]

His Majesty is also expected to appoint her soon to become a member of his Privy Council, the ancient body that formally advises the monarch. It will mean, as the future Queen, she will be able to attend the Accession Council, the ceremonial body that assembles upon the monarch's death to proclaim the accession of successor and therefore in the room at St James's Palace when William becomes King.

On the eve of King Charles's Coronation, Catherine confided to a well-wisher in the crowd that she felt 'excitement and nerves, all mixed up'. But when the big day came, on 6 May 2023, she seemed to have left any nerves behind. She was the embodiment of a royal princess, wearing her formal robe, adorned with the Royal Victorian Order mantle of the Dame Grand Cross. The Alexander McQueen gown she wore, with motifs from the four UK countries, and her headpiece, a creation by Jess Collett, showcased the red, white and blue of the Union Flag. She stood tall and radiated confidence, a beautiful symbol of the Crown.

A deep curtsy to King Charles during the crowning ceremony highlighted the profound respect she has for him personally, as well as to tradition and her loyalty to the Crown itself. The King, those close to him say, has unwavering faith in Catherine, seeing her as a lynchpin for the modern monarchy. The princess has demonstrated that she possesses all the qualities needed in these challenging and changing times for the monarchy, with her presence, gravitas and regal aura. She has grown into the role, her poise today in stark contrast to her timid performance at her first state banquet for President Xi Jinping in 2015. Today, her authenticity and dedication set her apart.

On St George's Day, 23 April 2024, King Charles appointed Catherine to be a Companion of Honour, a prestigious title traditionally bestowed upon individuals who have demonstrated exceptional achievement in the arts, medicine or science. Current members of the order include Sir David Attenborough, Dame Judi Dench, Sir Ian McKellen, Dame Maggie Smith, Sir Roy Strong, Sir Paul McCartney and JK Rowling.

However, the appointment raised eyebrows, promoting more discourse about the criteria used for such honours. The former Liberal Democrat MP Norman Baker, writing the day after in the *Guardian*, questioned whether it could be argued that the monarchy had been modernised when such archaic titles were still being handed out. 'The honours in themselves are absurd,' he declared, 'and make the mythical Ruritania look like a beacon of modernity.' Conversely, sources said the honour showed the high regard the King has for Catherine and it marked her dedication to the Crown.

The princess, once so unfairly deemed a mere mannequin for fancy attire, now stands as a pillar of stability in a monarchy often shaken by scandal. She has had to walk a fine line, captivating the media's appetite for news without stoking controversy. She has found her place at the heart of the family, embodying the essence of a traditional mother and enjoying outdoor adventures with her children, while also embracing her role to raise a future king, Prince George. It is a role that feels genuine, rooted in simplicity and domestic bliss.

Critics may label her bland, but her popularity remains strong as she wields a quiet influence, much like the late Queen, rather than challenging its essence. 'She's not just liked, she's not disliked,' remarks Victoria Murphy, a seasoned observer of royal affairs as a royal contributor for America's *ABC News*.

Catherine appears to navigate her role with natural grace, always seeking consensus rather than asserting dominance. In a world where the Royal Family must demonstrate purpose without overstepping constitutional boundaries, the princess has proved herself to be a leader who unites, a listener who guides and a model of quiet strength.

Commander Patrick Jephson RN, the Irish-born author who was previously the private secretary and equerry to Princess Diana, believes the monarchy needs what he calls 'reassuringly conventional royal performers' such as Catherine. She holds this royal dynasty's future in her hands, he has said, adding, 'It helps that Catherine, like Diana, has that indefinable but essential royal quality: "presence".'[145]

Like the late Queen Elizabeth, the Queen Mother, Catherine is a calming influence on her sometimes headstrong husband. He does not always take advice – hers or anyone else's, not even his father's. When King Charles raised concerns about William piloting his helicopter to fly his entire family around in early 2024, the prince was inflexible. An experienced pilot, he had previously upset Queen Elizabeth when he defied her by piloting his family the 115 miles from Kensington Palace to Anmer Hall in Norfolk. The Queen, haunted by the 1967 crash that killed Air Commodore John Blount, who was Captain of the Queen's Flight, later cautioned William, particularly about flying with his heir Prince George, telling her grandson that he should always be aware of the line of succession. 'She did not hold back,' one aide said.

After his cancer diagnosis, King Charles echoed his late mother's concerns, urging William to curb his helicopter use. When he refused, the King insisted that he sign a formal acknowledgement of the risks involved and take full responsibility for his actions, a grim reminder of the weight of succession.

The King sees the challenges ahead. He knows the monarchy must adapt, but also that after his cancer diagnosis the clock is ticking, not only for him but for the institution. The survival of the monarchy is not guaranteed by tradition alone, but by its capacity to engage with and reflect the evolving values and attitudes of the people it exists to serve. Integrity and authenticity matter.

In an era where every photo, especially an officially issued manipulated one, can spark global rumours, King Charles recognises that the monarchy's future looks less certain for the first time in decades. Queen Elizabeth, a selfless monarch and a symbol of stability and continuity, was respected around the world. She and her consort Prince Philip left large shoes to fill. Charles and Camilla, then William and Catherine, must find a way to steady the ship in stormy seas. William may want to focus on family, drawing boundaries around his duty. He is seen by critics – unfairly in my view – as a part-time prince. But can he and Catherine navigate the royal duties and their personal life in a world that watches their every move?

There is no doubt that Catherine has a strong, positive aura that surrounds her, 'an aura of perfection'.[146] Over the past thirteen years, she has undergone a remarkable transformation – evolving from a hesitant 29-year-old bride into a confident royal duchess, an accomplished orator and performer in public even before becoming the Princess of Wales, the second most senior female member of the Royal Family. Her extraordinary rise is, of course, still not over.

For William, the King and Catherine's cancer diagnosis in 2024 has served as a stark reminder of his own mortality. Looming like a shadow over their lives, it has emphasised their date with destiny.

As King Charles's eldest son and direct heir, Prince William's ascent to the throne follows a well-trodden path. When he is monarch, he will be supported by a cadre of officials who aid in the governance and administration of the realm. Catherine's role, however, is imbued with nuance. Unwavering, she stands ready to walk alongside her husband, offering love and steadfast support at every turn.

When the time arrives, she will be coronated as Queen Consort, standing by his side within the hallowed halls and gothic architecture of Westminster Abbey. Together, they will forge a resilient, glamorous and impactful partnership, shaping the course of twenty-first-century Great Britain and at the head of its ever-evolving modern monarchy.

The Princesses of Wales

The title, The Princess of Wales, was first used in 1361 by Joan Plantagenet, who was entitled the Countess of Kent in her own right. Her husband was the warrior hero of the battle of Crecy, the Black Prince, eldest son and heir of King Edward III. He was also Joan's half-first cousin as her father, Edward of Woodstock, the 1st Earl of Kent, was the sixth son of King Edward I by his second wife, Margaret of France, who was the daughter of King Philip III of France.

One of the most important and influential women of her age, Joan was dubbed the 'Fair Maid of Kent'. A controversial figure, she had been twice-married before her union with the prince, so at the King's request, Pope Innocent VI granted the four dispensations needed for their legal wedding at Windsor on 10 October 1361. Later, she became Dowager, Princess of Wales on the death of her husband in 1376, aged just forty-five; meaning he never reigned as he predeceased his father Edward III, who died the following year. She played an influential role at court after her second son was crowned King Richard II in July 1377, when he was only ten years old. Joan died aged fifty-eight on 7 August 1385.

The Princesses of Wales that followed her were either of royal blood, foreign princesses, distant royal cousins, or at least noble and high-born. The next woman to hold the title was Anne Neville, daughter of Richard Neville, the influential 16th Earl of Warwick, who was dubbed 'The Kingmaker'. He was a first cousin of Edward IV and had access to a large personal army, as well as being one of the wealthiest landowners and predominant men of his time. Warwick, a scheming Machiavellian figure, went on to betray the Crown and was killed at the decisive War of the Roses battle at Barnet in 1471. Edward IV's victory was followed by fourteen years of Yorkist rule over England.

Despite Warwick's treachery, his daughter Anne holds a unique place in history as wife to both the last Lancastrian heir to the English throne and later, the last Yorkist Plantagenet king, Richard III. She became the Princess of Wales when she married Edward of Westminster, who was also Prince of Wales, and the only son and heir apparent of the pious but incompetent monarch Henry VI.

The next to hold the title was Catherine of Aragon, the Spanish first wife of Henry VIII. She became the Princess of Wales while married to Henry's elder brother, Arthur, Prince of Wales, for a short period before his sudden death in March 1502, probably from consumption. The daughter of Isabella I of Castile and Ferdinand II of Aragon, Catherine was only three years old when she was betrothed to the Tudor prince Arthur, heir apparent to the English throne.

She later married Arthur's brother Prince Henry, who had been created Duke of Cornwall and the new Prince of Wales and Earl of Chester in February 1504, aged ten. Catherine did not get the title for a second time because she wed seventeen-year-old Henry VIII, who had only just acceded to the throne, on 11 June 1509, when she was aged twenty-three.

Wilhelmina Charlotte Caroline of Brandenburg-Ansbach, King George II's wife, was the next to hold the title. Known as Caroline Wilhelmina, she was the daughter of John Frederick, Margrave of Brandenburg-Ansbach.[147] Her parents died while she was still a child and she spent her early life in Berlin, before marrying Prince George of Hanover, the future King George II, in 1705. She accompanied him to England as Princess of Wales in 1714.

Princess Augusta of Saxe-Gotha-Altenburg was the Princess of Wales by marriage to Frederick, Prince of Wales, the eldest son and heir apparent of King George II. However, she never became Queen Consort, as Frederick predeceased his father in 1751. Her eldest son succeeded her father-in-law as George III in 1760.

The next to hold the title was Caroline of Brunswick-Wolfenbüttel, who was loathed by her husband and first cousin the Prince Regent, George IV. She became the Princess of Wales in April 1795 on her marriage to George, Prince of Wales, whom she had never met when they became engaged a year earlier. Although she was never crowned, she was Queen of the United Kingdom of Great Britain and Ireland and Queen of Hanover from 29 January 1820 until her death, aged fifty-three, on 25 August, just three weeks after her husband had barred her from his coronation.

Princess Alexandra of Denmark, wife of Edward VII, was the eldest daughter of Christian IX of Denmark and was the Princess of Wales from 1863 to 1901, the longest anyone has ever held that title. Hugely popular with the British public and renowned for her beauty, her style of dress and bearing were copied by fashion-conscious women of the age. Like Catherine, the current Princess of Wales, Alexandra was an enthusiastic and prolific amateur photographer, who learned how to use a hand-held camera and loved creating albums of family photographs. She was famously very tolerant of her husband's infidelities.

Princess Mary of Teck, a great-granddaughter of George III and wife of George V, was born at Kensington Palace on 26 May 1867, the daughter of Francis Paul, Duke of Teck, and Mary Adelaide, formerly a Princess of Cambridge. Due to her father's morganatic descent from the House of Württemberg, she was known by the title Serene Highness. Queen Victoria and the Prince of Wales (the future Edward VII) stood as godparents.

Her mother was the first cousin of Queen Victoria, being the younger daughter of Prince Adolphus, Duke of Cambridge, the youngest surviving son of King George III and Augusta of Hesse-Cassel. Queen Mary was the matriarch who stood firm during the abdication crisis in 1936, her strong sense of duty ingrained in her by Queen Victoria. She won plaudits for championing issues that concerned women's welfare and children.

Today, the ancient title of Princess of Wales carries a legacy of glamour, controversy and enduring fame, largely due to the last person to be known by it, Lady Diana Spencer. Diana was styled Her Royal Highness The Princess of Wales from her wedding day to Prince Charles until their divorce. After that, until her tragic death in a car accident in Paris in August 1997, she was stripped of her HRH rank on the orders of Queen Elizabeth II and was known until her death as Diana, Princess of Wales. Had she remarried, she would have lost that title too.

An aristocrat of noble and royal lineage before she married, Diana could trace her blood line back to the Stuart dynasty. She was descended from two illegitimate children of King Charles II, Henry Fitzroy and Charles Lennox, via two of her great-grandmothers, Adelaide Seymour and Rosalind Bingham. It means that when her son William, Prince of Wales, accedes to the throne, he will be the first British king to descend directly from the Stuart rulers as well as the Hanoverian monarchs. Diana was, of course, also the last person to use the title HRH The Princess of Wales until Catherine.

Appendix

Honours and titles granted to HRH The Duchess of Cambridge / HRH The Princess of Wales

Dame Grand Cross of the Royal Victorian Order, April 2019
The Tuvalu Order of Merit, 2016
(Both the Duke and Duchess of Cambridge were nominated by the Government of Tuvalu for the Order of Merit and approved by the Queen in October 2016.)
Royal Companion of the Order of the Companions of Honour, April 2024

Charities

As well supporting the King by undertaking duties at home and abroad, the Princess of Wales supports several charitable causes and organisations, several of which are focused on giving children the best possible start in life.

Early Years Support

For several years Catherine has been working with experts and organisations to highlight the importance of giving a solid psychological, social and emotional platform for children in their early formative years – pre-birth to five – to support their mental health.

Children's Mental Health

The princess champions issues related to children's mental health and emotional wellbeing. She has worked hard to bring wider appreciation to issues facing children today, such as addiction, poverty, abuse, neglect, loss and illness of family members and how it can have a long-lasting and traumatic impact if left unsupported. She has encouraged open and honest conversations about the subject of mental health to try and combat stigma.

Heads Together

In 2017 Catherine championed the Heads Together mental health campaign with the Duke of Cambridge and the Duke of Sussex. The coalition of eight mental health charity partners helped change the national conversation on mental health. The charities were: Anna Freud National Centre for Children and Families; Best Beginnings; CALM – The Campaign Against Living Miserably; Contact (a military mental health coalition); Mind; Place2Be; The Mix and YoungMinds. The campaign aimed to tackle stigma and raise awareness for people with mental health problems. In 2017 Heads Together was Virgin Money London Marathon Charity of the Year.

Sport and the Outdoors

The princess is a keen sportswoman and believes physical health complements mental health, but also that being outdoors inspires people and improves lives. She enjoys playing tennis and sailing and was an accomplished school hockey player.

Visual Arts

The princess is very interested in the visual arts, photography, design and textiles. She is a keen and accomplished amateur photographer and an Honorary Member of the Royal Photographic Society.

The Royal Foundation of The Prince and Princess of Wales

The Princess of Wales and Prince William direct their philanthropic work through The Royal Foundation of The Prince and Princess of Wales. It develops programmes and charitable projects based on the royal couple's interests and works with established organisations, giving investment, mentoring and support to help bolster the impact of their good work.

The Princess of Wales' Royal Patronages

Action for Children

The charity runs over 400 projects for some of the UK's most vulnerable young people. The Duchess of Cambridge became its patron in December 2016. Founded in 1868, it helps neglected children and their families throughout the UK, helping with areas such as foster care, adoption, child neglect and disability respite therapy.

Action on Addiction/The Forward Trust

Catherine became the charity patron in January 2012, meaning it was one of her first charities. Established in 2007 after merging three addiction charities – Action on Addiction, the Chemical Dependency Centre and Clouds – Action on Addiction exists to 'disarm addiction' through research, prevention, treatment, family support, professional education and training. She became patron of The Forward Trust when the charity merged with Action on Addition in June 2021.

All England Lawn Tennis and Croquet Club

The princess became patron of the All-England Lawn Tennis and Croquet Club when she took over from Her Majesty in December 2016. The All England Club is the tennis club where the Wimbledon Tennis Tournament is held every year. Catherine is an amateur tennis player and supports the club's initiative to promote tennis among youngsters.

Anne Freud Centre for Children and Families

Catherine became patron of the Anna Freud Centre in February 2016. The charity offers a wide range of services to children, families and schools. They provide training for mental health professionals and carry out research. The charity mission is to transform the experience of children, young people and their families with mental health issues by carrying out research, developing and offering services, teaching and training. The Princess of Wales has been the patron of the Anna Freud Centre since February 2016.

East Anglia Children's Hospices (EACH)

Catherine became patron of East Anglia Children's Hospices (EACH) in January 2012. It supports families and cares for children and young people with life-threatening conditions across Cambridgeshire, Essex, Norfolk and Suffolk.

Evelina London Children's Hospital

The princess became the patron of the hospital in December 2018. The Evelina London Hospital is part of Guy's and St Thomas' NHS Foundation Trust, of which Her Majesty the Queen is patron. Evelina London cares for children and young people from before birth, throughout childhood and into adult life.

Family Action

Catherine became patron of Family Action in December 2019, in line with her work in the Early Years Intervention. Her late Majesty the Queen passed the patronage to Catherine, having held the role for over sixty-five years. Queen Elizabeth II took over the patronage from Queen Mary in 1953. Established in 1869, Family Action helps families in difficulty by giving them practical help and support. It helps thousands with financial assistance through education and welfare grants programmes.

Foundling Museum

Catherine became patron of the Foundling Museum in March 2019. The princess has a longstanding interest in both the arts and supporting vulnerable families, and this patronage will further highlight the beneficial impact that art and creativity have on emotional wellbeing. The Foundling Museum tells the history of the Foundling Hospital, the UK's first children's charity and public art gallery. The Foundling Hospital, which continues today as the children's charity Coram, was established in 1739 by the philanthropist Thomas Coram to care for babies at risk of abandonment.

National Portrait Gallery
For a History of Art graduate, being patron of the National Portrait Gallery is a good fit. It opened in 1896 and features portraits of the most famous people in British history. Catherine became patron in January 2012 and supports the gallery's education and outreach programmes.

Natural History Museum
Catherine became patron in April 2013. The Natural History Museum's mission is to advance their knowledge of the natural world, inspiring better care of our planet.

NHS Charities (Joint patron with the Duke of Cambridge)
The princess became the joint patron of the National Health Service Charities (NHS Charities) with her husband William. There are more than 240 NHS Charities throughout the United Kingdom focused on helping hospitals. Collectively, these charities give £1 million every day to the NHS.

Nursing Campaign
The campaign aimed to raise the status and profile of nursing for a three-year period. It was run by the Burdett Trust in collaboration with the World Health Organization and the International Council of Nurses, Nursing Now, and was set up to empower nurses. The Princess of Wales became patron of the campaign in February 2018.

Place2Be

This charity provides early intervention mental health support without stigmatising children, young people or families at schools. The princess became patron in April 2013. It currently supports over 200 schools nationwide.

SportsAid

The charity, of which Catherine became patron in April 2013, is designed to assist our future sports stars now by giving them cash awards as they start out in their sporting careers.

The 1851 Trust

The Trust aims to inspires a new generation of sailors, developing their skills and training to become innovators of the maritime technology of the future. The princess, who became patron in October 2014, joined with sailing legend Sir Ben Ainslie to help promote sailing to young people and to get them involved with sailing and the marine industry.

Air Cadet Organisation

The Princess of Wales took over the role of patron of the Air Cadet Organisation in 2016 from Prince Philip, who was the patron for sixty-three years. It is a youth aviation organisation sponsored by the Royal Air Force in the UK.

Lawn Tennis Association

Catherine became patron of the Lawn Tennis Association in December 2016. The governing body of tennis in the UK, it promotes the sport of tennis through funding training, competitions and facilities.

The Royal College of Obstetricians and Gynaecologists

Founded in 1929 for people working in the field of obstetrics and gynaecology, the College was granted its royal charter in 1947 when the Queen Mother became patron. The princess took over as patron in February 2018.

English Rugby

In February 2022, the Princess of Wales became the patron of English rugby, a role previously held by Prince Harry. The BBC reported at the time that she 'becomes the figurehead for both the Rugby Football Union and Rugby Football League'.

The Royal Photographic Society

Catherine became patron after the late Queen asked her to take over the role after she had held it for sixty-seven years. It is one of the world's oldest photographic societies, founded in 1853 with the objective of promoting the art and science of photography.

Victoria and Albert Museum

With a mission to be the world's leading museum of art, design and performance, and to enrich people's lives by promoting the 'designed world', the V&A holds over 2.3 million objects that span over 5,000 years of human creativity of different mediums. In March 2018, Catherine became its first royal patron.

Official overseas visits by Catherine as Duchess of Cambridge and later, Princess of Wales

Solo visits

Denmark, February 2022
France, September 2023

Luxembourg, May 2017

Netherlands, October 2016

Joint official visits with Prince William

One visit:

Akrotiri and Dhekelia, December 2018

Australia, April 2014

Bahamas, March 2022

Belize, March 2002

Bhutan, April 2016

Denmark, November 2011

Germany, July 2017

India, April 2016

Ireland, March 2020

Jamaica, March 2022

Malaysia, September 2012

New Zealand, April 2014

Norway, February 2018

Pakistan, October 2019

Poland, July 2017

Singapore, September 2012

Solomon Islands, September 2012

Sweden, February 2018

Tuvalu, September 2012

Two visits:

Belgium, July 2017

Canada, June/July 2011 and September 2016

Three visits:
France, June 2014, June/July 2016 and March 2017
United States of America, July 2011, September 2016 and
December 2022

Selected Bibliography

Andersen, Christopher, *William and Kate: A Royal Love Story*, Gallery Books, 2010.

Bower, Tom, *Revenge*, Blink Publishing, 2023.

Brown, Tina, *The Palace Papers*, Century, 2022.

Dimbleby, Jonathan, *The Prince of Wales: A Biography*, Little, Brown, 1994.

Hardman, Robert, *Charles III: New King. New Court. The Inside Story*, MacMillan, 2024.

Hoey, Brian, *Prince William*, The History Press, 2003.

Holt, Bethan, *The Duchess of Cambridge*, Ryland, Peters & Small, 2021.

Jobson, Robert, *The New Royal Family*, John Blake, 2014.

Jobson, Robert, *Diana's Legacy: William and Harry*, MpressMedia, 2019.

Jobson, Robert, *Charles: Our Future King*, John Blake, 2019

Jobson, Robert, *William at 40*, AdLib, 2022.

Jobson, Robert, *Our King: Charles III, The Man and the Monarch*, 2023.

Joseph, Claudia, *Kate: The Making of a Princess*, William Morrow & Co., 2011.

Junor, Penny, *Prince William: Born to be King*, Hodder & Stoughton, 2012.

Lacey, Robert, *Battle of Brothers*, William Collins, 2020.

Low, Valentine, *Courtiers: The Hidden Power Behind the Crown*, Headline, 2023.

Morton, Andrew, *Diana: Her True Story – In Her Own Words*, Michael O'Mara, 2017.

Morton, Andrew, *Meghan: A Hollywood Princess*, Michael O'Mara, 2018.

Nicholl, Katie, *Kate: The Future Queen*, Hachette, 2015.

Scobie, Omid & Durand, Carolyn, *Finding Freedom*, HQ, 2020.

Scobie, Omid, *Endgame*, HQ, 2023.

Seward, Ingrid, *William & Harry: A Portrait of Two Princes*, Arcade, 2003.

Seward, Ingrid, *William and Harry: The People's Princes*, Welbeck, 2008.

Seward, Ingrid, *My Mother and I*, Simon & Schuster, 2024.

Wharfe, Ken, *Diana: Closely Guarded Secret*, John Blake, 2016.

Wharfe, Ken, *Guarding Diana*, John Blake, 2017.

Acknowledgements

I would first like to thank Perminder Mann, CEO of Bonnier Books UK, and now Honorary Visiting Professor of Publishing Studies at City University of London, for coming up with the idea for this book over a convivial lunch. I truly value her vision and support. I also really appreciate the support of Ciara Lloyd, Publishing Director for Blink and John Blake, for her wise counsel and expertise, and the entire editorial team for their unwavering hard work and professionalism. A big shoutout too to the editor of this book, Barry Johnston. He is a joy to work with and I thank him for his invaluable contribution – I cannot recommend him enough.

During my career as a royal correspondent and for the extensive research for this book, I have spoken to several invaluable inside sources and built relationships based on mutual trust. These people remain anonymous for obvious reasons, but I would like to acknowledge them here and thank them for their candid contributions that I believe have enriched this book.

Covering many royal engagements in the UK and on official overseas tours as an accredited royal correspondent and member of the UK royal rota for many years has given me excellent access to the Royal Family. It has facilitated my meeting Royal Family members, including Catherine, The Princess of Wales herself on a several occasions, and witnessed them up close as they carry out their official duties, which has broadened my appreciation of what our monarchy does and how it functions in a modern society.

For my background research I have also read many news articles and books about Catherine and the people whose lives she has impacted. They include books by my peers, writers whom I respect and acknowledge, including Ingrid Seward, Andrew Morton, Tom Bower, Katie Nicholl, Claudia Joseph, Robert Hardman, Bethan Holt, Valentine Low, Omid Scobie, Christopher Anderson and Penny Junor.

I have also drawn on several on the record interviews/podcasts that the princess has given as important secondary sources. These include interviews with Catherine conducted by Giovanna Fletcher, Alexandra Shulman and Max Foster's insightful broadcast and television interviews with Catherine that have served as valuable resources that I have credited in my extensive endnotes. I would also like to acknowledge Mike Tindall's podcast, *The Good, The Bad and The Rugby*, in a special episode ahead of the Rugby World Cup in September 2023, which featured the Prince and Princess of Wales and the Princess Royal.

I would like to thank fellow friends, colleagues and royal correspondents and photojournalists past and present who have helped with this book, but also whose counsel, company and most importantly, friendship I value deeply. These include *Daily Mail* editor-at-large Richard Kay, Ian Walker, executive editor of *MailOnline*, Inspector Ken Wharfe MVO, the former Scotland

Yard royalty protection officer to Princes William and Harry and of course the late Diana, Princess of Wales.

Thanks also to PA Media's highly respected court correspondent Alan Jones, the award-winning *Times* journalist Kate Mansey, the *Sun's* royal editor Matt Wilkinson, *Daily Mirror* executive Russell Myers and other members of the UK royal rota, past and present.

I would like to thank my colleagues at *ABC News*, particularly Zoe Magee, Victoria Murphy, Andrew Laurence, Dimitrije Stejic and Katie den Dass, Marc Bernstein and *ABC News* President Kim Goodwin for the opportunity to work alongside such a professional team of journalists and producers. Thanks also to my colleagues at Australia's top brekkie show on Channel 7's *Sunrise*, Sarah Stinson, Sean Power, David 'Dougie' Walters and the team, presenters Natalie Barr, Matt Shirvington, Edwina Bartholomew, Mark Beretta and past presenter David 'Kochie' Koch and Sam Armytage. Of course, a big shout-out too to the London-based bureau, Hugh Whitfield and Jimmy Cannon. I would also like to thank my good friends, the acclaimed royal photographers Robin Nunn, Kent Gavin and Arthur Edwards MBE, for their friendship, help and guidance over many years.

Last, but not least, I would like to thank my family, particularly my mother Jean, my late father Vic and my beloved son Charlie for their love and support.

Source Notes

Introduction

1   Queen Elizabeth, the Queen Mother, could trace her ancestry back through generations of Scottish nobility from her mother's family, the Bowes-Lyons, Earls of Strathmore, to Sir John Lyon, Thane of Glamis, who married King Robert II's daughter in the fourteenth century.

2   Some historians put the number of Princesses of Wales at eleven by including Queen Camilla in the list, even though she did not to use the title and chose instead to be known as the Duchess of Cornwall before becoming Queen.

Chapter 1: A Happy Childhood

3   The church is now owned by Bradfield College after they bought it from the Oxford Diocese and Church Commissioners in September 2021.

4   Princess Diana told journalist Andrew Morton for his book *Diana: Her True Story*, Michael O'Mara, 1992.

5   By the 1990s, Jordan saw a movement towards political liberalisation. King Hussein reinstated parliamentary elections and made steps towards greater democratisation. As expatriates, the Middleton family were largely insulated from these disturbances, but they were not blind to them.

6   From an article by Fay Schlesinger, *Daily Mail*, 26 April 2011.

7   Fay Schlesinger, *Daily Mail*, 26 April 2011.

8   From an interview in 2011 with *The National* newspaper.

9 *The National* newspaper, 2011.

10 In May 2023, following a downturn in profits caused by the COVID-19 pandemic, Party Pieces Holdings was sold to entrepreneur James Sinclair for £180,000 after it failed to avoid collapsing into administration.

11 From an interview with *People* magazine.

12 Catherine speaking on Giovanna Fletcher's *Happy Mum, Happy Baby* podcast, 15 February 2020.

13 From an interview with Downe House headteacher Susan Cameron by author Katie Nicholl.

14 From a conversation on a special episode of *The Good, The Bad & The Rugby* podcast to mark the Rugby World Cup 2023 with Mike Tindall, with Alex Payne (the Good), James Haskell (the Bad), featuring the Prince and Princess of Wales and the Princess Royal.

15 Willem Marx married an Italian TV presenter named Johanna Botta in 2014 and they have a son.

16 Her school friend Jessica Hay claimed this to be true.

17 The most famous Levi's guy in the UK was Nick Kamen, a handsome English model who appeared in TV commercials in the 1980s for Levi's 501 jeans.

18 From the podcast *Happy Mum, Happy Baby*, 15 February 2020.

19 From a report by Ffion Haff, MailOnline, 25 November 2023, and an interview with Ian Henry for the MailOnline.

Chapter 2: From Friendship to Love

20 From an interview by Katie Nicholl, *Vanity Fair*, 4 November 2010.

21 From their royal engagement interview with Tom Bradby, ITV, 2010.

22 Bradby engagement interview, ITV, 2010.

23 Bradby engagement interview, ITV, 2010.

24 As part of a charitable cookbook project benefiting The Passage, a homeless charity he supports, William shared his recipe for Bolognese sauce.

25 Katie Nicholl, *Kate: The Future Queen*, Hachette, 2013.

26 When the couple returned to their former university in May 2021, they stayed overnight in St Andrews before carrying out engagements in the area. With his wife watching on, William romantically thanked St Andrews 'for the woman he loves'.

SOURCE NOTES

Chapter 3: The Waiting Game

27 From a *Guardian* article, 25 March 2007.

Chapter 4: Our Way

28 From Katie Nicholl's book, *The Making of a Royal Romance*. Preface, 2011. Nicholl wrote that Catherine excused herself from a meeting and shut herself in a room for more than an hour to take the call.

29 The half-sister of Harry's one-time girlfriend Cressida Bonas, who dated him for two years from 2012. They share a mother.

30 Catherine and Pippa first got the nickname the Sizzler Sisters from society magazine *Tatler* because of their speedy rise to the top of the heap of British society. But they were also dubbed the 'Wisteria Sisters' by those in aristocratic circles in the media and accused of being social climbers.

31 Sir Henry is now a director at Thorp Perrow Arboretum in North Yorkshire and married Natasha Sinclair in 2011.

32 From an interview with Sam Waley-Cohen in the *Mail on Sunday*.

33 George VI was the first Royal Family member to be certified as a fully qualified pilot in 1919.

34 From an article by Richard Kay and Geoffrey Levy in the *Daily Mail*, 19 September 2008.

35 Now RaSP, the Met's Royal and Specialist Protection.

36 Mike Tindall, husband of William's cousin Zara, revealed in his podcast released in December 2023 that his nickname for the prince was 'One Pint Willy' because he rarely drinks more than one pint.

37 On an engagement to a children's centre in Cardiff in 2020.

38 From William and Catherine's ITV engagement interview in 2010. At the time, William always publicly called her Kate, not Catherine.

39 Gyles Brandreth, *Elizabeth: An Intimate Portrait*, Michael Joseph, 2022.

40 From Cheryl Cole's autobiography *Cheryl: My Story*, Harper, 2012.

Chapter 6: First Steps

41 From an interview given by the duchess for the 2016 ITV documentary, *Our Queen at Ninety*.

42 Equivalent to £1.8 million today.

43 In the 2016 ITV documentary *Our Queen at Ninety*, the Duchess of Cambridge spoke about the 'art of walkabouts' and her own difficulties. The interview was Catherine's first on television since getting engaged to Prince William in 2011.

44 *Cosmopolitan* magazine, April 2016.

Chapter 7: The Cynical Hunt

45 Bethan Holt, *The Duchess of Cambridge: A Decade of Modern Royal Style*, Ryland, Peters & Small, 2020.

Chapter 8: Boy George

46 From a pooled royal rota interviewed in the *Daily Mail*, 21 March 2013.

47 From the *Happy Mum, Happy Baby* podcast in February 2020.

48 *Happy Mum, Happy Baby* podcast.

49 There has been at least one HRH Prince of Cambridge before: Prince George of Cambridge, born in 1819, grandson of King George III.

50 The couple acquired Lupo in the New Year, 2012 and the English Cocker Spaniel dog kept Catherine company at their Welsh home while William was on RAF duty.

51 *Time* magazine, 18 April 2013.

Chapter 9: New Royal Family

52 From an interview with *Harper's Bazaar*.

53 Guy Thorpe-Beeston delivered the baby.

54 Sarah Vine's article in the *Daily Mail*, December 2015.

55 The *Independent*, 15 April 2016.

56 Award-winning author Hilary Mantel had sparked a row in 2013 when she cruelly described the duchess as appearing 'gloss-varnished', with a perfect, plastic smile. Her final barbed comment in the lecture at the British Museum was to call Catherine a 'shop-window mannequin' with no personality, whose only purpose is to breed.

Chapter 10: We Five

57 Quote from the *Daily Mail* online, 11 October 2011.

58 The Dutch masterpiece had been made more famous again by the film *Girl with a Pearl Earring*, starring Colin Firth, Scarlett Johansson and Tom Wilkinson, which was out at the time.

59 From an interview with the *Mail Online*, 11 October 2016 and the author's own notes as he covered the engagement in person.

60 From an article in the *Guardian* by Gaby Hinsliff, 6 May 2023. Gary Goldsmith was a victim of an entrapment sting in July 2009 by the now defunct *News of the World's* so-called 'fake sheikh' Mazher Mahmood. No charges were brought against him and Mahmood was later jailed in 2016 after being convicted of conspiracy to pervert the course of justice in a case involving the singer Tulisa Contostavlos.

61 Catherine shared this candid thought during her 2017 mental health campaign, 'Heads Together', in which the goal was to reduce the stigma surrounding mental health issues.

62 On a visit to Brent, North London, in 2022, Catherine said, 'I keep thinking Louis is my baby, but he's a proper boy now.'

Chapter 11: Family Feud

63 From an interview with Cressida Bonas by BBC Radio Four. She later married Harry Wentworth-Stanley, the son of the Marchioness of Milford Haven and her first husband, Nicholas Wentworth-Stanley, in 2020.

64 In an interview with ITV's Tom Bradby to publicise his book *Spare* (Bantam, 2023), Harry said that William was so frustrated during an argument in 2019 that he saw 'the red mist in him'. Harry said of his brother, 'He wanted me to hit him back, but I chose not to.'

65 The *Sun*, 13 October 2018.

66 The *Sun*, 24 January 2020.

67 The *Sun*, 4 April 2019.

68 *Spare*, Bantam, 2023.

69 In a 2014 video filmed in Soho House in Toronto, Meghan was filmed saying, 'Oh, I can do that so well,' when asked if she can make herself cry.

70 From an interview with Tom Bradby for the ITV documentary *Harry & Meghan: An African Journey*, 2019.

71 An interview with Tom Bradby in *The Times*, May 2021.

72 ibid.

Chapter 12: Varying Recollections

73 Quotes from two confidential sources, both former members of the Royal Household, interviewed by the author in August and September 2022.

74 The exclusive was broken by Dan Wootton, who went on to present his own show on *GB News*.

75 Omid Scobie and Carolyn Durand, *Finding Freedom*, HQ, 2020.

76 Valentine Low, *Courtiers: The Hidden Power Behind the Crown*, paperback edition published by Headline, October 2022.

Chapter 13: Sweet Charity

77 From an interview with Queen Rania on *CNN*, September 2022.

78 Arthur Edwards on ITV's *This Morning*, 12 May 2020.

79 From a speech by the Duchess of Cambridge at Place2Be Wellbeing in Schools Awards ceremony in London, 2016.

80 A speech by the Duchess of Cambridge, February 2015.

81 A speech by the Duchess of Cambridge at the Institute of Contemporary Arts, London, January 2017.

82 Queen Margrethe announced she would abdicate on 14 January 2022, the 52nd anniversary of her accession, leaving the throne to her son, Crown Prince Frederik, meaning Australian-born Mary would be his Queen.

83 From a documentary about the Queen's Jubilee.

84 An interview with the *Sun*, 9 January 2022.

85 The *Sun*, 9 January 2022.

86 Giovanna Fletcher's *Happy Mum, Happy Baby* podcast.

Chapter 14: We'll Meet Again

87 A report in the *Sun*, 2 November 2020.

88 From a BBC interview with Prince William in April 2020.

89 From a July 2020 BBC *Breakfast* interview.

90 Dr Jorie Lagerwey is an Associate Professor and head of film studies at University College Dublin and author of *Postfeminist Celebrity and Motherhood: Brand Mom*, Routledge, 2016.

91   From an article by Camilla Tominey, *Daily Telegraph*, 6 December 2020.

92   An article by Alexandra Shulman, British *Vogue*, January 2022.

93   From an interview by reporter Richard Palmer with Claudia Acott Williams for the *Sunday Express*, 6 March 2022.

94   Arthur Edwards in an interview with the author.

95   She shared this relatable story during a phone call with photographer Ceri A. Edwards for her 'Hold Still' project, which the Cambridges shared in a video on their YouTube channel.

96   From the introduction of the book, *Hold Still: A Portrait of Our Nation in 2020*, National Portrait Gallery, 2021.

97   From a royal reporter's pool, May 2021.

Chapter 15: The End of an Era

98   From an interview by the author with an anonymous member of the Royal Household.

99   From an article by Emily Hodgkin, *Express* Online, 21 April 2021.

100   The headline from the *Independent* article by Nadine White, 23 March 2023.

101   From an article by Jonny Dymond for BBC Online, 25 March 2022.

102   From an article in the *Guardian* by Rachel Hall and Amelia Gentleman, 25 March 2022.

103   This was never revealed officially, but Gyles Brandreth, who was close to Prince Philip, stated in his November 2022 book, *Elizabeth: An Intimate Portrait*, that the Queen had bone marrow cancer, with bone pain being the most prevalent symptom.

104   An interview with the Princess Royal in a documentary, *Charles III: The Coronation Year*, by Oxford Films for BBC One and iPlayer marking the first year of King Charles' reign, broadcast on 26 December 2023.

105   Robert Hardman, *Charles III: New King. New Court. The Inside Story*, Macmillan, 2024. It referred to a memorandum now housed in the Royal Archives.

106   An interview with a senior source and the author, first published in the book *Our King: Charles III: The Man and The Monarch Revealed*, John Blake Books, 2023.

Chapter 16: Tough Act to Follow

107   Andrew Morton, *Diana: Her True Story – In Her Words*, Michael O'Mara, 2003.

108   Prince William started referring to his wife as Catherine publicly soon after the ITV Tom Bradby engagement interview in 2010.

109   From her interview with Martin Bashir, BBC *Panorama*, 20 November 1995.

Chapter 17: No Place Like Home

110   Matt Wilkinson in the *Sun*, 27 May 2021.

111   The royal engagement numbers are from *Daily Telegraph*, 9 December 2023.

112   Kensington Palace YouTube Channel, 'Shaping Our Society' for the Early Years Campaign, February 2023.

113   BBC Radio One interview by Scott Mills and Chris Stark with the Duke and Duchess of Cambridge, 21 April 2017.

114   Matt Wilkinson, the *Sun*, 23 August 2022.

115   Richard Kay, *Daily Mail*, 23 August 2022.

116   The Cambridges' homes are Adelaide Cottage, Windsor, Apartment 1A, Kensington Palace, London, and Anmer Hall, Sandringham, Norfolk. It is not clear if they still have use of a fourth property, Tam-Na-Ghar, a cottage on the Balmoral Estate that the Queen gave William when he was a student at St Andrews University, which some commentators included in the list to make four. It is understood it is now let commercially.

117   Conversation with the author and a former member of the Royal Household.

118   From the *Happy Mum, Happy Baby* podcast in 2020.

119   From a Zoom chat during lockdown between Catherine and the pupils of Casterton Primary Academy, according to Anita Ghidotti, chief executive of the Pendle Trust in *Hello!* magazine.

Chapter 18: Shaping Up

120   Police Constable Wayne Couzens was jailed for life at the Old Bailey for murder of Sarah Everard in September 2021. He used his position as a police officer to trick her into his car as she walked home after visiting a friend in South London on 3 March 2021. Her body was found in woodland around fifty miles away. On appeal against the whole life term, Lord Chief Justice, Lord Burnett, said former

P.C. Couzens' crime was so exceptional the sentence should stand. On 14 September 2023 it was announced that two women, Dania Al-Obeid and Patsy Stevenson, who were arrested while attending the Sarah Everard vigil, had been paid damages and received an apology from the Metropolitan Police.

121 From the *Guardian* newspaper.

122 The results were released in an online forum hosted by the Royal Foundation on 26 November 2020.

123 *Happy Mum, Happy Baby* podcast.

124 *Hello!* magazine, 17 August 2021.

125 The Earthshot Prize offers £1 million grants to eco-innovators helping to find solutions to environmental problems and guests were asked not to buy any new outfits for the occasion.

Chapter 19: Dissenting Voices

126 The term 'Megxit' refers to the withdrawal of the Duke and Duchess of Sussex from royal duties, announced in January 2020, according to the Collins Dictionary.

127 Sarah Vine in the *Daily Mail* on Catherine's fashion sense.

128 Dr Jorie Lagerwey, head of film studies at University College Dublin and author of *Postfeminist Celebrity and Motherhood: Brand Mom*, describes Catherine as 'the anti-professional', having forfeited her career aspirations for a subservient royal role that demands she walk a pace behind her husband in public.

129 Comments made about the duchess by the writer Hilary Mantel in a lecture at the British Museum, February 2013.

130 Wendy Holden, *Independent*, 20 January 2013.

131 The estimate was first recorded in an article in *Newsweek* in 2012.

132 The *Sun*, 2012.

133 From the ITV documentary, *Anne: The Princess Royal at 70*, 2020.

Chapter 20: The Royal Labyrinth

134 Revealed in the *Daily Mail* by the newspaper's diary columnist Richard Eden, September 2023. This new boss, he said, would report directly to them and would not answer to the private secretaries who have long held power behind the scenes at the palaces. 'They are overthrowing the traditional, hierarchical structure in which staff answer to private secretaries. It has really set the cat among the pigeons,' he reported.

135   Catherine spoke to the *Daily Mail* royal editor Rebecca English about how she still does her motherly duties while on royal tour.

136   James Middleton was a guest on *GMB* on 20 July 2023 and was invited onto the show to talk about his clinical depression. In his interview he praised the Prince and Princess of Wales for how they have helped with his mental health struggles.

137   An interview with an anonymous Royal Household source.

138   An interview with the author by a former courtier.

Chapter 21: A Cause for Concern

139   The *Sun*, 23 January 2024.

140   Special information given by a senior source to the author.

141   Matt Wilkinson, the *Sun*, 23 January 2024.

Chapter 22: The Heart of the Family

142   Julie Burchill, *Daily Mail,* 27 March 2024.

143   The King's longstanding commitment to cancer support is highlighted by his role with Macmillan Cancer Support, a relationship that spans over two decades. Furthermore, it has been disclosed that he recently took on the mantle of patron for Cancer Research UK. This organisation is devoted to saving lives through research, influence and information, and finds a significant ally in King Charles.

144   Rebecca English, *Daily Mail*, 6 January 2024.

145   Page Six, the *New York Post*'s renowned gossip column, a world leader in celebrity and entertainment news.

146   The phrase 'aura of perfection' was coined by royal expert Duncan Larcombe, who said she has grown into her role and made it her own in an interview with *OK!* Magazine, 25 August 2021.

The Princesses of Wales

147   A Margrave is the hereditary title of some princes of the Holy Roman Empire and is the equivalent in rank to a British Duke.